JAPANESE CANDLESTICK CHARTING TECHNIQUES

ローソクは身を減らして人を照らす

"Candles Exhaust Themselves to Give Light to Men"

. . . .

JAPANESE CANDLESTICK CHARTING TECHNIQUES

A Contemporary Guide to the Ancient
Investment Techniques of the Far East

STEVE NISON

NEW YORK INSTITUTE OF FINANCE

New York   London   Toronto   Sydney   Tokyo   Singapore

Library of Congress Cataloging-in-Publication Data

Nison, Steve.
    Japanese candlestick charting techniques : a contemporary guide to
the ancient investment technique of the Far East / Steve Nison.
      p. cm.
    Includes bibliographical references and index.
    ISBN 0-13-931650-7
    1. Stocks—Charts, diagrams, etc. 2. Investment analysis.
  I. Title.
HG4638.N57 1991   90-22736
    332.63'22—dc20   CIP
This publication is designed to provide accurate and authoritative information in regard to the subject matter covered. It is sold with the
understanding that the publisher is not engaged in rendering legal,
accounting, or other professional service. If legal advice or other expert
assistance is required, the services of a competent professional
person should be sought.

From a Declaration of Principles Jointly Adopted by
a Committee of the American Bar Association
and a Committee of Publishers and Associations

NYIF and NEW YORK INSTITUTE OF FINANCE
are trademarks of Executive Tax Reports, Inc.
used under license by Prentice Hall Direct, Inc.

Printed in the United States of America

20 19 18 17 16 15 14

Acknowledgements

· ·

Like having ice cream after a tonsillectomy, this section is my treat after the book's completion.

Some of those who deserve recognition for their help are addressed in Chapter 1 in my discussion of my candlestick education. There are many others whom I would like to thank for their help along my candlestick path. Candles might help light the way, but without the assistance and insights of many others it would have been almost impossible to do this book. There were so many who contributed in one way or another to this project that if I have forgotten to mention anyone I apologize for this oversight.

The Market Technicians Association (MTA) deserves special mention. It was at the MTA's library that I first discovered candlestick material written in English. This material, albeit scant, was extremely difficult to obtain, but the marvelously complete MTA library had it. This information provided the scaffolding for the rest of my candlestick endeavors.

Besides the two English references on candlesticks I mention in Chapter 1, I also obtained a wealth of information from books published in Japanese. I would like to thank the following Japanese publishers and authors for these books that I used as references:

Kabushikisouba no Technical Bunseki (Stock Market Technical Analysis) by Gappo Ikutaro, published by Nihon Keizai Shinbunsha

Kabuka Chato no Tashikana Yomikata (A Sure Way to Read Stock Charts) by Katsutoshi Ishii, published by Jiyukokuminsha

Keisen Kyoshitsu Part 1 (Chart Classroom Part 1), published by Toshi Rader

Hajimete Kabuka Chato wo Yomu Hito no Hon (A Book for Those Reading Stock Charts for the First Time) by Kazutaka Hoshii, published by Asukashuppansha

Nihon Keisenshi (The History of Japanese Charts), Chapter 2 by Kenji Oyama, published by Nihon Keisai Shimbunsha

Shinpan Jissen Kabushiki Chart Nyumon (Introduction to Stock Charts) by Okasan Keisai Kenkyusho, published by Diamond-sha

Sakata Goho Wa Furinkazan (Sakata's Five Rules are Wind, Forest, Fire and Mountain), published by Nihon Shoken Shimbunsha

Yoshimi Toshihiko no Chato Kyoshitsu (Toshihiko Yoshimi's Chart Classroom) by Toshihiko Yoshimi, published by Nihon Chart

Then there's the team at Merrill Lynch who were so helpful in looking over the manuscript, making suggestions, and providing ideas. John Gambino, one of the best colleagues anyone can work with provided all the Elliott Wave counts in this book. Chris Stewart, Manager of Futures Research, not only read the entire manuscript but provided valuable suggestions and finely dissected the many, many charts I used. I also want to thank Jack Kavanagh in compliance who also read the manuscript. Yuko Song provided extra insights by conveying some of my candlestick questions to her Japanese customers who use candlesticks.

I have included hundreds of charts in this book from various services. Before I thank all the services that have generously provided use of their candlestick charts, I want to give plaudits to Bloomberg L.P. and CQG (Commodity Quote Graphics).

Bloomberg L.P. was among the first on-line services to provide candlestick charts on the American markets. It's too bad I didn't discover this earlier. I was drawing candlestick charts on my own for years before I found out about Bloomberg. CQG, an on-line futures charting service, was also among the first to see the potential of candlestick charts. Within a few weeks of my first candlestick article, they sent me an alpha test (this is a high-tech term for the very early stages of software prototype testing) of their candlestick software for my CQG System One™. Once I had this software, my candlestick research progressed exponentially. Most of the charts in this book are courtesy of CQG.

Besides Bloomberg L.P. and CQG, other services that were kind enough to provide charts are:

Commodity Trend Service Charts (North Palm Beach, FL), CompuTrac™ (New Orleans, LA), Ensign Software (Idaho Falls, ID), Future-Source™ (Lombard, Ill), and Quick 10-E Financial Information System (New York, N.Y.).

I want to thank those who took time from their busy schedules to review the introductions for Part Two of the book. These are: Dan

Gramza for the chapter on Market Profile®; Jeff Korzenik for the chapters on options and hedging; John Murphy for the chapter on volume and open interest; once again, John Gambino for the chapter on Elliott Wave; Charles LeBeau for the chapter on oscillators; Gerard Sanfilippo and Judy Ganes for the chapter on hedging; and Bruce Kamich for the English language glossary.

The Nippon Technical Analysts Association (NTAA) deserves utmost praise for their assistance. Mr. Kojiiro Watanabe at the Tokyo Investment Information Center helped me to contact NTAA members who have been especially helpful. They are: Mr. Minoru Eda, Manager, Quantative Research, Kokusai Securities Co.; Mr. Yasushi Hayashi, Senior Foreign Exchange Trader at Sumitomo Life Insurance; and Mr. Nori Hayashi, Senior Analyst, Fidelity Management and Research (Far East). When I asked them questions via fax I expected just brief answers. But these three NTAA members took their valuable time to write pages of explanations, complete with drawings. They were wonderful about sharing their candlestick experiences and insights with me. I also want to thank them for reading over and providing information for Chapter 2 on the history of Japanese technical analysis. If there are any mistakes that remain, they are those that I failed to correct.

I want to thank again "idea a day" Bruce Kamich. Bruce is a friend and a fellow futures technician. Throughout our 15-year friendship he has provided me with many valuable ideas and suggestions. Probably two of the most important were his suggestion that I join the MTA and his constant haranguing until I agreed to write a book about candlesticks.

Then there's the publishing staff of the New York Institute of Finance. They were all great, but those with whom I worked most closely deserve extra praise. Susan Barry and Sheck Cho patiently, skillfully and affably guided a neophyte author through the labyrinth of the book publishing business.

Of course there is my family. At the time that I was writing this book, our newborn son Evan entered the picture (with all the excitement about candlesticks, I came close to calling him Candlesticks Nison). Try writing a book with a newborn and a rambunctious four-year-old daughter, Rebecca, and you start to get an idea of how much my wife, Bonnie, contributed to this book. She cared for the children while I maladroitly pummeled away at the keyboard. Obviously, she had the harder job.

For each chapter's heading, and throughout the book, I used Japanese proverbs or sayings. Many times proverbs in the United States are considered trite and are rarely used. This is not so in Japan where proverbs are respected. Besides being enjoyable to read, the Japanese proverbs offer insights into Japanese beliefs and perspectives. I would like to thank the following publishers for the use of their material for the proverbs and sayings used in this book: University of Oklahoma Press, Charles E. Tuttle, and Kenkyusha Ltd.

Finally, I must give proper and legal acknowledgements to many of the services I relied upon during my writing and research. Tick Volume Profile™ is a registered trademark of CQG. Market Profile® and Liquidity Data Bank® are registered trademarks of the Chicago Board of Trade. The CBOT holds exclusive copyrights to the Market Profile® and Liquidity Data Bank® graphics. Graphics reproduced herein under the permission of the Chicago Board of Trade. The views expressed in this publication are solely those of the author and are not to be construed as the views of the Chicago Board of Trade nor is the Chicago Board of Trade in any way responsible for the contents thereof.

PREFACE

···

能ある鷹は爪を隠す

"A clever hawk hides his claws"

Would you like to learn a technical system refined by centuries of use, but virtually unknown here? A system so versatile that it can be fused with any Western technical tool? A system as pleasurable to use as it is powerful? If so, this book on Japanese candlestick charting techniques is for you. You should find it valuable no matter what your background in technical analysis.

Japanese candlestick charts are older than bar charts and point and figure charts. Candlesticks are exciting, powerful, and fun. Using candlesticks will help improve your market analysis. My focus will be mainly on the U.S. markets, but the tools and techniques in this book should be applicable to almost any market.

Candlestick techniques can be used for speculation and hedging. They can be used for futures, equities, options, or anywhere technical analysis is applied. By reading this book you will discover how candlesticks will add another dimension of analysis.

Do not worry if you have never seen a candlestick chart. The assumption of this book is that they are new to you. Indeed, they are new to the vast majority of the American and European trading and investing community.

If you are a seasoned technician, you will discover how joining Japanese candlesticks with your other technical tools can create a powerful synergy of techniques. The chapters on joining Japanese candlestick techniques with Western technical tools will be of strong interest to you.

If you are an amateur technician, you will find how effective candlestick charts are as a stand alone charting method. To help guide you, I have included a glossary of all the western and Japanese candlestick terms used.

The Japanese technicals are honed by hundreds of years of evolution. Yet, amazingly, we do not know how the Japanese analyze our markets with their traditional technical tool called *candlesticks*. This is disconcerting if you consider that they are among the biggest players in the financial markets. The Japanese are big technical traders. Knowing how the Japanese use candlestick charts to analyze both our markets and theirs may help you answer the question "What are the Japanese going to do?"

The Japanese use a combination of western chart and candlestick techniques to analyze the markets. Why shouldn't we do the same? If you do not learn about Japanese candlestick charts, your competition will!

If you like reading about colorful terminology like "hanging-man lines," "dark-cloud covers," and "evening stars" then this book is for you. If you subscribe to one of the multitude of services now providing candlestick charts and would like to learn how to use these charts, then this book is for you.

In the first part of the book, you learn how to draw and interpret over 50 candlestick lines and formations. This will slowly and clearly lay a solid foundation for the second part where you will learn to use candlesticks in combination with Western technical techniques.

This book will not give you market omniscience. It will, however, open new avenues of analysis and will show how Japanese candlesticks can "enlighten" your trading.

Contents

· ·

PART TWO: THE RULE OF MULTIPLE TECHNICAL TECHNIQUES

CHAPTER 1

INTRODUCTION

....

始めは大事

"The beginning is most important"

SOME BACKGROUND

Some of you may have already heard of candlecharts. Probably, many more of you have not. In December 1989, I wrote an introductory article on candlesticks that precipitated an immediate groundswell of interest. It turned out that I was one of the few Americans familiar with this centuries-old Japanese technique. I wrote follow-up articles, gave numerous presentations, taught classes, and was interviewed on television and by newspapers across the country. In early 1990, I wrote a short reference piece for my Chartered Market Technician thesis about candlestick charts. It contained very basic introductory material, but it was the only readily available information on candlestick charts in the United States. This handout became very popular. Within a few months, Merrill Lynch, the publisher of the booklet, received over 10,000 requests.

HOW I LEARNED ABOUT CANDLESTICK CHARTS

"Why," I have often asked myself, "has a system which has been around so long almost completely unknown in the West?" Were the Japanese trying to keep it secret? Was it the lack of information in the United States? I don't know the answer, but it has taken years of research to fit all the pieces together. I was fortunate in several ways.

Perhaps my perseverance and serendipity were the unique combination needed that others did not have.

In 1987, I became acquainted with a Japanese broker. One day, while I was with her in her office, she was looking at one of her Japanese stock chart books (Japanese chart books are in candlestick form). She exclaimed, "look, a window." I asked what she was talking about. She told me a *window* was the same as a *gap* in Western technicals. She went on to explain that while Western technicians use the expression "filling in the gap" the Japanese would say "closing the window." She then used other expresions like, "doji" and "dark-cloud cover." I was hooked. I spent the next few years exploring, researching, and analyzing anything I could about candlestick charts.

It was not easy. There are scant English publications on the subject. My initial education was with the help of a Japanese broker and through drawing and analyzing candlestick charts on my own. Then, thanks to the Market Technicians Association (MTA) library, I came across a booklet published by the Nippon Technical Analysts Association called *Analysis of Stock Price in Japan.* It was a Japanese booklet which had been translated into English. Unfortunately, there were just ten pages on interpreting candlestick charts. Nonetheless, I finally had some English candlestick material.

A few months later, I borrowed a book that has had a major influence on my professional life. The MTA office manager, Shelley Lebeck, brought a book entitled *The Japanese Chart of Charts* by Seiki Shimizu and translated by Greg Nicholson (published by the Tokyo Futures Trading Publishing Co.) back from Japan. It contains about 70 pages on candlestick charts and is written in English. Reading it was like finding an oasis in a desert.

As I discovered, while the book yielded a harvest of information, it took some effort and time to get comfortable with its concepts. They were all so new. I also had to become comfortable with the Japanese terminology. The writing style was sometimes obscure. Part of this might have resulted from the translation. The book was originally written in Japanese about 25 years ago for a Japanese audience. I also found out, when I had my own material translated, that it is dreadfully difficult to translate such a specialized subject from Japanese to English. Nonetheless, I had some written reference material. This book became my "Rosetta Stone."

I carried the book with me for months, reading and rereading, taking copious notes, applying the candlestick methods to the scores of my hand-drawn candlestick charts. I chewed and grinded away at the new ideas and terminology. I was fortunate in another sense. I had the help of the author, Seiki Shimizu, to answer my many questions. Although Mr. Shimizu does not speak English, the translator of the book, Greg Nicholson, graciously acted as our intermediary via fax messages. The *Japanese Chart of Charts* provided the foundation for the rest of my investigation into candlesticks. Without that book, this book would not have been possible.

In order to continually develop my abilities in candlestick charting techniques, I sought out Japanese candlestick practitioners who would have the time and inclination to speak with me about the subject. I met a Japanese trader, Morihiko Goto who had been using candlestick charts and who was willing to share his valuable time and insights. This was exciting enough! Then he told me that his family had been using candlestick charts for generations! We spent many hours discussing the history and the uses of candlestick charts. He was an invaluable storehouse of knowledge.

I also had an extensive amount of Japanese candlestick literature translated. Obtaining the original Japanese candlestick information was one problem. Getting it translated was another. Based on one estimate there are probably fewer than 400 full-time Japanese-to-English translators in America (this includes part-time translators)[1] I had to find a translator who could not only translate routine material, but also the highly specialized subject of technical analysis. In this regard I was lucky to have the help of Languages Services Unlimited in New York. The director, Richard Solberg, provided indispensable help to this project. He was a rarity. He was an American fluent in Japanese who understood, and used, technical analysis. Not only did Richard do a wonderful job of translating, but he helped me hunt down and obtain Japanese candlestick literature. Thanks to his help I might have the largest collection of Japanese books on candlesticks in the country. Without Richard this book would have been much less extensive.

Before my introductory article on candlestick charts appeared in late 1989, there were few services offering candlestick charts in the United States. Now a plethora of services offer these charts. These include:

Bloomberg L.P. (New York, NY);

Commodity Trend Service Charts (North Palm Beach, FL);

CompuTrac™ (New Orleans, LA);

CQG (Glenwood Springs, CO);

Ensign Software (Idaho Falls, ID);

FutureSource™ (Lombard, IL); and

Knight Ridder–Commodity Perspective (Chicago, IL).

By the time you read this book, there probably will be additional services providing candlestick charts. Their popularity grows stronger every day. The profusion of services offering the candlestick charts attests to both their popularity and their usefulness.

WHY HAVE CANDLESTICK CHARTING TECHNIQUES CAPTURED THE ATTENTION OF TRADERS AND INVESTORS AROUND THE WORLD?

I have had calls and faxes from around the world requesting more information about candlestick techniques. Why the extensive interest? There are many reasons and a few are:

1. Candlestick charts are flexible. Users run the spectrum from first-time chartists to seasoned professionals. This is because candlestick charts can be used alone or in combination with other technical analysis techniques. A significant advantage attributed to candlestick charting techniques is that these techniques can be used in addition to, not instead of, other technical tools. I am not trying to convince veteran technicians that this system is superior to whatever else they may be using. That is not my claim. My claim is that candlestick charting techniques provide an extra dimension of analysis.

2. Candlestick charting techniques are for the most part unused in the United States. Yet, this technical approach enjoys a centuries-old tradition in the Far East, a tradition which has evolved from centuries of trial and error.

3. Then there are the picturesque terms used to describe the patterns. Would the expression "hanging-man line" spark your interest? This is only one example of how Japanese terminology gives candlesticks a flavor all their own and, once you get a taste, you will not be able to do without them.

4. The Japanese probably know all the Western methods of technical analysis, yet we know almost nothing about theirs. Now it is our turn to benefit from their knowledge. The Japanese use a combination of candlestick charting techniques along with Western technical tools. Why shouldn't we do the same?

5. The primary reason for the widespread attention aroused by candlestick charts is that using them instead of, or in addition to, bar charts is a win–win situation.

As we will see in Chapter 3 on drawing candlestick lines, the same data is required in order to draw the candlestick charts as that which is needed for our bar charts (that is, the open, high, low, and close). This is very significant since it means that any of the technical analysis used with bar charting (such as moving averages, trendlines, Elliott Wave, retracements, and so on) can be employed with candlestick charts. But, and this is the key point, candlestick charts can send signals not available from bar charts. In addition, there are some patterns that may allow you to get the jump on those who use traditional Western charting techniques. By employing candlestick charting instead of bar charting you have the ability to use all the same analyses as you would with bar charting. But candlestick charts provide a unique avenue of analysis not available anywhere else.

WHAT IS IN THIS BOOK?

Part I of the book reveals the basics on constructing, reading, and interpreting over 50 candlestick chart lines and patterns. Part II explains how to meld candlestick charts with Western technical analysis techniques. This is where the true power of candlecharts is manifested. This is how I use them.

I have drawn illustrations of candlestick patterns to assist in the educational process. These illustrations are representative examples only. The drawn exhibits should be viewed in the context that they show certain guidelines and principles. The actual patterns do not have to look exactly as they do in the exhibits in order to provide the reader with a valid signal. This is emphasized throughout the book in the many chart examples. You will see how variations of the patterns can still provide important clues about the state of the markets.

Thus, there is some subjectivity in deciding whether a certain candlestick formation meets the guidelines for that particular formation, but this subjectivity is no different than that used with other charting techniques. For instance, is a $400 support area in gold considered broken if prices go under $400 intra-day, or do prices have to close under $400? Does a $.10 penetration of $400 substantiate broken support or is a larger penetration needed? You will have to decide these answers based on your trading temperment, your risk adversity, and your market philosophy. Likewise, through text, illustrations and real examples I will provide the general principles and guidelines for recognizing the candlestick formations. But you should not expect the real-world examples to always match their ideal formations.

I believe that the best way to explain how an indicator works is through marketplace examples. Consequently, I have included many such examples. These examples span the entire investment spectrum from futures, fixed-income, equity, London metal markets and foreign exchange markets. Since my background is in the futures markets, most of my charts are from this arena. I also look at the entire time spectrum—from intra-day to daily, weekly, and monthly candlestick charts. For this book, when I describe the candlestick lines and patterns, I will often refer to daily data. For instance, I may say that in order to complete a candlestick pattern the market has to open above the prior day's high. But the same principles will be valid for all time frames.

Two glossaries are at the end of the text. The first includes candlestick terms and the second Western technical terms used in the book. The candlestick glossary includes a visual glossary of all the patterns.

As with any subjective form of technical analysis, there are, at times, variable definitions which will be defined according to the users' experience and background. This is true of some candlestick patterns. Depending on my source of information, there were instances in which I came across different, albeit usually minor, definitions of what constitutes a certain pattern. For example, one Japanese author writes that the open has to be above the prior close in order to complete a dark-cloud cover pattern (see Chapter 4). Other written and oral sources say that, for this pattern, the open should be above the prior high.

In cases where there were different definitions, I chose the rules that increased the probability that the pattern's forecast would be correct. For example, the pattern referred to in the prior paragraph is a reversal signal that appears at tops. Thus, I chose the definition that the market has to open above the prior day's high. It is more bearish if the market opens above the prior day's high and then fails, then it would be if the market just opens above the prior day's close and then failed.

Much of the Japanese material I had translated is less than specific. Part of this might be the result of the Japanese penchant for being vague. The penchant may have its origins in the feudal ages when it was acceptable for a samurai to behead any commoner who did not treat him as expected. The commoner did not always know how a samurai expected him to act or to answer. By being vague, many heads were spared. However, I think the more important reason for the somewhat ambiguous explanations has to do with the fact that technical analysis is more of an art than a science. You should not expect rigid rules with most forms of technical analysis—just guideposts.

Yet, because of this uncertainty, some of the ideas in this book may be swayed by the author's trading philosophy. For instance, if a Japanese author says that a candlestick line has to be "surpassed" to signal the next bull move, I equate "surpassed" with "on a close above." That is because, to me, a close is more important than an intra-day move above a candlestick line. Another example of subjectivity: In the Japanese literature many candlestick patterns are described as important at a high-price area or at a low-price area. Obviously what constitutes a "high-price" or "low-price" area is open to interpretation.

SOME LIMITATIONS

As with all charting methods, candlestick chart patterns are subject to the interpretation of the user. This could be viewed as a limitation. Extended experience with candlestick charting in your market specialty will show you which of the patterns, and variations of these patterns, work best. In this sense, subjectivity may not be a liability. As you gain experience in candlestick techniques, you will discover which candlestick combinations work best in your market. This may give you an advantage over those who have not devoted the time and energy in tracking your markets as closely as you have.

As discussed later in the text, drawing the individual candlestick chart lines requires a close. Therefore, you may have to wait for the close to get a valid trading signal. This may mean a market on close order may be needed or you may have to try and anticipate what the close will be and place an order a few minutes prior to the close. You may also prefer to wait for the next day's opening before placing an order.

This aspect may be a problem but there are many technical systems (especially those based on moving averages of closing prices) which require a closing price for a signal. This is why there is often a surge in activity during the final few minutes of a trading session as computerized trading signals, based on closing prices, kick into play. Some technicians consider only a close above resistance a valid buy signal so they have to wait until the close for confirmation. This aspect of waiting for a close is not unique to candlestick charts.

On occasion, I can use the hourly candlestick charts to get a trade signal rather than waiting for the close of that day. For instance, there could be a potentially bullish candlestick pattern on the daily chart. Yet, I would have to wait for the close before the candlestick pattern is completed. If the hourly charts also show a bullish candlestick indicator during that day, I may recommend buying (if the prevalent trend is up) even before the close.

The opening price is also important in the candlestick lines. Equity traders, who do not have access to on-line quote machines, may not be able to get opening prices on stocks in their newspapers. I hope that, as candlestick charts become more common, more newspapers will include openings on individual stocks.

Candlestick charts provide many useful trading signals. They do not, however, provide price targets. There are other methods to forecast targets (such as prior support or resistance levels, retracements, swing objectives, and so on). Some Japanese candlestick practitioners place a trade based on a candlestick signal and stay with that trade until another candlestick pattern tells them to offset. Candlestick patterns should always be viewed in the context as to what occurred before and in relation to other technical evidence.

With the hundreds of charts throughout this book, do not be surprised if you see patterns that I have missed within charts. There will also be examples of patterns that, at times, did not work. Candlesticks will not provide an infallible trading tool. They do, however, add a vibrant color to your technical palette.

Candlestick charts allow you to use the same technical devices that you use with bar charts. But the candlestick charts give you signals not available with bar charts. So why use a bar chart? In the near future, candlestick charts may become as standard as the bar chart. In fact, I am going to make a bold prediction: *As more technicians become comfortable with candlestick charts, they will no longer use bar charts.* I have been a technical analyst for nearly 20 years. And now, after discovering all their benefits, I only use candlestick charts. I still use all the traditional Western technical tools, but the candlesticks have given me a unique perspective into the markets.

Before I delve into the topic of candlestick charts, I will briefly discuss the importance of technical analysis as a separate discipline. For those of you who are new to this topic, the following section is meant to emphasize why technical analysis is so important. It is not an in-depth discussion. If you would like to learn more about the topic, I suggest you read John Murphy's excellent book *Technical Analysis of the Futures Markets* (The New York Institute of Finance).

If you are already familiar with the benefits of technical analysis, you can skip this section. Do not worry, if you do not read the following section, it will not interfere with later candlestick chart analysis information.

THE IMPORTANCE OF TECHNICAL ANALYSIS

The importance of technical analysis is five-fold. First, while fundamental analysis may provide a gauge of the supply/demand situations, price/earnings ratios, economic statistics, and so forth, there is no psychological component involved in such analysis. Yet the markets are influenced at times, to a major extent, by emotionalism. An ounce of emotion can be worth a pound of facts. As John Manyard Keynes stated, "there is nothing so disastrous as a rational investment policy in an irrational world."[2] Technical analysis provides the only mechanism to measure the "irrational" (emotional) component present in all markets.

Here is an entertaining story about how strongly psychology can affect a market. It is from the book *The New Gatsbys*.[3] It takes place at the Chicago Board of Trade.

> Soybeans were sharply higher. There was a drought in the Illinois Soybean Belt. And unless it ended soon, there would be a severe shortage of beans. . . . Suddenly a few drops of water slid down a window. "Look," someone shouted, "rain!". More than 500 pairs of eyes [the traders—editor's note] shifted to the big windows. . . . Then came a steady trickle which turned into a steady downpour. It was raining in downtown Chicago.

> Sell. Buy. Buy. Sell. The shouts cascaded from the traders' lips with a roar that matched the thunder outside. And the price of soybeans began to slowly move down. Then the price of soybeans broke like some tropic fever.

> It was pouring in Chicago all right, but no one grows soybeans in Chicago. In the heart of the Soybean Belt, some 300 miles south of Chicago the sky was blue, sunny and very dry. But even if it wasn't raining on the soybean fields it was in the *heads of the traders, and that is all that counts* [emphasis added]. To the market nothing matters unless the market reacts to it. *The game is played with the mind and the emotions* [emphasis added].

In order to drive home the point about the importance of mass psychology, think about what happens when you exchange a piece of paper called "money" for some item like food or clothing? Why is that paper, with no intrinsic value, exchanged for something tangible? It is because of a shared psychology. Everyone believes it will be accepted, so it is. Once this shared psychology evaporates, when people stop believing in money, it becomes worthless.

Second, technicals are also an important component of disciplined trading. Discipline helps mitigate the nemesis of all traders, namely, emotion. As soon as you have money in the market, emotionalism is in the driver's seat and rationale and objectivity are merely passengers. If you doubt this, try paper trading. Then try trading with your own funds. You will soon discover how deeply the counterproductive aspects of tension, anticipation, and anxiety alter the way you trade and view the markets—usually in proportion to the funds committed. Technicals can put objectivity back into the drivers seat. They provide a mechanism to set entry and exit points, to set risk/reward ratios, or stop/out levels. By using them, you foster a risk and money management approach to trading.

As touched upon in the previous discussion, the technicals contribute to market objectivity. It is human nature, unfortunately, to see the market as we want to see it, not as it really is. How often does the following occur? A trader buys. Immediately the market falls. Does he take a loss. Usually no. Although there is no room for hope in the market, the trader will glean all the fundamentally bullish news he can in order to buoy his hope that the market will turn in his direction. Meanwhile prices continue to descend. Perhaps the market is trying to tell him something. The markets communicate with us. We can monitor these messages by using the technicals. This trader is closing his eyes and ears to the messages being sent by the market.

If this trader stepped back and objectively viewed price activity, he might get a better feel of the market. What if a supposedly bullish story is released and prices do not move up or even fall? That type of price action is sending out volumes of information about the psychology of the market and how one should trade in it.

I believe it was the famous trader Jesse Livermore who expressed the idea that one can see the whole better when one sees it from a distance. Technicals make us step back and get a different and, perhaps, better perspective on the market.

Third, following the technicals is important even if you do not fully believe in their use. This is because, at times, the technicals are the major reason for a market move. Since they are a market moving factor, they should be watched.

Fourth, random walk proffers that the market price for one day has no bearing on the price the following day. But this academic view leaves out an important component—people. People remember prices from one day to the next and act accordingly. To wit, peoples' reactions indeed affect price, but price also affects peoples' reactions. Thus, price, itself, is an important component in market analysis. Those who disparage technical analysis forget this last point.

Fifth, and finally, the price action is the most direct and easily accessible method of seeing overall supply/demand relationships. There may be fundamental news not known to the general public but you can expect it is already in the price. Those who have advance knowledge of some market moving event will most likely buy or sell until current prices reflect their information. This knowledge, at times, consequently, may be discounted when the event occurs. Thus, current prices should reflect all available information, whether known by the general public or by a select few.

NOTES

[1]Hill, Julie Skur. "That's Not What I Said," *Business Tokyo*, August 1990, pp. 46–47.
[2]Smith, Adam. *The Money Game*, New York, NY: Random House, 1986, p. 154.
[3]Tamarkin, Bob. *The New Gatsbys*, Chicago, IL: Bob Tamarkin, 1985, pp. 122–123.

CHAPTER 2

A HISTORICAL BACKGROUND

. . . .

古きを訪ねて新しきを知る

"Through Inquiring of the Old We Learn the New"

This chapter provides the framework through which Japanese technical analysis evolved. For those who are in a rush to get to the "meat" of the book (that is, the techniques and uses of candlesticks), you can skip this chapter, or return to it after you have completed the rest of the book. It is an intriguing history.

Among the first and the most famous people in Japan to use past prices to predict future price movements was the legendary Munehisa Homma.[1] He amassed a huge fortune trading in the rice market during the 1700s. Before I discuss Homma, I want to provide an overview of the economic background in which Homma was able to flourish. The time span of this overview is from the late 1500s to the mid-1700s. During this era Japan went from 60 provinces to a unified country where commerce blossomed.

From 1500 to 1600, Japan was a country incessantly at war as each of the *daimyo* (literally "big name" meaning "a feudal lord") sought to wrestle control of neighboring territories. This 100-year span between 1500 and 1600 is referred to as "Sengoku Jidai" or, literally, "Age of Country at War." It was a time of disorder. By the early 1600s, three extraordinary generals—Nobunaga Oda, Hideyoshi Toyotomi, and Ieyasu Tokugawa—had unified Japan over a 40-year period. Their prowess and achievements are celebrated in Japanese history and folklore.

There is a Japanese saying: "Nobunaga piled the rice, Hideyoshi kneaded the dough, and Tokugawa ate the cake." In other words, all three generals contributed to Japan's unification but Tokugawa, the last of these great generals, became the shogun whose family ruled Japan from 1615 to 1867. This era is referred to as the *Tokugawa Shogunate*.

The military conditions that suffused Japan for centuries became an integral part of candlestick terminology. And, if you think about it, trading requires many of the same skills needed to win a battle. Such skills include strategy, psychology, competition, strategic withdrawals, and yes, even luck. So it is not surprising that throughout this book you will come across candlestick terms that are based on battlefield analogies. There are "night and morning attacks", the "advancing three soldiers pattern", "counter attack lines", the "gravestone", and so on.

The relative stability engendered by the centralized Japanese feudal system lead by Tokugawa offered new opportunities. The agrarian economy grew, but, more importantly, there was expansion and ease in domestic trade. By the 17th century, a national market had evolved to replace the system of local and isolated markets. This concept of a centralized marketplace was to indirectly lead to the development of technical analysis in Japan.

Hideyoshi Toyotomi regarded Osaka as Japan's capital and encouraged its growth as a commercial center. Osaka's easy access to the sea, at a time where land travel was slow, dangerous, and costly, made it a national depot for assembling and disbursing supplies. It evolved into Japan's greatest city of commerce and finance. Its wealth and vast storehouses of supplies provided Osaka with the appellation the "Kitchen of Japan." Osaka contributed much to price stability by smoothing out regional differences in supply. In Osaka, life was permeated by the desire for profit (as opposed to other cities in which money making was despised). The social system at that time was composed of four classes. In descending order they were the Soldier, the Farmer, the Artisan, and the Merchant. It took until the 1700s for merchants to break down the social barrier. Even today the traditional greeting in Osaka is "Mokari-makka" which means, "are you making a profit?".

In Osaka, Yodoya Keian became a war merchant for Hideyoshi (one of the three great military unifiers). Yodoya had extraordinary abilities in transporting, distributing, and setting the price of rice. Yodoya's front yard became so important that the first rice exchange developed there. He became very wealthy—as it turned out, too wealthy. In 1705, the *Bakufu* (the military government led by the Shogun) confiscated his entire fortune on the charge that he was living in luxury not befitting his social rank. The Bakufu was apprehensive about the increasing amount of power acquired by certain merchants. In 1642, certain officials and merchants tried to corner the rice market. The punishment was severe: their children were executed, the merchants were exiled, and their wealth was confiscated.

The rice market that originally developed in Yodoya's yard was institutionalized when the Dojima Rice Exchange was set up in the late 1600s in Osaka. The merchants at the Exchange graded the rice and bargained to set its price. Up until 1710, the Exchange dealt in actual rice. After 1710, the Rice Exchange began to issue and accept rice warehouse receipts. These warehouse receipts were called *rice coupons*. These rice receipts became the first futures contracts ever traded.

Rice brokerage became the foundation of Osaka's prosperity. There were more than 1,300 rice dealers. Since there was no currency standard (the prior attempts at hard currency failed due to the debasing of the coins), rice became the defacto medium of exchange. A daimyo needing money would send his surplus rice to Osaka where it would be placed in a warehouse in his name. He would be given a coupon as a receipt for this rice. He could sell this rice coupon whenever he pleased. Given the financial problems of many daimyos, they would also often sell rice coupons against their next rice tax delivery (taxes to the daimyo were paid in rice—usually 40% to 60% of the rice farmer's crop). Sometimes the rice crop of several years hence was mortgaged.

These rice coupons were actively traded. The rice coupons sold against future rice deliveries became the world's first futures contracts. The Dojima Rice Exchange, where these coupons traded, became the world's first futures exchange. Rice coupons were also called "empty rice" coupons (that is, rice that was not in physical possession). To give you an idea of the popularity of rice futures trading, consider this: In 1749, there were a total of 110,000 bales (rice used to trade in bales) of empty-rice coupons traded in Osaka. Yet, throughout all of Japan there were only 30,000 bales of rice.[2]

Into this background steps Homma, called "god of the markets." "Munehisa Homma was born in 1724 into a wealthy family. The Homma family was considered so wealthy that there was a saying at that time, "I will never become a Homma, but I would settle to be a local lord." When Homma was given control of his family business in 1750, he began trading at his local rice exchange in the port city of Sakata. Sakata was a collections and distribution area for rice. Since Homma came from Sakata, you will frequently come across the expression "Sakata's Rules" in Japanese candlestick literature. These refer to Homma.

When Munehisa Homma's father died, Munehisa was placed in charge of managing the family's assets. This was in spite of the fact that he was the youngest son. (It was usually the eldest son who inherited the power during that era.) This was probably because of Munehisa's market savvy. With this money, Homma went to Japan's largest rice exchange, the Dojima Rice Exchange in Osaka, and began trading rice futures.

Homma's family had a huge rice farming estate. Their power meant that information about the rice market was usually available to them. In addition, Homma kept records of yearly weather conditions. In order to learn about the psychology of investors, Homma analyzed rice prices going back to the time when the rice exchange was in Yodoya's yard. Homma also set up his own communications system. At prearranged times he placed men on rooftops to send signals by flags. These men stretched the distance from Osaka to Sakata.

After dominating the Osaka markets, Homma went to trade in the regional exchange at Edo (now called Tokyo). He used his insights to amass a huge fortune. It was said he had 100 consecutive winning trades.

His prestige was such that there was the following folk song from Edo: "When it is sunny in Sakata (Homma's town), it is cloudy in Dojima (the Dojima Rice Exchange in Osaka) and rainy at Kuramae (the Kuramae exchange in Edo)." In other words when there is a good rice crop in Sakata, rice prices fall on the Dojima Rice Exchange and collapse in Edo. This song reflects the Homma's sway over the rice market.

In later years Homma became a financial consultant to the government and was given the honored title of samurai. He died in 1803. Homma's books about the markets (*Sakata Senho* and *Soba Sani No Den*) were said to have been written in the 1700s. His trading principles, as applied to the rice markets, evolved into the candlestick methodology currently used in Japan.

NOTES

[1]His first name is sometimes translated as Sokyu and his last name is sometimes translated as Honma. This gives you an idea of the difficulty of translating Japanese into English. The same Japanese symbols for Homma's first name, depending on the translator, can be Sokyu or Munehisa. His last name, again depending on the translator, can be either Homma or Honma. I chose the English translation of Homma's name as used by the Nippon Technical Analysts Association.

[2]Hirschmeier, Johannes and Yui, Tsunehiko. *The Development of Japanese Business 1600–1973*, Cambridge, MA: Harvard University Press, 1975, p. 31.

PART 1

THE BASICS

千里の道も一歩から

"Even a Thousand Mile Journey Begins with the First Step"

CHAPTER 3

CONSTRUCTING THE CANDLESTICKS

. . . .

櫓櫂がなくて舟で渡れぬ

"Without Oars You Cannot Cross in a Boat"

A comparison between the visual differences of a bar chart and a candlestick chart is easy to illustrate. Exhibit 3.1 is the familiar Western bar chart. Exhibit 3.2 is a candlestick chart of the same price information as that in the bar chart. On the candlestick chart, prices seem to jump off the page presenting a stereoscopic view of the market as it pushes the flat, two-dimensional bar chart into three dimensions. In this respect, candlecharts are visually exciting.

DRAWING THE CANDLESTICK LINES

Since candlestick charts are new to most Western technicians, the most common Western chart, the bar chart, is used throughout this chapter as an instructional tool for learning how to draw the candlestick lines.

Drawing the daily bar chart line requires open, high, low, and close. The vertical line on a bar chart depicts the high and low of the session. The horizontal line to the left of the vertical line is the opening price. The horizontal line to the right of the vertical line is the close.

Exhibit 3.3 shows how the same data would be used to construct a bar chart and a candlestick chart. Although the daily bar chart lines and candlestick chart lines use the same data, it is easy to see that they are drawn differently. The thick part of the candlestick line is called the *real*

EXHIBIT 3.1. Cocoa—March, 1990, Daily Bar Chart

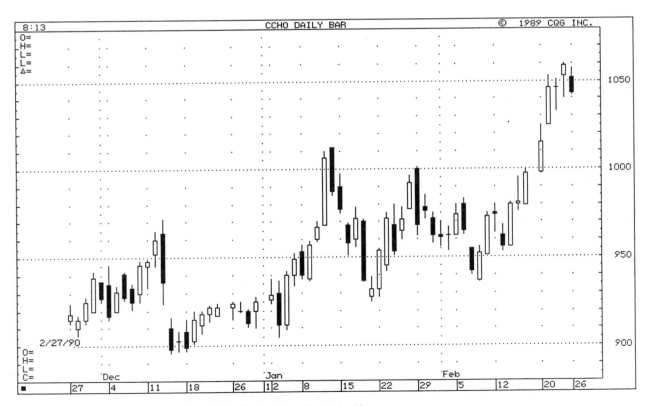

EXHIBIT 3.2. Cocoa—March, 1990, Daily Candlestick Chart

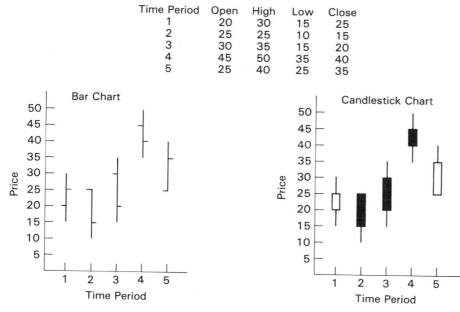

Time Period	Open	High	Low	Close
1	20	30	15	25
2	25	25	10	15
3	30	35	15	20
4	45	50	35	40
5	25	40	25	35

EXHIBIT 3.3 Bar Chart and Candlestick Chart

body. It represents the range between that session's opening and closing. When the real body is black (i.e., filled in) it means the close of the session was lower than the open. If the real body is white (i.e., empty), it means the close was higher than the open.

The thin lines above and below the real body are the *shadows*. These shadows represent the session's price extremes. The shadow above the real body is called the *upper shadow* and the shadow under the real body is known as the *lower shadow*. Accordingly, the peak of the upper shadow is the high of the session and the bottom of the lower shadow is the low of the session. It is easy to see why these are named candlestick charts since the individual lines often look like candles and their wicks. If a candlestick line has no upper shadow it is said to have a *shaven head*. A candlestick line with no lower shadow has a *shaven bottom*. To the Japanese, the real body is the essential price movement. The shadows are usually considered as extraneous price fluctuations.

Exhibits 3.4 through 3.7 demonstrate some common candlestick lines. Exhibit 3.4 reveals a long black candlestick reflecting a bearish period in which the market opened near its high and closed near its low. Exhibit 3.5 shows the opposite of a long black body and, thus, represents a bullish period. Prices had a wide range and the market opened near the low and closed near the high of the session. Exhibit 3.6 shows candlesticks having small real bodies and, as such, they represent a tug of war between the bulls and the bears. They are called *spinning tops* and are neutral in lateral trading bands. As shown later in this book (in the sec-

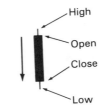

EXHIBIT 3.4. Black Candlestick

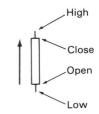

EXHIBIT 3.5. White Candlestick

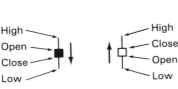

EXHIBIT 3.6. Spinning Tops

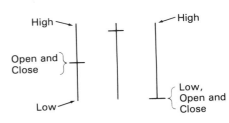

EXHIBIT 3.7. Doji Examples

tions on stars and harami patterns), these spinning tops do become important when part of certain formations. The spinning top can be either white or black. The lines illustrated in Exhibit 3.6 have small upper and lower shadows, but the size of the shadows are not important. It is the diminutive size of the real body that makes this a spinning top. Exhibit 3.7 reveals no real bodies. Instead, they have horizontal lines. These are examples of what are termed *doji lines.*

A doji occurs when the open and close for that session are the same or very close to being the same (e.g., two- or three-thirty-seconds in bonds, a ¼ cent in grains, and so on.). The lengths of the shadows can vary. Doji are so important that an entire chapter is devoted to them (see Chapter 8 *The Magic Doji*).

Candlestick charts can also be drawn more colorfully by using the classical Japanese candlestick chart colors of red and black. Red can be used instead of the white candlestick. (This could be especially useful for computer displays of the candlestick charts.) The obvious problem with this color scheme is that photo copies and most computer printouts will not be useful since all the real bodies would come out as black.

Some readers may have heard the expression *yin* and *yang lines.* These are the Chinese terms for the candlestick lines. The yin line is another name for the black candlestick and the yang line is equivalent to the white candlestick. In Japan, a black candlestick is called *in-sen* (black line) and the white candlestick is called *yo-sen* (white line).

The Japanese place great emphasis on the relationship between the open and close because they are the two most emotionally charged points of the trading day. The Japanese have a proverb that says, "the first hour of the morning is the rudder of the day." So is the opening the rudder for the trading session. It furnishes the first clue about that day's direction. It is a time when all the news and rumors from overnight are filtered and then joined into one point in time.

The more anxious the trader, the earlier he wants to trade. Therefore, on the open, shorts may be scrambling for cover, potential longs may want to emphatically buy, hedgers may need to take a new or get out of an old position, and so forth.

After the flurry of activity on the open, potential buyers and sellers have a benchmark from which they can expect buying and selling. There are frequent analogies to trading the market and fighting a battle. In this sense, the open provides an early view of the battlefield and a provisional indication of friendly and opposing troops. At times, large traders may try to move the market on the open by executing a large buy or sell order. Japanese call this a *morning attack*. Notice that this is another military analogy. The Japanese use many such military comparisons as we shall see throughout the book.

CANDLESTICK TERMINOLOGY AND MARKET EMOTION

Technicals are the only way to measure the emotional component of the market. The names of the Japanese candlestick charts make this fact evident. These names are a colorful mechanism used to describe the emotional health of the market at the time these patterns are formed. After hearing the expressions "hanging man" or "dark-cloud cover," would you think the market is in an emotionally healthy state—of course not! These are both bearish patterns and their names clearly convey the unhealthy state of the market.

While the emotional condition of the market may not be healthy at the time these patterns form, it does not preclude the possibility that the market will become healthy again. The point is that at the appearance of, say, a dark-cloud cover, longs should take defensive measures or, depending on the general trend and other factors, new short sales could be initiated.

There are many new patterns and ideas in this book, but the descriptive names employed by the Japanese not only make candlestick charting fun, but easier to remember if the patterns are bullish or bearish. For example, in Chapter 5 you will learn about the "evening star" and the "morning star." Without knowing what these patterns look like or what they imply for the market, just by hearing their names which do you think is bullish and which is bearish? Of course, the evening star which comes out before darkness sets in, sounds like the bearish signal—and so it is! The morning star, then, is bullish since the morning star appears just before sunrise.

The other pivotal price point is the close. Margin calls in the futures markets are based on the close. We can thus expect heavy emotional involvement into how the market closes. The close is also a pivotal price point for many technicians. They may wait for a close to confirm a break-out from a significant chart point. Many computer trading systems (for example, moving average systems) are based on closes. If a large buy or sell order is pushed into the market at, or near, the close, with the intention of affecting the close, the Japanese call this action a *night attack*.

Exhibits 3.4 to 3.7 illuminate how the relationship between a period's open, high, low, and close alters the look of the individual candlestick line. Now let us turn our attention to how the candlestick lines, alone or in combination, provide clues about market direction.

CHAPTER 4

REVERSAL PATTERNS

....

一寸先は闇

"Darkness Lies One Inch Ahead"

Technicians watch for price clues that can alert them to a shift in market psychology and trend. *Reversal patterns* are these technical clues. Western reversal indicators include double tops and bottoms, reversal days, head and shoulders, and island tops and bottoms.

Yet the term "reversal pattern" is somewhat of a misnomer. Hearing that term may lead you to think of an old trend ending abruptly and then reversing to a new trend. This rarely happens. Trend reversals usually occur slowly, in stages, as the underlying psychology shifts gears.

A trend reversal signal implies that the prior trend is likely to change, but not necessarily reverse. This is very important to understand. Compare an uptrend to a car traveling forward at 30 m.p.h. The car's red brake lights go on and the car stops. The brake light was the reversal indicator showing that the prior trend (that is, the car moving forward) was about to end. But now that the car is stationary will the driver then decide to put the car in reverse? Will he remained stopped? Will he decide to go forward again? Without more clues we do not know.

Exhibits 4.1 through 4.3 are some examples of what can happen after a top reversal signal appears. The prior uptrend, for instance, could convert into a period of sideways price action. Then a new and opposite trend lower could start. (See Exhibit 4.1.) Exhibit 4.2 shows how an old uptrend can resume. Exhibit 4.3 illustrates how an uptrend can abruptly reverse into a downtrend.

It is prudent to think of reversal patterns as trend change patterns. I was tempted to use the term "trend change patterns" instead of "reversal patterns" in this book. However, to keep consistent with other tech-

EXHIBIT 4.1. Top Reversal   **EXHIBIT 4.2.** Top Reversal   **EXHIBIT 4.3.** Top Reversal

nical analysis literature, I decided to use the term reversal patterns. Remember that when I say "reversal pattern" it means only that the prior trend should change but not necessarily reverse.

Recognizing the emergence of reversal patterns can be a valuable skill. Successful trading entails having both the trend and probability on your side. The reversal indicators are the market's way of providing a road sign, such as "Caution—Trend in Process of Change." In other words, the market's psychology is in transformation. You should adjust your trading style to reflect the new market environment. There are many ways to trade in and out of positions with reversal indicators. We shall discuss them throughout the book.

An important principle is to place a new position (based on a reversal signal) only if that signal is in the direction of the major trend. Let us say, for example, that in a bull market, a top reversal pattern appears. This bearish signal would not warrant a short sale. This is because the major trend is still up. It would, however, signal a liquidation of longs. If there was a prevailing downtrend, this same top reversal formation could be used to place short sales.

I have gone into detail about the subject of reversal patterns because most of the candlestick indicators are reversals. Now, let us turn our attention to the first group of these candlestick reversal indicators, the hammer and hanging-man lines.

HAMMER AND HANGING-MAN LINES

Exhibit 4.4 shows candlesticks with long lower shadows and small real bodies. The real bodies are near the top of the daily range. The variety of candlestick lines shown in the exhibit are fascinating in that either line can be bullish or bearish depending on where they appear in a trend. If either of these lines emerges during a downtrend it is a signal that the downtrend should end. In such a scenario, this line is labeled a *hammer*,

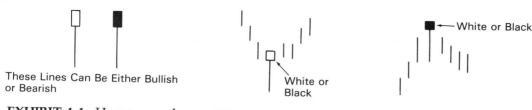

EXHIBIT 4.4. Hammer and Hanging Man Candlesticks

EXHIBIT 4.5. Hammer

EXHIBIT 4.6. Hanging Man

as in "the market is hammering out" a base. See Exhibit 4.5. Interestingly, the actual Japanese word for this line is *takuri*. This word means something to the affect of "trying to gauge the depth of the water by feeling for its bottom."

If either of the lines in Exhibit 4.4 emerge after a rally it tells you that the prior move may be ending. Such a line is ominously called a *hanging man* (see Exhibit 4.6). The name hanging man is derived from the fact that it looks like a hanging man with dangling legs.

It may seem unusual that the same candlestick line can be both bullish and bearish. Yet, for those familiar with Western island tops and island bottoms you will recognize that the identical idea applies here. The island formation is either bullish or bearish depending on where it is in a trend. An island after a prolonged uptrend is bearish, while the same island pattern after a downtrend is bullish.

The hammer and hanging man can be recognized by three criteria:

1. The real body is at the upper end of the trading range. The color of the real body is not important.
2. A long lower shadow should be twice the height of the real body.
3. It should have no, or a very short, upper shadow.

The longer the lower shadow, the shorter the upper shadow and the smaller the real body the more meaningful the bullish hammer or bearish hanging man. Although the real body of the hammer or hanging man can be white or black, it is slightly more bullish if the real body of the hammer is white, and slightly more bearish if the real body of the hanging man is black. If a hammer has a white real body it means the market sold off sharply during the session and then bounced back to close at, or near, the session's high. This could have bullish ramifications. If a hanging man has a black real body, it shows that the close could not get back to the opening price level. This could have potentially bearish implications.

It is especially important that you wait for bearish confirmation with the hanging man. The logic for this has to do with how the hanging-man line is generated. Usually in this kind of scenario the market is full of bullish energy. Then the hanging man appears. On the hanging-man day, the market opens at or near the highs, then sharply sells off, and then rallies to close at or near the highs. This might not be the type of price action that would let you think the hanging man could be a top reversal. But this type of price action now shows once the market starts to sell off, it has become vulnerable to a fast break.

If the market opens lower the next day, those who bought on the open or close of the hanging-man day are now left "hanging" with a losing position. Thus, the general principle for the hanging man; the greater the down gap between the real body of the hanging-man day and the opening the next day, the more likely the hanging man will be a top. Another bearish verification could be a black real body session with a lower close than the hanging-man sessions close.

Exhibit 4.7 is an excellent example of how the same line can be bearish (as in the hanging-man line on July 3) or bullish (the hammer on July 23). Although both the hanging man and hammer in this example have black bodies, the color of the real body is not of major importance.

Exhibit 4.8 shows another case of the dual nature of these lines. There is a bearish hanging man in mid-April that signaled the end of the

EXHIBIT 4.7. Soybean Oil—December, 1990, Daily (Hanging Man and Hammer)

EXHIBIT 4.8. Dow Jones Industrials—1990, Daily (Hanging Man and Hammer)

rally which had started with the bullish hammer on April 2. A variation of a hanging man emerged in mid-March. Its lower shadow was long, but not twice the height of the real body. Yet the other criteria (a real body at the upper end of the daily range and almost no upper shadow) were met. It was also confirmed by a lower close the next day. This line, although not an ideal hanging man, did signal the end of the upturn which started a month earlier. Candlestick charting techniques, like other charting or pattern recognition techniques, have guidelines. But, they are not rigid rules.

As discussed above, there are certain aspects that increase the importance of hanging-man and hammer lines. But, as shown in the hanging man of mid-March, a long lower shadow may not have to be twice the height of the real body in order to give a reversal signal. The longer the lower shadow, the more perfect the pattern.

Exhibit 4.9 shows a series of bullish hammers numbered 1 to 4 (hammer 2 is considered a hammer in spite of its minute upper shadow). The interesting feature of this chart is the buy signal given early in 1990. New lows appeared at hammers 3 and 4 as prices moved under the July lows at hammer 2. Yet, there was no continuation to the downside. The bears had their chance to run with the ball. They fumbled. The two bullish

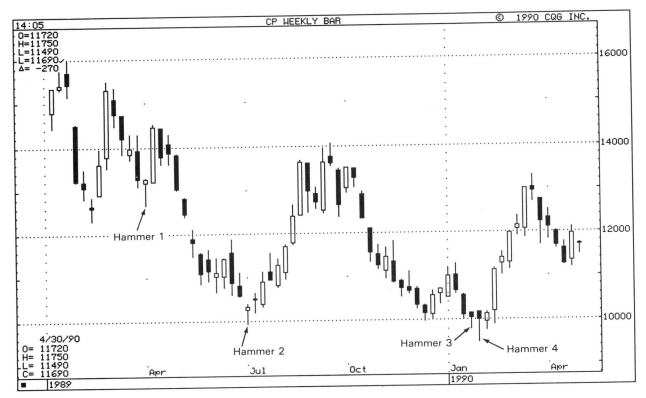

EXHIBIT 4.9. Copper—Weekly (Hammers)

hammers (3 and 4) show the bulls regained control. Hammer 3 was not an ideal hammer since the lower shadow was not twice the height of the real body. This line did reflect, however, the failure of the bears to maintain new lows. The following week's hammer reinforced the conclusion that a bottom reversal was likely to occur.

In Exhibit 4.10 hammers 1 and 3 are bottoms. Hammer 2 signaled the end of the prior downtrend as the trend shifted from down to neutral. Hammer 4 did not work. This hammer line brings out an important point about hammers (or any of the other patterns I discuss). They should be viewed in the context of the prior price action. In this context, look at hammer 4. The day before this hammer, the market formed an extremely bearish candlestick line. It was a long, black day with a shaven head and a shaven bottom (that is, it opened on its high and closed on its low). This manifested strong downside momentum. Hammer 4 also punctured the old support level of January 24. Considering the afore-mentioned bearish factors, it would be prudent to wait for confirmation that the bulls were in charge again before acting on hammer 4. For example, a white candlestick which closed higher than the close of hammer 4 might have been viewed as a confirmation.

Drawing the intra-day chart using candlesticks shows the high, low, open, and close of the session (see Exhibit 4.11). For example, an hourly

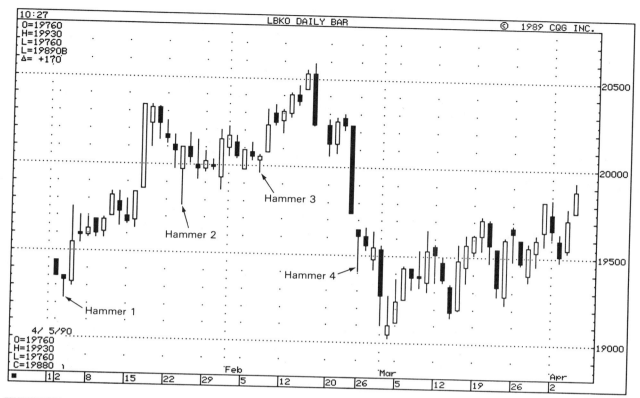

EXHIBIT 4.10. Lumber—May, 1990, Daily (Hammers)

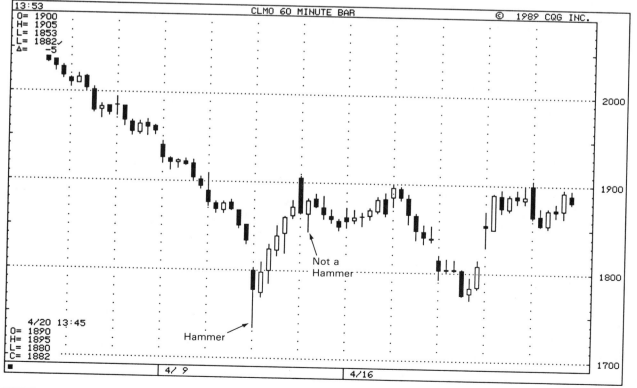

EXHIBIT 4.11. Crude Oil—June, 1990, Intra-day (Hammer)

session would have a candlestick line that uses the opening and close for that hour in order to determine the real body. The high and low for that hour would be used for the upper and lower shadows. By looking closely at this chart, one can see that a hammer formed during the first hour on April 11. Like hammer 4 in Exhibit 4.10, prices gapped lower but the white candlestick which followed closed higher. This helped to confirm a bottom.

The second hourly line on April 12, although in the shape of a hammer, was not a true hammer. A hammer is a bottom reversal pattern. One of the criterion for a hammer is that there should be a downtrend (even a minor one) in order for the hammer to reverse that trend. This line is not a hanging man either since a hanging man should appear after an uptrend. In this case, if this line arose near the highs of the prior black candlestick session, it would have been considered a hanging man.

Exhibit 4.12 shows a hammer in early April that successfully called the end of the major decline which had began months earlier. The long lower shadow, (many times the height of the real body) a small real body, and no upper shadow made this a classic hammer.

Exhibit 4.13 shows a classic hanging-man pattern. New highs were made for the move via an opening gap on the hanging-man day. The

EXHIBIT 4.12. Nikkei—1990, Daily (Hammer)

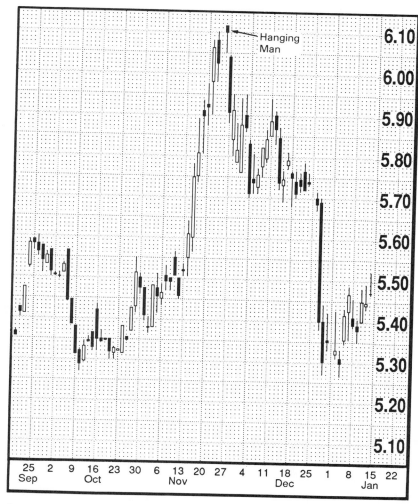

EXHIBIT 4.13. Silver—May 1990, Daily (Hanging Man)

market then gaps lower leaving all those new longs, who bought on the hanging man's open or close, left "hanging" with a losing position.

In Exhibit 4.14 we see that the rally, which began in early February, terminated with the arrival of two consecutive hanging-man lines. The importance of bearish confirmation after the hanging-man line is reflected in this chart. One method of bearish confirmation would be for the next day's open to be under the hanging man's real body. Note that after the appearance of the first hanging man, the market opened higher. However, after the second hanging man, when the market opened under the hanging man's real body, the market backed off.

Exhibit 4.15 illustrates that a black real body day, with a lower close after a hanging-man day, can be another method of bearish confirmation. Lines 1, 2, and 3 were a series of hanging-man lines. Lack of bearish confirmation after lines 1 and 2 meant the uptrend was still in force.

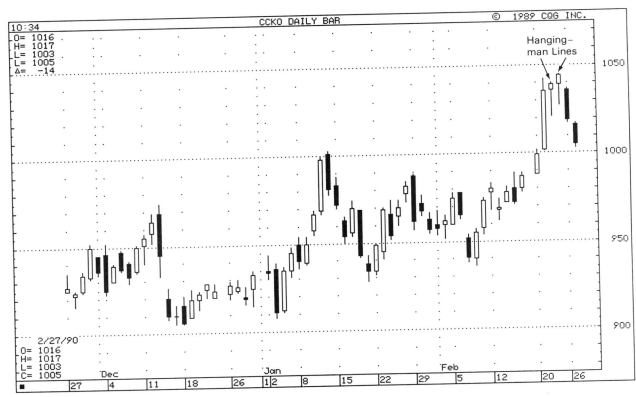

EXHIBIT 4.14. Cocoa—May 1990, Daily (Hanging Man)

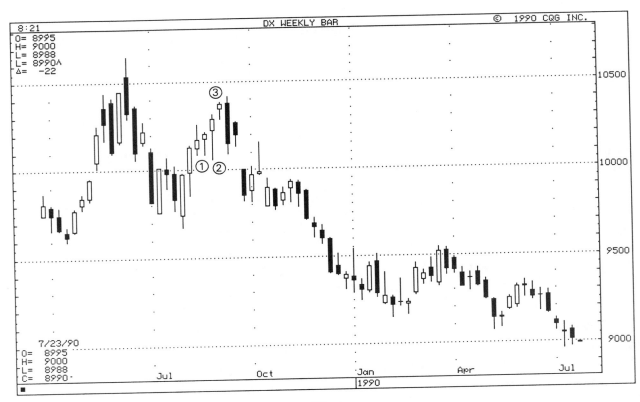

EXHIBIT 4.15. Dollar Index—Weekly (Hanging Man)

Observe hanging man 3. The black candlestick which followed provided the bearish confirmation of this hanging man line. Although the market opened about unchanged after hanging man 3, by the time of its close, just about anyone who bought on the opening or closing of hanging man 3 was "hanging" in a losing trade. (In this case, the selloff on the long black candlestick session was so severe that anyone who bought on the hanging-man day—not just those who bought on the open and close—were left stranded in a losing position.)

Exhibit 4.16 shows an extraordinary advance in the orange juice market from late 1989 into early 1990. Observe where this rally stopped. It stopped at the hanging man made in the third week of 1990. This chart illustrates the point that *a reversal pattern does not mean that prices will reverse*, as we discussed in Chapter 3. A reversal indicator implies that the prior trend should end. That is exactly what happened here. After the appearance of the hanging-man reversal pattern, the prior uptrend ended with the new trend moving sideways.

Another hanging man appeared in July. This time prices quickly reversed from up to down. But, as we have discussed previously, this scenario should not always be expected with a top trend reversal.

Exhibit 4.17 illustrates a classic hanging-man pattern in May. It shows

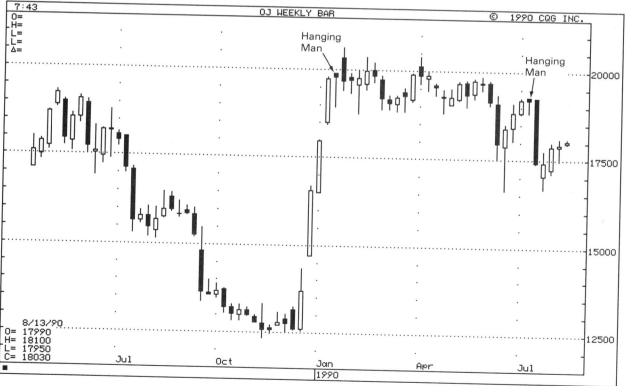

EXHIBIT 4.16. Orange Juice—Weekly (Hanging Man)

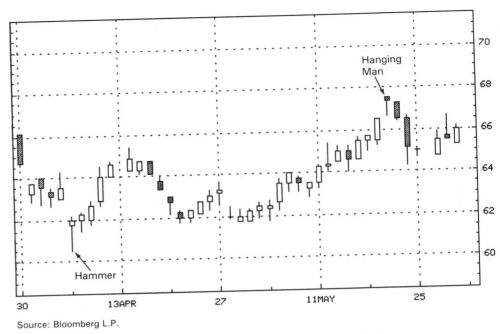

Source: Bloomberg L.P.

EXHIBIT 4.17. American Airlines—1989, Daily (Hanging Man)

a very small real body, no upper shadow, and a long lower shadow. The next day's black real body confirmed this hanging man and indicated a time to vacate longs. (Note the bullish hammer in early April.)

ENGULFING PATTERN

The hammer and hanging man are individual candlestick lines. As previously discussed, they can send important signals about the market's health. Most candlestick signals, however, are based on combinations of individual candlestick lines. The *engulfing pattern* is the first of these multiple candlestick line patterns. The engulfing pattern is a major reversal signal with two opposite color real bodies composing this pattern.

Exhibit 4.18 shows a *bullish engulfing pattern*. The market is in a downtrend, then a white bullish real body wraps around, or engulfs, the prior period's black real body. This shows buying pressure has overwhelmed selling pressure. Exhibit 4.19 illustrates a *bearish engulfing pattern*. Here the market is trending higher. The white real body engulfed by a black body is the signal for a top reversal. This shows the bears have taken over from the bulls.

There are three criteria for an engulfing pattern:

1. The market has to be in a clearly definable uptrend or downtrend, even if the trend is short term.

EXHIBIT 4.18. Bullish Engulfing Pattern

EXHIBIT 4.19. Bearish Engulfing Pattern

2. Two candlesticks comprise the engulfing pattern. The second real body must engulf the prior real body (it need not engulf the shadows).

3. The second real body of the engulfing pattern should be the opposite color of the first real body. (The exception to this rule is if the first real body of the engulfing pattern is so small it is almost a doji (or is a doji). Thus, after an extended downtrend, a tiny white real body engulfed by a very large white real body could be a bottom reversal. In an uptrend, a minute black real body enveloped by a very large black real body could be a bearish reversal pattern).

The closest analogy to the Japanese candlestick engulfing pattern is the *Western reversal day.* A Western reversal day occurs when, during an uptrend (or downtrend), a new high (or low) is made with prices closing under (or above) the prior day's close. You will discover that the engulfing pattern may give reversal signals not available with the Western reversal day. This may allow you to get a jump on those who use traditional reversal days as a reversal signal. This is probed in Exhibits 4.21, 4.22, and 4.23.

Some factors that would increase the likelihood that an engulfing pattern would be an important reversal indicator would be:

1. If the first day of the engulfing pattern has a very small real body and the second day has a very long real body. This would reflect a dissipation of the prior trend's force and then an increase in force behind the new move.

2. If the engulfing pattern appears after a protracted or very fast move. A protracted trend increases the chance that potential buyers are already long. In this instance, there may be less of a supply of new longs in order to keep the market moving up. A fast move makes the market overextended and vulnerable to profit taking.

3. If there is heavy volume on the second real body of the engulfing pattern. This could be a blow off (volume using candlestick charts is discussed in Chapter 15).

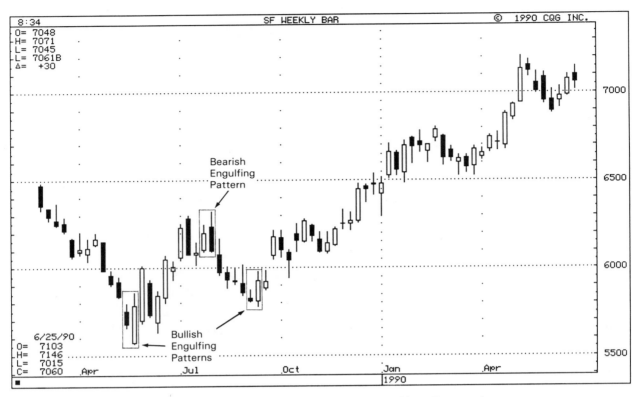

EXHIBIT 4.20. Swiss Franc—Weekly (Bullish and Bearish Engulfing Patterns)

4. If the second day of the engulfing pattern engulfs more than one real body.

Exhibit 4.20 shows that the weeks of May 15 and May 22 formed a bullish engulfing pattern. During the last two weeks of July, a bearish engulfing pattern emerged. September's bullish engulfing pattern was the bottom of the selloff prior to the major rally.

In Exhibit 4.21 a monthly crude oil chart with both the bullish and bearish engulfing patterns can be seen. In late 1985, a precipitous $20 decline began. The third and fourth month of 1986 showed the two candlestick lines of the bullish engulfing pattern. It signaled an end to this downtrend. The rally that began with this bullish engulfing pattern concluded with the bearish engulfing pattern in mid-1987. The small bullish engulfing pattern in February and March of 1988 terminated the downtrend that started with the mid-1987 bearish engulfing pattern. After this bullish engulfing pattern, the trend went from down to sideways for five months.

The black candlestick of February 1990 came within 8 ticks of engulfing the January 1990 white candlestick. Consequently, this was not a perfect bearish engulfing pattern but, with candlesticks, as with other

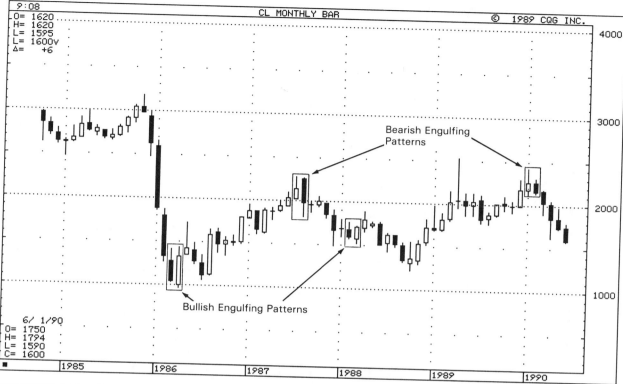

EXHIBIT 4.21. Crude Oil—Monthly (Bullish and Bearish Engulfing Pattern)

charting techniques, there should be some latitude allowed. It is safer to view this as a bearish engulfing pattern with all its inherently bearish implications than to ignore that possibility just because of 8 ticks. As with all charting techniques, there is always room for subjectivity.

The bearish engulfing patterns in 1987 and in 1990 convey an advantage provided by the engulfing pattern—it may give a reversal signal not available using the criteria for a reversal day in Western technicals. A rule for the Western top reversal day (or, in this case, reversal month) is that a new high has to be made for the move. New highs for the move were not made by the black real body periods in the bearish engulfing patterns. Thus, using the criteria for the Western reversal they would not be recognized as reversal patterns in the United States. Yet, they were reversals with the candlestick techniques.

Exhibit 4.22 shows another instance where the candlestick charts may allow one to get a jump on regular bar charting tools. Observe the price action on July 7 and 8. Here again, since there was no new high made, there was no sign of a top reversal by using the traditional Western reversal day as a gauge. Yet, with candlesticks, there is a bearish reversal signal, namely the bearish engulfing pattern, does show itself.

The two candlestick lines 1 and 2 in early June look like a bullish

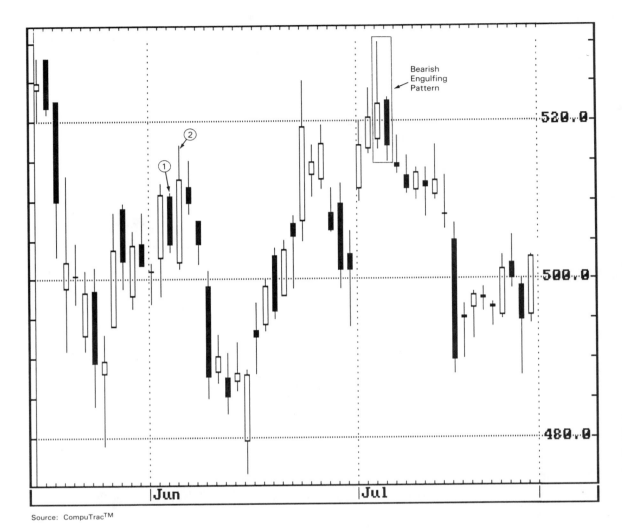

EXHIBIT 4.22. Platinum—October, 1989, Daily (Bearish Engulfing Pattern)

engulfing pattern. However, the bullish engulfing pattern is a bottom trend reversal indicator. This means it must appear after a downtrend (or sometimes at the bottom of a lateral band). In early June, when the bullish engulfing pattern appeared it did not warrant action since it did not appear in a downtrend.

Exhibit 4.23 is a series of bearish engulfing patterns. Pattern 1 dragged the market into a multi-month lateral band from its prior uptrend. Engulfing pattern 2 only called a temporary respite to the rally. Bearish engulfing patterns 3, 4, and 5 all gave reversal signals that were not available with Western technical techniques (that is, since no new highs were made for the move they were not considered reversal weeks).

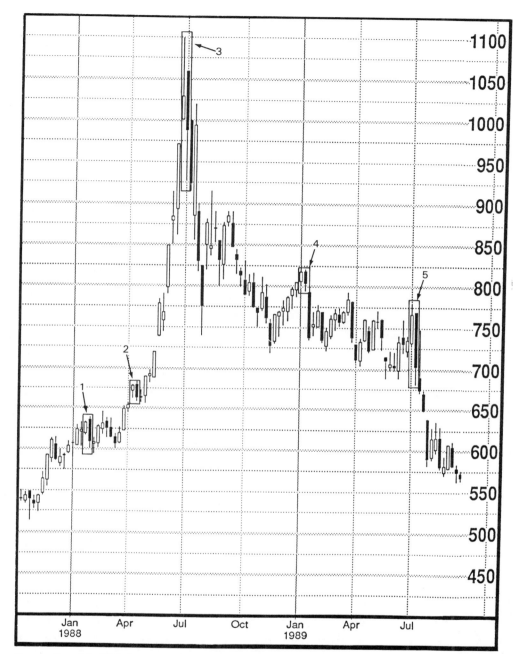

EXHIBIT 4.23.
Soybeans—Weekly
(Bearish Engulfing
Patterns)

DARK-CLOUD COVER

Our next reversal pattern is the *dark-cloud cover* (see Exhibit 4.24). It is a
two candlestick pattern that is a top reversal after a uptrend or, at times,
at the top of a congestion band. The first day of this two candlestick pattern is a strong white real body. The second day's price opens above the

EXHIBIT 4.24. Dark-cloud Cover

prior session's high (that is, above the top of the upper shadow). However, by the end of the second day's session, the market closes near the low of the day and well within the prior day's white body. The greater the degree of penetration into the white real body the more likely a top will occur. Some Japanese technicians require more than a 50% penetration of the black session's close into the white real body. If the black candlestick does not close below the halfway point of the white candlestick it may be best to wait for more bearish confirmation following the dark cloud cover.

The rationale behind this bearish pattern is readily explained. The market is in an uptrend. A strong white candlestick is followed by a gap higher on the next session's opening. Thus far, the bulls are in complete control. But then no continuation of the rally occurs! In fact, the market closes at or near the lows of the day moving well within the prior day's real body. In such a scenario, the longs will have second thoughts about their position. Those who were waiting for selling short now have a benchmark to place a stop—at the new high of the second day of the dark-cloud cover pattern.

The following is a list of some factors that intensify the importance of dark-cloud covers:

1. The greater the degree of penetration of the black real body's close into the prior white real body, the greater the chance for a top. If the black real body covers the prior day's entire white body, a bearish engulfing pattern would occur. The dark-cloud cover's black real body only gets partially into the white body. Think of the dark-cloud cover as a partial solar eclipse blocking out part of the sun (that is, covers only part of the prior white body). The bearish engulfing pattern can be viewed as a total solar eclipse blocking out the entire sun (that is, covers the entire white body). A bearish engulfing pattern, consequently, is a more meaningful top reversal. If a long, white real body closes above the highs of the dark-cloud cover, or the bearish engulfing pattern, it could presage another rally.

2. During a prolonged uptrend, if there is a strong white day which opens on its low (that is, a shaven bottom) and closes on its high (that is, a shaven head) and the next day reveals a long black real body day, opening on its high and closing on its low, then a shaven head and shaven bottom black day have occurred.

3. If the second body (that is, the black body) of the dark-cloud cover opens above a major resistance level and then fails, it would prove the bulls were unable to take control of the market.

4. If, on the opening of the second day there is very heavy volume, a buying blow off could have occurred. For example, heavy volume at a new opening high could mean that many new buyers have decided to jump aboard ship. Then the market sells offs. It probably won't be too long before this multitude of new longs (and old longs who have ridden the uptrend) realize that the ship they jumped onto is the *Titanic.* For futures traders, very high opening interest can be another warning.

Exhibit 4.25 demonstrates the difference between the dark-cloud cover and the bearish engulfing pattern. The two candlesticks in June 1989 constitute a dark-cloud cover. A long, white real body is followed by a long, black real body. The black real body opened on a new high for the move and then closed near its lows and well into the prior day's

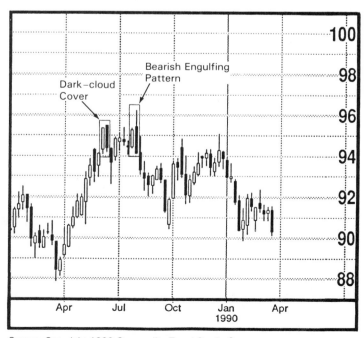

EXHIBIT 4.25. Municipal Bonds—Weekly (Dark-cloud Cover and Bearish Engulfing Pattern)

EXHIBIT 4.26. Crude Oil—July 1990, Daily (Dark-cloud Cover)

white real body. The municipal bond market backed off after this top reversal appeared. The final *coup de grace* came a few weeks later when the bearish engulfing pattern materialized. We see how the dark-cloud cover's black real body covered only part of the prior white real body. The black real body of the bearish engulfing pattern enveloped the entire previous white real body.

In Exhibit 4.26 three dark-cloud covers can be seen. Other bearish signals confirmed each of these patterns. Let us look at them on an individual basis.

1. *Dark-cloud cover 1.* This is a variation on the ideal dark-cloud cover pattern. In this dark-cloud cover, the second day's black real body opened at the prior day's high instead of above it. It was still only a warning sign but it was viewed as a negative factor. This dark-cloud cover also signified a failed attempt by the bulls to take out resistance at the mid-February highs.

2. *Dark-cloud cover 2.* Besides this dark-cloud cover, there was another reason for caution at this $21 level. A technical axiom is that a prior support level, once broken, can convert to new resistance. That is what happened at $21. Note how the old $21 support, once breached

on March 9, converted to resistance. The failed rally attempt during the dark-cloud cover pattern during the first two days of April proved this resistance. (Chapter 11 examines this concept of the interchangeability of support and resistance.)

3. *Dark-cloud cover 3.* This shows that there was also a failure at a resistance zone made during the late April highs.

These are instances where the bearish dark-cloud cover coincided with resistance levels. This concept, where more than one technical indicator corroborates another, is important. It is the main focus of the second half of this book where the combination of candlestick techniques with other technical tools is discussed.

Exhibit 4.27 shows that during the early part of March, dark-cloud cover 1 halted a two-week rally. A week-long correction ensued. Two more dark-cloud covers formed in April. Dark-cloud cover 2 hinted that the prior sharp two-day rally was probably over. Dark-cloud cover 3, in mid-April, was especially bearish. Why did this dark-cloud cover turn out to be so negative? The reason has to do with the psychology of this pattern.

As noted previously, the rationale behind the negative aspect of the

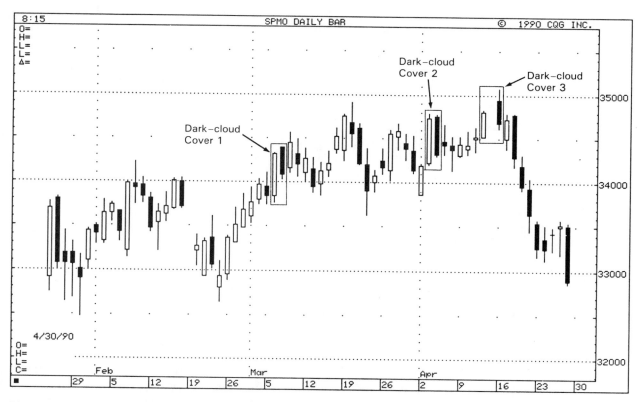

EXHIBIT 4.27. S&P—June 1990 (Dark-cloud Covers)

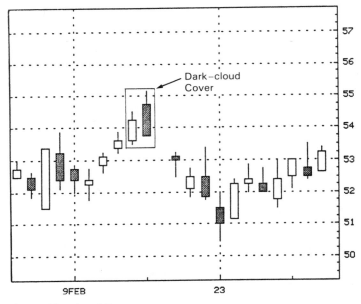

EXHIBIT 4.28. Bristol Myers—1990, Daily   Source: Bloomberg L.P.

dark-cloud cover is the result of a new high on the open, with the market closing deeply into the prior white real body. What would happen, though, if, on the second day of the dark-cloud cover, the open penetrates the highs not from days, or even weeks ago, but from months ago and then fails at these new highs? This would produce very negative connotations. This is the scenario that unfolded in April. The highest levels in at least three months were touched on the black candlestick session of dark-cloud cover 3. This high failed to hold and prices closed well within the prior white real body.

In Exhibit 4.28, we see that the price incline commencing February 10 came to an abrupt halt with the mid-February dark-cloud cover.

PIERCING PATTERN

During many of my speaking engagements, after I have discussed the bearish dark-cloud cover pattern, it's not too long before I am asked if there is an opposite formation. Yes, there is and it is called a *piercing pattern.* Just as a dark-cloud cover is a top reversal, its opposite, the piercing pattern, is a bottom reversal (see Exhibit 4.29). It is composed of two candlesticks in a falling market. The first candlestick is a black real body day and the second is a long, white real body day. This white day opens sharply lower, under the low of the prior black day. Then prices

EXHIBIT 4.29. Piercing Pattern

push higher, creating a relatively long, white real body that closes above the mid-point of the prior day's black real body.

The bullish piercing pattern is akin to the bullish engulfing pattern. In the bullish engulfing pattern the white real body engulfs the previous black real body. With the bullish piercing pattern, the white real body only pierces the prior black body. In the piercing pattern, the greater the degree of penetration into the black real body, the more likely it will be a bottom reversal. An ideal piercing pattern will have a white real body that pushes more than halfway into the prior session's black real body. If the market closes under the lows of the bullish engulfing pattern or the piercing pattern by way of a long black candlestick, then another downleg should resume.

The psychology behind the piercing pattern is as follows: The market is in a downtrend. The bearish black real body reinforces this view. The next day the market opens lower via a gap. The bears are watching the market with contentment. Then the market surges toward the close, managing not only to close unchanged from the prior day's close, but sharply above that level. The bears will be second guessing their position. Those who are looking to buy would say new lows could not hold and perhaps it is time to step in from the long side.

The piercing pattern signal increases in importance based on the same factors (1) through (4) as with the dark-cloud cover, but in reverse. (See previous section.) In the section on the dark-cloud cover, I mentioned that although some Japanese traders like to see the black real body close more that midway in the prior white candlestick, there is some flexibility to this rule. With the piercing pattern, there is less flexibility. The piercing pattern's white candlestick should push more than halfway into the black candlestick's real body. The reason for less latitude with the bullish piercing pattern than with the bearish dark-cloud cover pattern is the fact that the Japanese have three other patterns called the *on-neck,* the *in-neck,* and the *thrusting pattern* (see Exhibits 4.30 to 4.32) that have the same basic formation as the piercing pattern, but which are viewed as bearish signals since the white real body gets less than halfway into the black's real body.

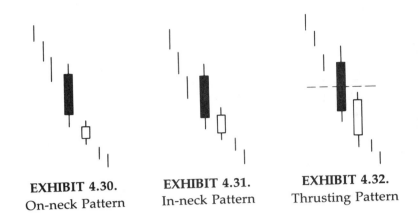

EXHIBIT 4.30.
On-neck Pattern

EXHIBIT 4.31.
In-neck Pattern

EXHIBIT 4.32.
Thrusting Pattern

Thus these three potentially bearish patterns (Exhibits 4.30 to 4.32) and the bullish piercing pattern (Exhibit 4.29) all have the same form. The difference between them is in the degree of penetration by the white candlestick into the black candlestick's real body. The on-neck pattern's white candlestick (usually a small one) closes near the low of the previous session. The in-neck pattern's white candlestick closes slightly into the prior real body (it should also be a small white candlestick). The thrusting pattern should be a longer white candlestick that is stronger than the in-neck pattern but still does not close above the middle of the prior black real body.

With these patterns, as prices move under the white candlestick's low, the trader knows that it's time to sell. (Note that the thrusting pattern in Exhibit 4.32 is bearish in a declining market, but as part of a rising market, would be considered bullish. The thrusting pattern is also bullish if it occurs twice within several days of each other.)

It is not important to remember the individual patterns in Exhibits 4.30 to 4.32. Just remember the concept that the white candlestick should push more than halfway into the black candlestick's real body to send a bottom reversal signal.

In Exhibit 4.33, the bears successfully knocked the market to new lows for the move on April 27 as shown by the long black day. The next day the market opened lower. This opening turned out to be the low of the day and Boeing closed well within the prior day's black real body. The two candlesticks on April 27 and 28 created the bullish piercing pattern.

Exhibit 4.34 shows a classic piercing pattern during the week of March 26. Note how the white real body followed a very weak long, black real body. The white day opened on a new low for the move. The strong close that day, which pushed well into the previous black real body, was a powerful indication that the bears lost control of the market. The white day was a very strong session. It opened on its low (that

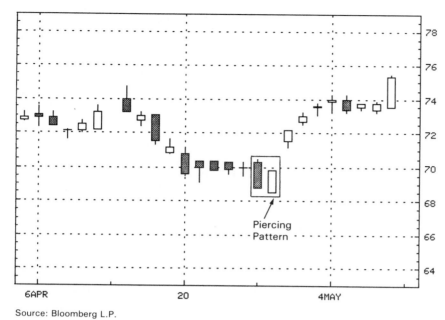

EXHIBIT 4.33. Boeing—1990, Daily (Piercing Pattern)

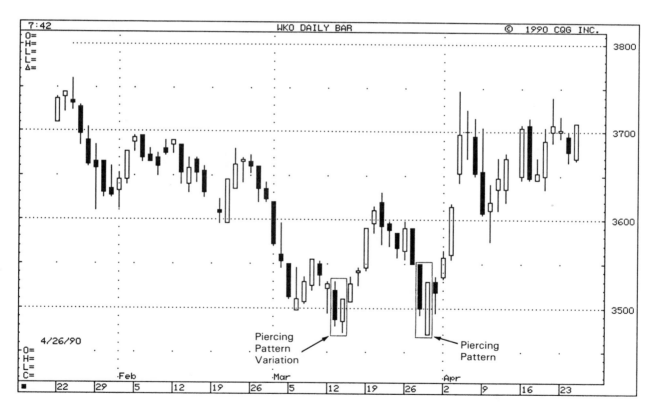

EXHIBIT 4.34. Wheat—May 1990, Daily (Piercing Pattern)

is, a shaven bottom) and closed its high (that is, a shaven head). Note how this bullish piercing pattern brought to an end the selloff that commenced with the bearish engulfing pattern of March 19 and 20.

On this Wheat chart there is also a variation of the piercing pattern during the week of March 12. The reason it is a variation is because the white real body opened under the prior day's real body, but not under the prior day's low. Nonetheless, because the white real body closed more than 50% into the prior day's black real body it was a warning sign that the prior downleg was running out of steam.

Exhibit 4.35 illustrates how candlestick patterns can help the analyst get a quick sense of the market's health. During the latter part of February 1990, a broker asked me what I thought of oats. I rarely monitor oats. Nonetheless, I retrieved the candlestick chart shown in Exhibit 4.35 and told him that the downtrend was probably over. Why? I had noticed that during the week of February 20, an almost classic piercing pattern appeared. I also saw this piercing pattern coincided with a successful test of the early February lows. This increased the chance that a double bottom had been built.

Exhibit 4.36 illustrates that the downtrend, which began with the bearish engulfing pattern in late 1984, ended in mid-1987 with the

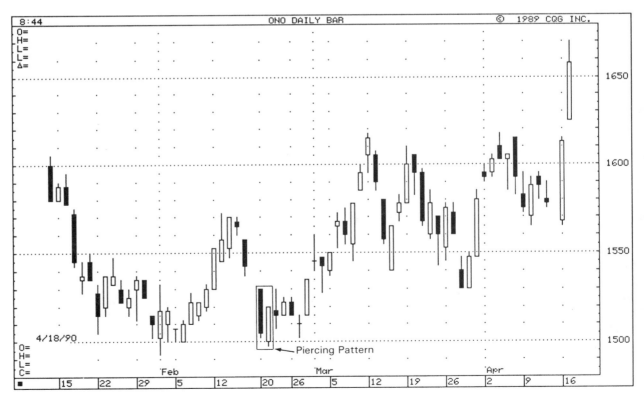

EXHIBIT 4.35. Oats—July 1990, Daily (Piercing Pattern)

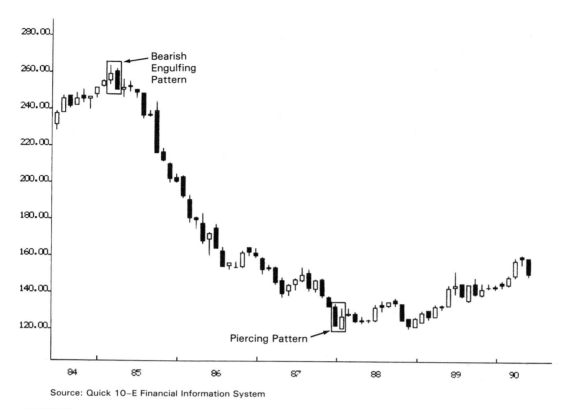

Source: Quick 10–E Financial Information System

EXHIBIT 4.36. Cash Yen, Monthly (Piercing Pattern)

appearance of this piercing pattern. Although the market did not rally after this bottom reversal signal, the signal did forecast the end of the selling pressure that had pulled the market down from mid-1984 to mid-1987. After the piercing pattern the market stabilized for a year, and then rallied.

CHAPTER 5

STARS

· ·

用人に飽きはない

"One cannot be too cautious"

One group of fascinating reversal patterns is that which includes stars. A *star* is a small real body that gaps away from the large real body preceding it (see Exhibit 5.1). It is still a star as long as the star's real body does not overlap the prior real body. The color of the star is not important. Stars can occur at tops or at bottoms (sometimes a star during a downtrend is labeled a *rain drop*). If the star is a doji instead of a small real body, it is called a *doji star* (see Exhibit 5.2).

The star, especially the doji star, is a warning that the prior trend may be ending. The star's small real body represents a stalemate in the tug of war between the bulls and bears. In a strong uptrend, the bulls are in charge. With the emergence of a star after a long white candlestick in an uptrend, it is a signal of a shift from the buyers being in control to a deadlock between the buying and selling forces. This deadlock may have occurred either because of a diminution in the buying force or an increase in the selling force. Either way, the star tells us the prior uptrend power has dissipated and the market is vulnerable to a setback.

The same is true, but in reverse, for a star in a downtrend. That is, if a star follows a long black candlestick in a downtrend, it reflects a change in the market environment. For example, during the downtrend the bears were in command but a change is seen in the advent of the star, which signals an environment in which the bulls and the bears are more in equilibrium. The downward energy has thus been cooled. This is not a favorable scenario for a continuation of the bear market.

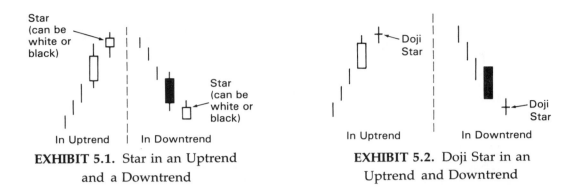

EXHIBIT 5.1. Star in an Uptrend and a Downtrend

EXHIBIT 5.2. Doji Star in an Uptrend and Downtrend

The star is part of four reversal patterns including:

1. the *evening star;*
2. the *morning star;*
3. the *doji star;* and
4. the *shooting star.*

In any of these star patterns the real body of the star can be white or black.

THE MORNING STAR

The *morning star* (see Exhibit 5.3) is a bottom reversal pattern. Its name is derived because, like the morning star (the planet Mercury) that foretells the sunrise, it presages higher prices. It is comprised of a tall, black real body followed by a small real body which gaps lower (these two lines comprise a basic star pattern). The third day is a white real body that moves well within the first period's black real body. This pattern is a signal that the bulls have seized control. I will break down this three-candlestick pattern into its components in order to understand the rationale behind this last statement.

EXHIBIT 5.3. Morning Star

The market is in a downtrend when we see a black real body. At this time the bears are in command. Then a small real body appears. This means sellers are losing the capacity to drive the market lower. The next day, the strong white real body proves that the bulls have taken over. An ideal morning star would have a gap before and after the middle line's real body (that is, the star). This second gap is rare, but lack of it does not seem to vitiate the power of this formation.

Exhibit 5.4 shows that a bullish morning star pattern developed during December 19 through 21. The rally that began with this pattern ran out of steam with the dark-cloud cover on December 26 and 27. Exhibit 5.5 shows that the October lows were made via a star (the small real body in the first week in October). The week after this star, the market had a strong white real body. This white real body completed the morning star pattern. The black candlestick after this white body formed a dark-cloud cover. The market then temporarily backed off. The morning star nonetheless became a major bottom. Exhibit 5.6 shows a variation on the morning star in which there is more than one star (in this case there are three "stars"). Note how the third small real body session (that is, the third star) was a hammer and a bullish engulfing line.

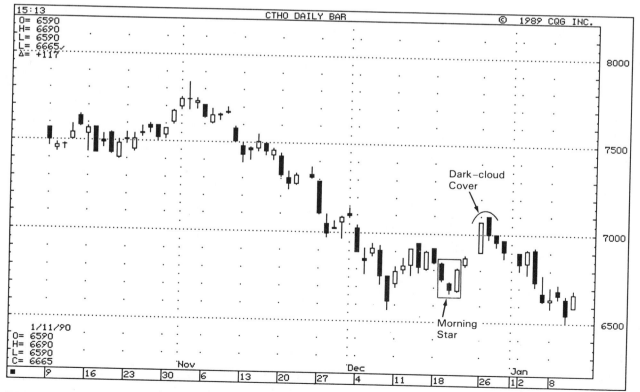

EXHIBIT 5.4. Cotton—March, 1990, Daily (Morning Star)

EXHIBIT 5.5. Crude Oil—Weekly (Morning Star)

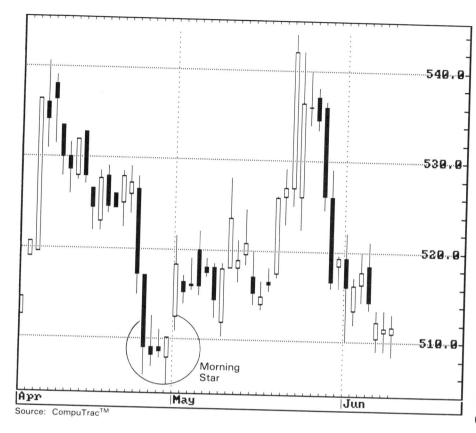

Source: CompuTrac™

EXHIBIT 5.6. Silver—September 1990, Daily (Morning Star)

THE EVENING STAR

The evening star is the bearish counterpart of the morning star pattern. It is aptly named because the evening star (the planet Venus) appears just before darkness sets in. Since the evening star is a top reversal it should be acted on if it arises after an uptrend. Three lines compose the evening star (see Exhibit 5.7). The first two lines are a long, white real body followed by a star. The star is the first hint of a top. The third line corroborates a top and completes the three-line pattern of the evening star. The third line is a black real body that moves sharply into the first periods white real body. I like to compare the evening star pattern to a traffic light. The traffic light goes from green (the bullish white real body)

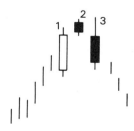

EXHIBIT 5.7. Evening Star

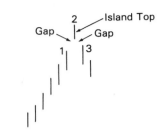

EXHIBIT 5.8. Western Island Top

EXHIBIT 5.9. Dow Jones Industrials—Weekly, 1987 (Evening Star)

to yellow (the star's warning signal) to red (the black real body confirms the prior trend has stopped).

In principle, an evening star should have a gap between the first and second real bodies and then another gap between the second and third real bodies. However, from my experience this second gap is rarely seen and is not necessary for the success of this pattern. The main concern should be the extent of the intrusion of the third day's black real body into the first day's white real body.

At first glance Exhibit 5.7 is like an island top reversal as used by Western technicians. Analyzing the evening star more closely shows it furnishes a reversal signal not available with an island top (see Exhibit 5.8). For an island top, the low of session 2 has to be above the highs of sessions 1 and 3. However, the evening star only requires the low of the real body 2 to be above the high of real body 1 to be a reversal signal.

The evening star pattern shown in Exhibit 5.9 reflects the Summer of 1987 which called the high of the Dow just before the crash. (I wonder if the Japanese technicians who use candlesticks were looking at this!)

Exhibit 5.10 provides an example of how candlestick indicators can transmit a reversal signal not easily found with Western tools. The last

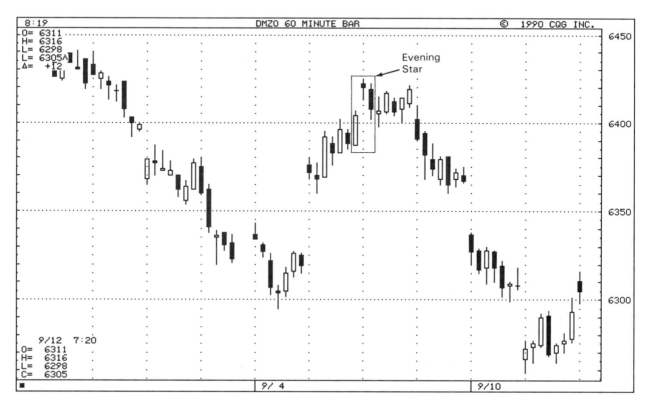

EXHIBIT 5.10. Deutschemark—December 1990, Intra-day (Evening Star)

hour on September 5 and the first two hours the next day formed an evening star pattern. The star portion of this evening star pattern would not have been an island top based on the aforementioned discussion. In this instance, candlesticks provided a top reversal indication not available with the Western island top. Also note how the rally that ended with this evening star began with the morning star on September 4.

Although more important after an uptrend, the evening star can be important at the top of a congestion band if it confirms another bearish signal. (See Exhibit 5.11.) That is what happened in the middle of April. The star portion (that is, the second day) of the evening star coincided with a resistance area. The basis for this resistance at $413 was that it was an old support level from late March. Old support often converts to new resistance. Try to remember this! It is a very useful trading rule. Chapter 11 discusses support and resistance in more detail. In any case,

Source: CompuTrac™

EXHIBIT 5.11. Gold—December 1989, Daily (Evening Star)

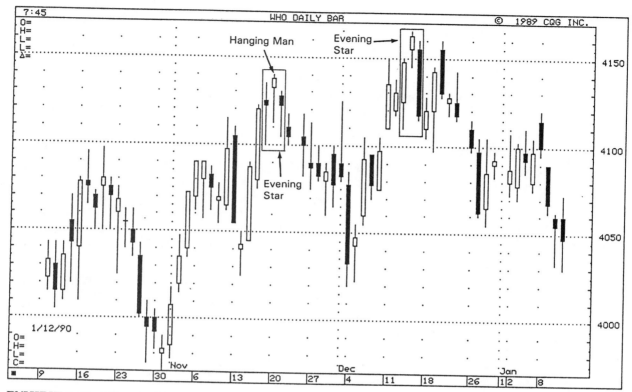

EXHIBIT 5.12. Wheat—March 1990, Daily (Evening Star)

the resistance level near $413 coincided with the appearance of the evening star thus reinforcing the negativeness of the pattern.

Exhibit 5.12 shows a well-defined evening star in mid-December. The star was preceded by a strong, white real body and followed by a weak, black real body. A variation of an evening star appeared in mid-November. The reason it was a variation is that the evening star usually has a long, white real body preceding the star, and then a black real body after the star. We did not see the long, white or black real body lines here. We view this as a top, however, not only because of its minor resemblance to an evening star pattern, but because of the hanging-man line on November 21 (the "star" portion of the evening star). The next day's opening under the hanging man's real body confirmed a top.

Some factors that would increase the likelihood that an evening or morning star could be a reversal would include:

1. If there is a gap between the first candlestick's and star's real bodies and then in the star's and third candlestick's real bodies;

2. If the third candlestick closes deeply into the first candlestick's real body;

A HISTORICAL NOTE

The full name of the evening and morning star patterns are *the three-river evening star* and the *three-river morning star*. I originally thought they were termed "three-river" evening and morning stars because each of these patterns had three candlestick lines—hence three rivers. I discovered that the origin is much more fascinating.

Nobunaga Oda, a major military figure of the late 16th century, was one of the three military leaders who unified feudal Japan (see Chapter 2). He fought a seminal battle that occurred in a very fertile rice growing province. Since rice was a gauge of wealth, Nobunaga was as determined to wrest this area as fervently as the owners were to defend it. This fertile rice area had three rivers. The heavily defended area made it difficult for Nobunaga to cross these three rivers. Victory was his when his forces finally forded these three rivers. Hence the name "three river" morning and evening star where it is difficult to change the trend. Yet, victory for the attacking army is assured when the hurdle of the "three rivers" is crossed.

3. If there is light volume on the first candlestick session and heavy volume on the third candlestick session. This would show a reduction of the force for the prior trend and an increase in the direction force of the new trend.

THE MORNING AND EVENING DOJI STARS

When a doji gaps above a real body in a rising market, or gaps under a real body in a falling market, that doji is called a *doji star*. Exhibit 5.2 shows doji stars. Doji stars are a potent warning that the prior trend is apt to change. The session after the doji should confirm the trend reversal. Accordingly, a doji star in an uptrend followed by a long, black real body that closed well into the white real body would confirm a top reversal. Such a pattern is called an *evening doji star* (see Exhibit 5.13). The evening doji star is a distinctive form of the regular evening star. The regular evening star pattern has a small real body as its star (that is, the second candlestick), but the evening doji star has a doji as its star. The evening doji star is more important because it contains a doji.

A doji star during an uptrend is often the sign of an impending top. It is important to note that if the session after the doji star is a white candlestick which gaps higher, the bearish nature of the doji star is negated.

EXHIBIT 5.13. Evening Doji Star

EXHIBIT 5.14. Morning Doji Star

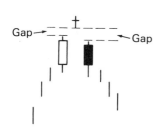

EXHIBIT 5.15. Abandoned Baby
in an Uptrend

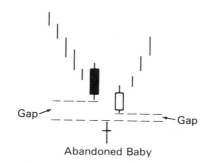

EXHIBIT 5.16. Abandoned Baby
in a Downtrend

In a downtrend, if there is a black real body, followed by a doji star, confirmation of a bottom reversal would occur if the next session was a strong, white candlestick which closed well into the black real body. That three candlestick pattern is called a *morning doji star* (see Exhibit 5.14). This type of morning star can be a meaningful bottom. If, during a downtrend, a black candlestick gaps under the doji star, the potentially bullish implications of the doji star is voided. This is why it is important to wait for confirmation in the next session or two with doji stars.

If there is an upside gap doji star (that is, the shadows do not touch) followed by a downside gap black candlestick where the shadows also do not touch, the star is considered a major top reversal signal. This is called an *abandoned baby top* (see Exhibit 5.15). This pattern is very rare!

The same is true, only in reverse, for a bottom. Specifically, if there is a doji star that has a gap before and after it (where the shadows do not touch) it should be a major bottom. This pattern is referred to as an *abandoned baby bottom* (see Exhibit 5.16). It is also extremely rare! The abandoned baby is like a Western island top or bottom where the island session would be a doji.

Exhibit 5.17 shows that a doji star in early June halted the prior price decline. It is still called a star although the shadow of the doji star bottom overlaps the prior day's black real body. When the white real body appeared after the star, confirmation of the downturn was over. The

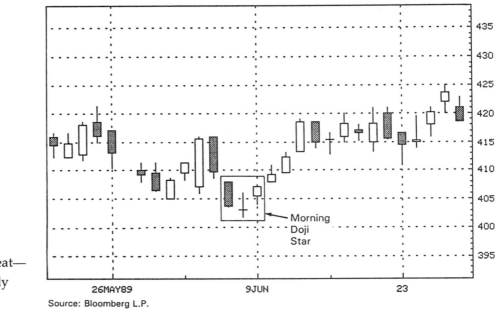

EXHIBIT 5.17. Wheat—December 1989, Daily (Morning Doji Star)

Source: Bloomberg L.P.

EXHIBIT 5.18. Coffee—September 1990, Daily (Morning Doji Star)

black real body before and the white real body after the doji star made this three-line pattern a morning doji star.

On the doji star candlestick of Exhibit 5.18, prices broke under $.85. This was a support area from early in July. The fact that the new lows could not hold is considered bullish. Add to this the morning doji star pattern and you have two reasons to suspect a bottom.

Exhibit 5.19 is an example of both an evening doji star and a regular evening star. Price action from March through May 1986 formed an evening doji star. This pattern halted a sharp rally which began just a few months previously. A selloff ensued after this evening doji star. It ended with the bullish engulfing pattern. The rally from that engulfing pattern topped during the evening star pattern of mid-1987.

In Exhibit 5.20, we see the three lines that form the evening doji star on March 17, 18, and 19. This pattern ended the rally that began with a hammer the prior week. This example again shows that certain candlestick configurations should have more latitude in the equity market. This is because, unlike futures, stock prices may open relatively unchanged from the prior close. This means that specific patterns that relate the open to the prior day's close may have to be adjusted for this fact.

In the case of Dow Chemical, note how the evening doji star was not

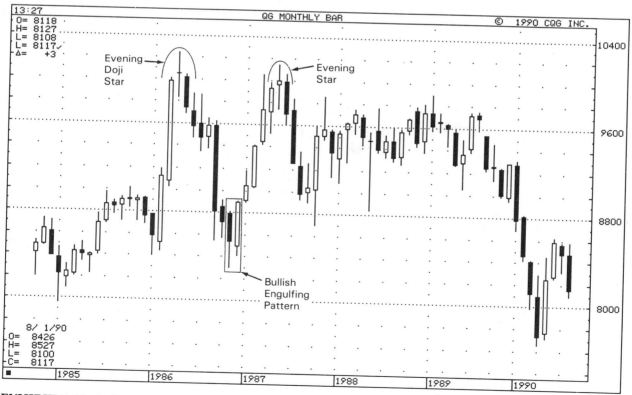

EXHIBIT 5.19. Liffe Long Gilt—Monthly (Evening Doji Star).

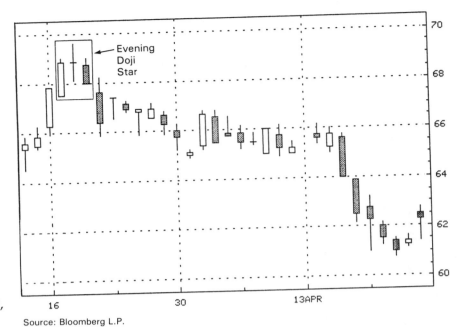

EXHIBIT 5.20. Dow
Chemical—Daily 1990,
(Evening Doji Star)

Source: Bloomberg L.P.

a true star. A doji star's real body (that is, its opening and closing price) should be over the prior day's real body. Here it was not. Therefore, allow more flexibility with candlestick indicators with equities. For those who monitor the equity markets, as you experiment with candlestick techniques, you should discover which patterns may have to be modified.

In Exhibit 5.21, one can see that a few weeks before 1987's major sell-off, an evening doji star top arose. The center candlestick of this pattern (the doji star) did not gap above the prior white candlestick as should a true star. However, as discussed in Exhibit 5.20, one should allow more latitude with this concept of gaps since stocks often open at, or very near, the prior session's close.

Exhibit 5.22 reveals a very unusual and ominous occurrence in that back-to-back evening doji patterns formed. Candlestick lines 1 through 3 formed an evening doji star. The next three sessions, lines 4 through 6, fashioned another evening doji star.

EXHIBIT 5.21.
NYSE—Weekly
(Evening Doji Star).

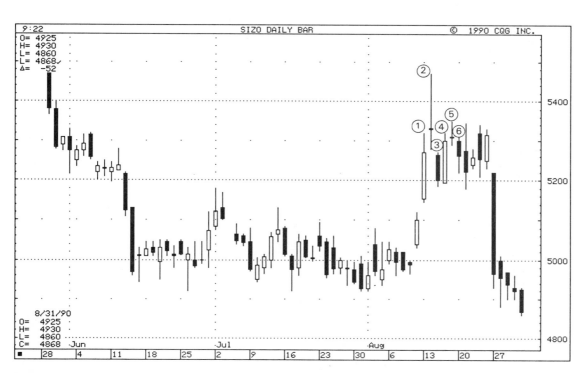

EXHIBIT 5.22. Silver—December 1990, Daily (Evening Doji Stars)

EXHIBIT 5.23. Shooting Star

THE SHOOTING STAR AND THE INVERTED HAMMER

A *shooting star* is a two-line pattern that sends a warning of an impending top. It looks like its name, a shooting star. It is usually not a major reversal signal as is the evening star. As shown in the Exhibit 5.23, the shooting star has a small real body at the lower end of its range with a long upper shadow. As with all stars, the color of the real body is not important. The shooting star pictorially tells us that the market opened near its low, then strongly rallied and finally backed off to close near the opening. In other words, that session's rally could not be sustained.

An ideal shooting star has a real body which gaps away from the prior real body. Nonetheless, as will be seen in several chart examples, this gap is not always necessary.

A shooting star shaped candlestick after a downturn could be a bullish signal. Such a line is called an *inverted hammer*. The inverted hammer line is discussed later in this chapter.

In Exhibit 5.24, one can see that on April 2, a bearish shooting star was signaling trouble overhead. Exhibit 5.25 well illustrates the shooting star and its variations. Shooting star variations include the following:

1. *Shooting star 1* is a variation on a shooting star. It is not an ideal star because there is no gap between the real bodies. It, nonetheless, proves the failure of the bulls to maintain their drive.

2. *Shooting star 2* is of little importance. It does meet part of the criteria of a shooting star (that is, a star with a small real body and long upper shadow). Yet, it fails to meet one important rule. It does not appear after an uptrend nor at the top of a congestion zone. As such, it should be viewed as a small real body day with little significance. A small real body (that is, a spinning top) reflects indecision. In the middle of a trading range indecision should be expected.

3. *Shooting star 3* has the shape of the shooting star but it is not a true star since it does not gap away from the prior real body. However, this day's shooting star should be viewed in context of the prior price action. The top of the upper shadow for shooting star 3 is an assault

EXHIBIT 5.24. Yen—24-Hour Spot, Daily, 1990 (Shooting Star)

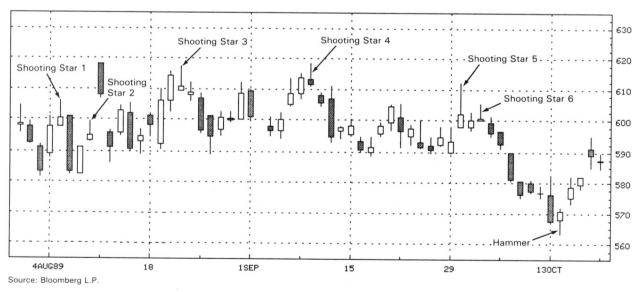

Source: Bloomberg L.P.

EXHIBIT 5.25. Soybeans—March 1990, Daily (Shooting Stars)

at the early August high at $6.18. The bulls exhausted themselves on the intra-day rally to that level. The soybeans then closed near the low of the day.

4. *Shooting star 4* is very similar to shooting star 3. It also is not an ideal shooting star since its real body did not gap away from the prior real body. Yet it was another rally attempt that faltered near $6.18. It proved that the bulls could not gain control.

(Shooting stars 3 and 4, although not ideal shooting star patterns, bring out an important point. As I said in the beginning of the book, the patterns do not have to be perfectly formed to provide a valid signal. Always view candlestick lines and patterns in the context of the other technical evidence. Thus, shooting stars 3 and 4 were not ideal, yet the shape of the shooting star line, itself, in context with the prior action, was bearish.)

5. *Shooting star 5* is another failure at resistance. You have to admire the bulls' tenacity, though, in trying to push this market higher. With each failure at the $6.18 resistance, one has to wonder how long will it be before the bulls give up. We get the answer with shooting star 6.

6. *Shooting star 6* was the final failed push. The bulls then gave way. The hammer then called the end of the selloff.

Exhibit 5.26 is another example where the shooting star pattern did not gap away from the prior real body. It was, nonetheless, a significant reversal signal. Here again let us look at the shooting star in context. It was another failure at the third quarter 1989 highs. The shooting star spelled the end of a rally that began with the hammer.

Exhibit 5.27 reveals that a classic shooting star made its appearance in the first hour of May 29. The ensuing price decline stopped at the bullish engulfing pattern on June 4.

Exhibit 5.28 illustrates two shooting stars that preceded meaningful price declines. Exhibit 5.29 shows that the shooting star was also a failure at the October/November 1989 highs. A double whammy! Exhibit 5.30 shows a pair of shooting stars. Each spelled the end of the preceding rally.

EXHIBIT 5.26. Bonds—Weekly (Shooting Star)

EXHIBIT 5.27. Corn—December 1990, Intra-day (Shooting Star)

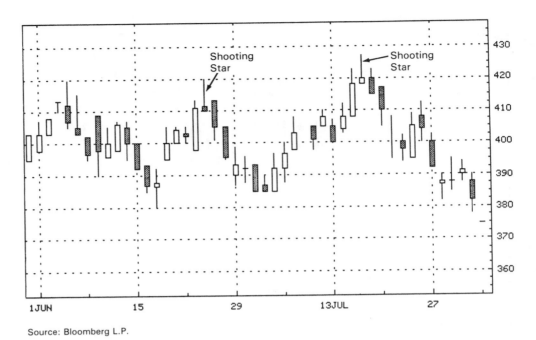

Source: Bloomberg L.P.

EXHIBIT 5.28. Barrett Resources—Daily, 1990 (Shooting Star)

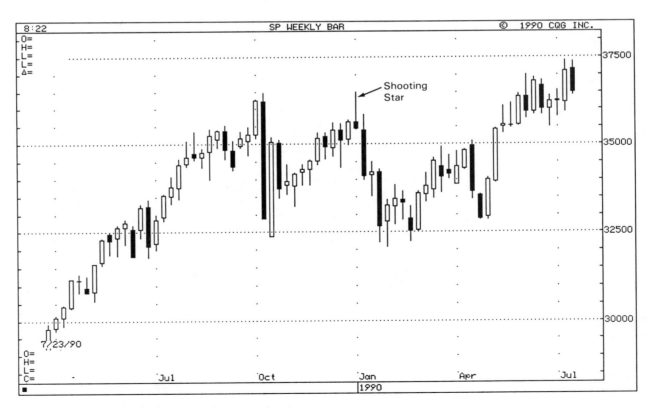

EXHIBIT 5.29. S&P—Weekly (Shooting Star)

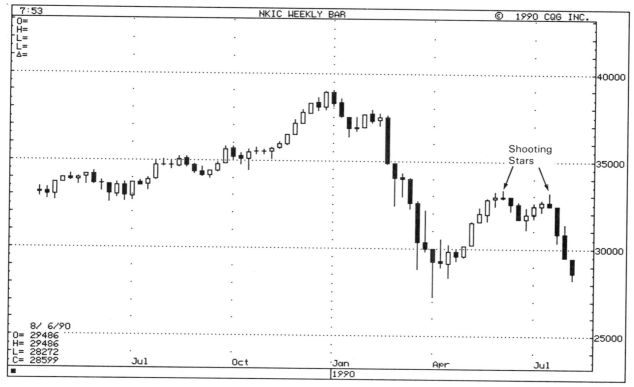

EXHIBIT 5.30. Nikkei—Weekly (Shooting Star)

THE INVERTED HAMMER

While not a star pattern, we'll discuss the inverted hammer in this section because of its resemblance to the shooting star. Exhibit 5.31 illustrates that an *inverted hammer* looks like a shooting star line with its long upper shadow and small real body at the lower end of the range. But, while the shooting star is a top reversal line, the inverted hammer is a bottom reversal line. As with a regular hammer, the inverted hammer is a bullish pattern after a downtrend.

Refer back to the corn chart discussed in Exhibit 5.27. Look at the first candlestick of the bullish engulfing pattern of June 4. It has the same appearance as the shooting star (the color of the real body does not mat-

EXHIBIT 5.31. Inverted Hammer

ter). In this instance, it appears during a downtrend and thus it becomes a potentially bullish inverted hammer.

It is important to wait for bullish verification on the session following the inverted hammer. Verification could be in the form of the next day opening above the inverted hammer's real body. The larger the gap the stronger the confirmation. A white candlestick with higher prices can also be another form of confirmation.

The reason bullish verification of the inverted hammer is important is because the price action that forms the inverted hammer appears bearish. To wit, on the inverted hammer session the market opens on, or near its low, then rallies. The bulls fail to sustain the rally and prices close at, or near, the lows of the session. Why should a line like this be a potentially bullish reversal signal? The answer has to do with what happens over the next session. If the next day opens above the real body of the inverted hammer, it means those who shorted at the opening or closing of the inverted hammer day are losing money. The longer the market holds above the inverted hammer's real body the more likely these shorts will cover. This could spark a short covering rally which could lead to bottom pickers going long. This could feed upon itself and a rally could be the result.

In the corn example, the inverted hammer was followed in the next session by a bullish engulfing line. That line served as confirmatory price action.

As seen in Exhibit 5.32, shooting star 1 eased the market into an essentially lateral band from its prior strong rallying mode. The black candlestick after shooting star 3 corroborated a top since it completed a bearish engulfing pattern. The decline that started with shooting star 3 ended with the March 27 and 28 piercing pattern. This pattern formed the foundation for a rally which terminated at shooting star 4. Observe where the decline after shooting 4 stopped—an inverted hammer on April 21 which was substantiated by the next day's higher white real body. If this white real body was longer, we could say there was a bullish morning star (the black real body before the inverted hammer, the inverted hammer, and the white real body after the hammer would make up this three candlestick morning star pattern if the third white line was longer). The rally initiated with the bullish inverted hammer pushed prices up, until another—you guessed it—shooting star at 5.

Exhibit 5.33 illustrates other examples of inverted hammers. Note how inverted hammers 1 and 2 were confirmed by stronger prices the following day. This is important. Inverted hammer 2 became part of a morning star pattern.

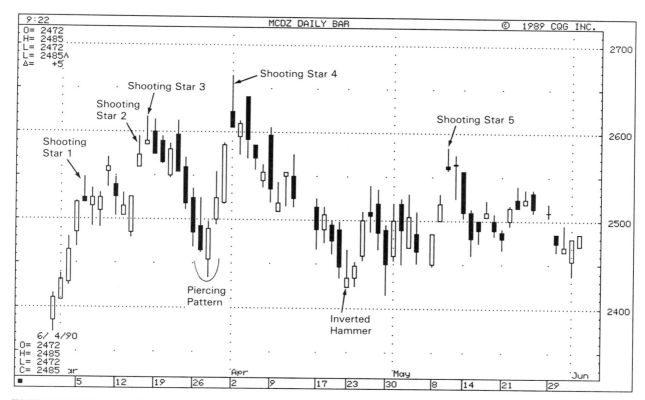

EXHIBIT 5.32. London Zinc—Three Month, 1990 (Shooting Stars and Inverted Hammer)

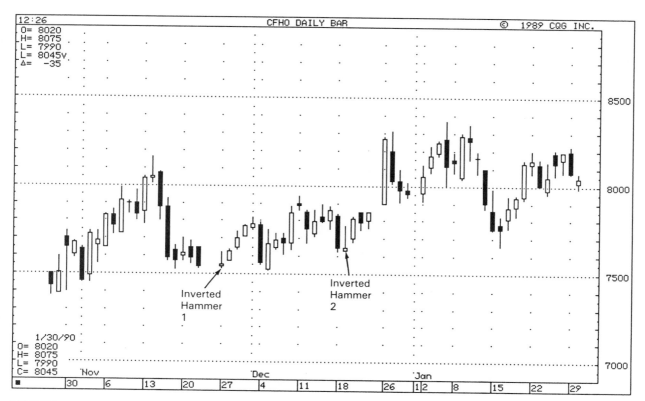

EXHIBIT 5.33. Coffee—March 1990, Daily (Inverted Hammers)

CHAPTER 6

MORE REVERSAL FORMATIONS

....

臭い物に蓋

"Put a Lid on What Smells Bad"

The reversal formations in Chapters 4 and 5 are comparatively strong reversal signals. They show that the bulls have taken over from the bears (as in the bullish engulfing pattern, a morning star, or a piercing pattern) or that the bears have wrested control from the bulls (as in the bearish engulfing pattern, the evening star, or the dark-cloud cover). This chapter examines more reversal indicators which are usually, but not always, less powerful reversal signals. These include the *harami pattern, tweezers tops* and *bottoms, belt-hold lines,* the *upside-gap two crows,* and *counter-attack lines.* This chapter then explores strong reversal signals that include three black crows, three mountains, three rivers, dumpling tops, fry pan bottoms, and tower tops and bottoms.

THE HARAMI PATTERN

The *harami pattern* (see Exhibit 6.1) is a small real body which is contained within a prior relatively long real body. "Harami" is an old Japanese word for "pregnant." The long candlestick is "the mother" candlestick and the small candlestick as the "baby" or "fetus." In Chapter 3, we discussed how spinning tops (that is, small real bodies) are useful in certain formations. The harami is one of these formations (the star, examined in Chapter 5, is another).

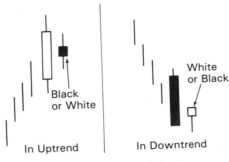

EXHIBIT 6.1. Harami   **EXHIBIT 6.2.** Inside Day

The harami pattern is the reverse of the engulfing pattern. In the engulfing pattern, a lengthy real body engulfs the preceding small real body. For the harami, a small real body follows an unusually long real body. For the two candlesticks of the engulfing pattern the color of the real bodies should be opposite to one another. This is not necessary for the harami. You will find, however, that in most instances, the real bodies in the harami are oppositely colored. Exhibit 6.7 displays the difference between the engulfing and harami patterns.

The harami formation is comparable to the Western inside day. An *inside day* occurs when the highs and lows are within the prior period's range (see Exhibit 6.2). Yet, while a Western inside day is usually thought of as having little, or no, forecasting importance, the harami pattern predicts that the market will separate from its previous trend. While a Western inside session requires the high and low be within the prior session's range, the harami requires a narrow opening and closing range (that is, a small real body) to be within the prior wide opening and closing range (that is, a tall real body).

The harami pattern is usually not as much of a significant reversal signal as are, say, the hammer, hanging man, or engulfing patterns. With the harami a brake has been applied to the market; the immediate preceding trend should end and the market will often come to a lull. At times, the harami can warn of a significant trend change—especially at market tops.

Exhibit 6.3 illustrates a distinctive type of harami called a *harami cross*. A harami cross has a doji for the second day of the harami pattern instead of a small real body. The harami cross, because it contains a potent doji (more about doji in Chapter 8), is viewed as a major reversal signal. The harami cross is sometimes referred to as the *petrifying pattern*.

As illustrated in Exhibit 6.1, the color of the second session is unimportant. The decisive feature of this pattern is that the second session has a minute real body relative to the prior candlestick and that this

EXHIBIT 6.3. Harami Cross

small real body is inside the larger one. The size of the shadows are usually not important in either a harami or harami cross.

The harami displays a disparity about the market's health. After a bull move, the long white real body's vitality is followed by the small real body's uncertainty. This shows the bulls' upward drive has weakened. Thus a trend reversal is possible. During a bear move, the heavy selling pressure reflected by a long, black real body is followed by the second day's vacillation. This could portend a trend reversal since the second day's small real body is an alert that the bears' power has diminished.

Exhibit 6.4 illustrates that a small rally started on April 18. Harami 1

EXHIBIT 6.4. Platinum—July 1990, Daily (Harami)

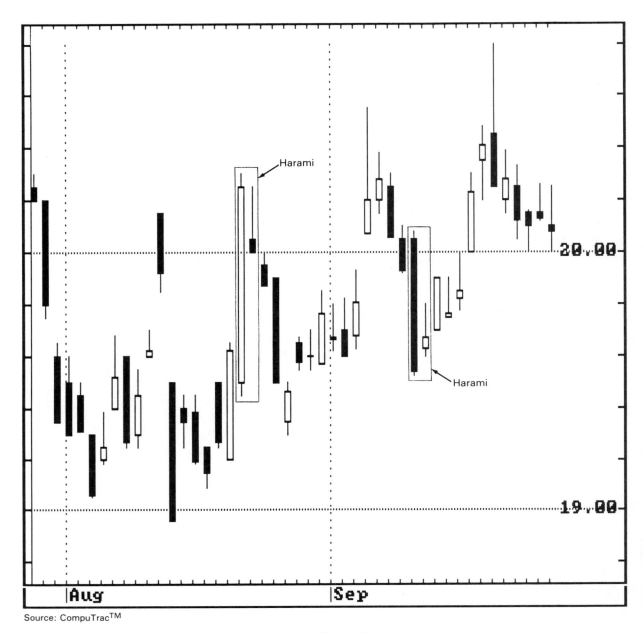

Source: CompuTrac™

EXHIBIT 6.5. Soybean Oil—March 1990, Daily (Harami)

called its end and the selloff that started with harami 1 stopped with harami 2. Harami 3 reflects how a harami pattern might be useful even if there is no evident trend before a harami pattern occurs. Note that there was no evident trend during the first few days of May. Then harami 3 arose with its long, white real body followed by a small, black real body (remember the color of the second day's real body is not important).

A trader could, nonetheless, use this pattern as a signal that the rally started on the strong, white day had failed. The market was now at a point of indecision. A buy would not be recommended until the indecision had been resolved via a close above the highs of harami 3.

Harami 4 was a classic. An uptrend was evident prior to the tall white candlestick. The next day's small real body completed the harami. This small real body also took on the negative aspects of a shooting star day (although not a perfect star since the real body was not above the prior real body).

Exhibit 6.5 illustrates exemplary harami. Each of the second day's real bodies are diminutive compared to the prior long real bodies. The first harami implied a lack of upside momentum; the second harami implied a drying up of selling pressure.

Exhibit 6.6 illustrates how the two candlestick harami pattern in late March spelled the top of the market. The selloff continued until the bullish hammer occurred on April 24. Notice how the shadow of the second session in the harami was outside the real body of the prior session. This demonstrates the importance of the relationship between the real bodies and not the shadows.

Exhibit 6.7 shows a steep decline which ensued from the bearish engulfing pattern of May 7 and 8. This harami marked the change of a downtrend into a lateral band.

Intra-day traders could use the harami in Exhibit 6.8 as a signal that the prior intra-day trend might be over. Appropriate action would then be warranted. In this example, the early April 17 precipitous price decline ended and the market went into a lull after the harami pattern. This harami could have been used by day traders to cover shorts. Like

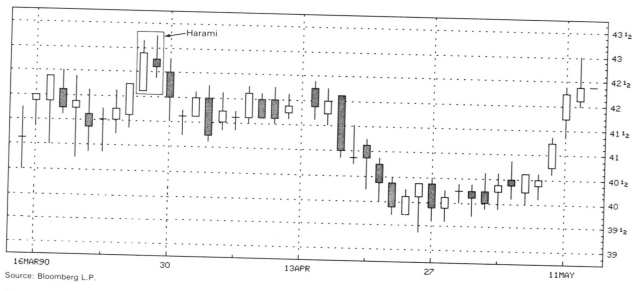

EXHIBIT 6.6. AT&T—1990, Daily (Harami)

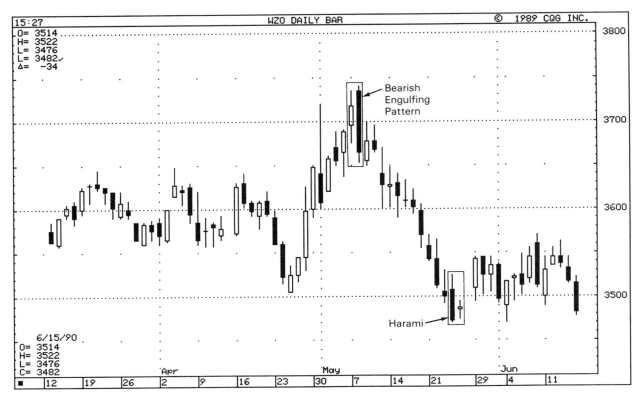

EXHIBIT 6.7. Wheat—December 1990, Daily (Harami)

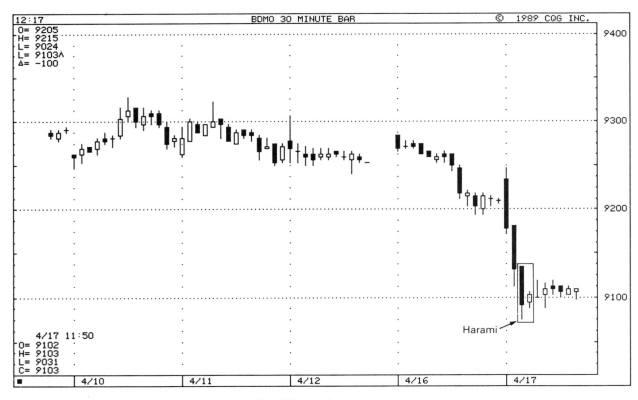

EXHIBIT 6.8. Bonds—June 1990, Intra-day (Harami)

EXHIBIT 6.9. Silver—September 1990, Daily (Harami).

any bottom reversal pattern, this harami did not preclude the possibility that the market would resume its downward course. Yet, this harami relayed a condition about the market. Specifically, it told us that, at least at the time of the harami, the downward pressure had subsided.

Exhibit 6.9 is a good example of a precipitous downtrend converted to a lateral trading environment after the advent of the harami. In this example we see how the prior downtrend, in which prices cascaded from $5.40 to $4.85, stopped at the harami. But the harami did not necessarily imply a rally. After a harami the market usually eases into a congestion band.

Harami Cross

The regular harami has a tall real body followed by a smaller real body. Yet, there are no rules as to what is considered a "small" candlestick. This, like many other charting techniques, is subjective. As a general principle, the smaller the second real body, the more potent the pattern. This is usually true because the smaller the real body, the greater the ambivalence and the more likely a trend reversal. In the extreme, as the

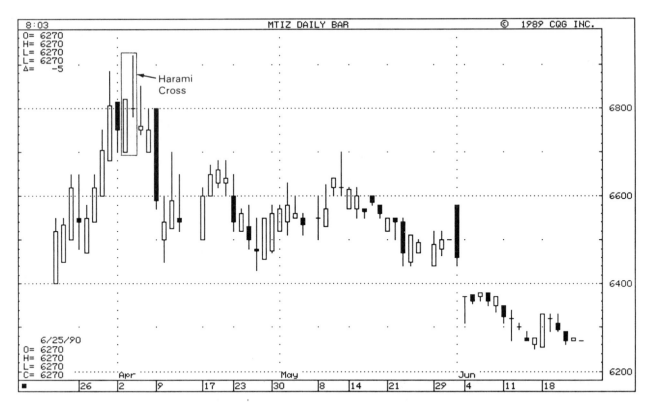

EXHIBIT 6.10. London Tin—Three Month, 1990 (Harami Cross)

real body becomes increasingly smaller as the spread between the open and close narrows, a doji is formed.

As mentioned, a doji preceded by a long real body is called a *harami cross*. The harami cross carries more significance than a regular harami pattern. Where the harami is not a major reversal pattern, the harami cross is a major reversal pattern. A harami cross occurring after a very long white candlestick is a pattern a long trader ignores at his own peril. Harami crosses also call bottoms, but they are more effective at tops.

Exhibit 6.10 illustrates how the rally from mid-March abruptly ended when the harami cross pattern formed on April 2 and 3. Exhibit 6.11 shows how the large upside gap made in mid-January shouted, "bull market." But, the harami cross said, "no bull market now." Exhibit 6.12 shows how an unusually large black candlestick session followed by a doji created a harami cross. It shows how the market had severed itself from the prior downtrend. A hammerlike session after the doji of the harami cross (that successfully tested the recent lows) gave further proof of a bottom.

EXHIBIT 6.11. Corn—May 1990, Daily (Harami Cross)

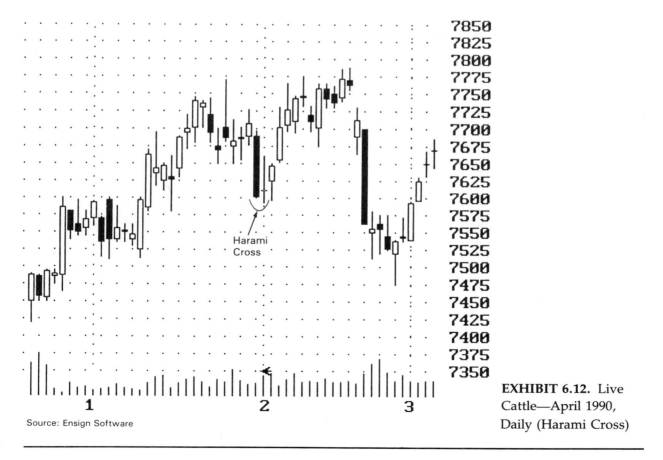

Source: Ensign Software

EXHIBIT 6.12. Live
Cattle—April 1990,
Daily (Harami Cross)

TWEEZERS TOPS AND BOTTOMS

Tweezers are two or more candlestick lines with matching highs or lows. They are called tweezers because they are compared to the two prongs of a tweezers. In a rising market, a *tweezers top* is formed when the highs match. In a falling market, a *tweezers bottom* is made when the lows are the same. The tweezers could be composed of real bodies, shadows, and/or doji. A tweezers occurs on nearby or consecutive sessions and as such are usually not a vital reversal signal. They take on extra importance when they occur after an extended move or contain other bearish (for a top reversal) or a bullish (for a bottom reversal) candlestick signals. Exhibits 6.13 through 6.18 elaborate on this idea.

Exhibit 6.13 shows how, in an uptrend, a long white line is followed by a doji. This two-candlestick pattern, a harami cross with the same high, can be a significant reversal signal. Exhibit 6.14 illustrates a tweezers top formed by a long white candlestick and a hanging-man line during the next session. If the market opens under the hanging-man's real body, odds are strong that a top has been reached. The market should not close above the tweezers top in order for this bearish view to prevail. This two-line mixture can also be considered a harami. As such, it would be a top reversal pattern during an uptrend. Exhibit 6.15 illustrates a tweezers top joined with the second period's bearish shooting-star line. Although not a true shooting star, the second line is bearish based on the price action which creates it; the market opens near its

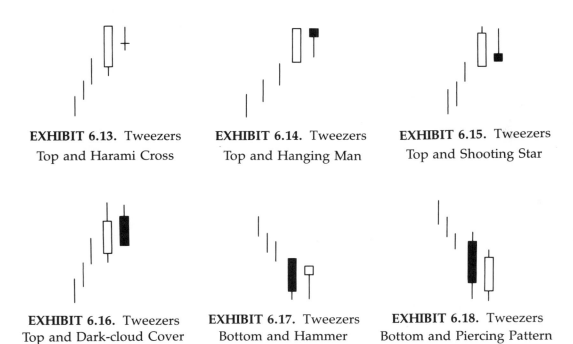

EXHIBIT 6.13. Tweezers Top and Harami Cross

EXHIBIT 6.14. Tweezers Top and Hanging Man

EXHIBIT 6.15. Tweezers Top and Shooting Star

EXHIBIT 6.16. Tweezers Top and Dark-cloud Cover

EXHIBIT 6.17. Tweezers Bottom and Hammer

EXHIBIT 6.18. Tweezers Bottom and Piercing Pattern

lows, rallies to the prior session's high, then closes near its low for the session. This would also be considered a harami pattern.

Exhibit 6.16 illustrates a variation on the dark-cloud cover. Here, the second day opens above the prior day's close (instead of above the prior day's high). The black candlestick day's high touches the prior period's high and then falls. This could be viewed as a combination of a dark-cloud cover and a tweezers top. Exhibit 6.17 shows a hammer session which successfully tests the prior long black candlestick's lows. The hammer, and the successful test of support, proves that the sellers are losing control of the market. This two-line combination can also be viewed as a harami. This would be another reason to view this action as important support. Exhibit 6.18 is a variation on the bullish piercing line with a tweezers bottom added in for good measure. A true piercing line would open under the prior day's low. Here it opened under the prior day's close.

These examples of tweezers are not inclusive. They are representative of how top and bottom tweezers should be confirmed by other candlestick indications so as to be valuable forecasting tools. For those who want a longer time perspective, tweezers tops and bottoms on the weekly and monthly candlestick charts made by consecutive candlesticks could be important reversal patterns. This would be true even without other candlestick confirmation because, on a weekly or monthly chart, for example, a low made the preceding session that is successfully tested this session could be an important base for a rally. Less important, and less likely to be a base for a rally, would be, on a daily chart, a low made yesterday that is successfully tested today.

Exhibit 6.19 illustrates tweezer tops and bottoms. The tweezers top was confirmed when the second day completed a bearish engulfing pattern. Tweezers bottom pattern 1 illustrates a star. Note also how this two-day tweezer bottom was a successful test of the piercing pattern from the prior week. Tweezers bottom 2 is a set of two hammers. The combination of these two bullish indications, the tweezers bottom and the hammers, set the stage for a rally.

Exhibit 6.20 shows that the lows made on January 24, near $.95, were retested a week later. The test was not only successful, but this test built a bullish engulfing pattern. Exhibit 6.21 shows that on February 14 and 15, a two-day tweezers bottom also established a bullish engulfing pattern. Exhibit 6.22 illustrates a hanging man following a long white candlestick. The highs on both of these weeks (as well as the next) were the same, thus creating a tweezers top. The two lines of the tweezers were also a harami pattern. Exhibit 6.23 shows that a variation of an evening star developed in late June. For a true evening star, we like to see a longer white candlestick as the first line in the pattern. Nonetheless, this

Source: CompuTrac™

EXHIBIT 6.19. Crude Oil—May 1990, Daily (Tweezers Tops and Bottoms)

became a resistance area as proved by the following week's hanging man. The hanging man touched the prior week's highs and failed. This created a tweezers top.

At the August 1987 peaks, as shown in Exhibit 6.24, the S&P's long white candlestick followed by a doji formed a tweezers top which acted as resistance the next week. Besides the tweezers top, a doji after a long white candlestick at high price levels is dangerous. This feature is discussed in detail in Chapter 8.

EXHIBIT 6.20. Copper—May 1990, Daily (Tweezers Bottom)

Source: CompuTrac™

EXHIBIT 6.21. Canadian Dollar—June 1990, Daily (Tweezers Bottom)

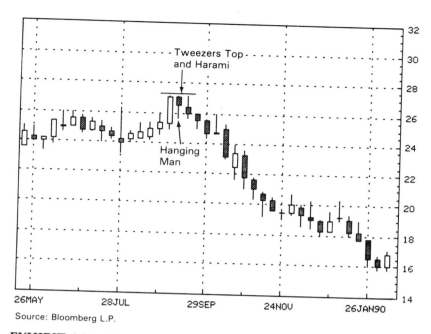

Source: Bloomberg L.P.

EXHIBIT 6.22. Chrysler—Weekly, 1989–1990, (Tweezers Top)

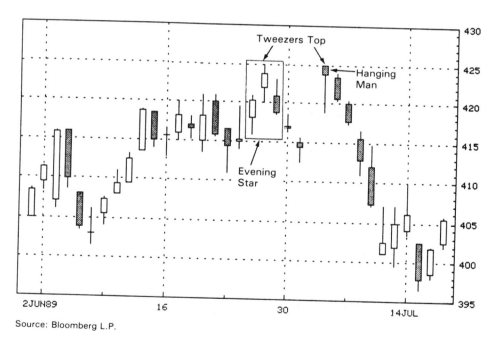

Source: Bloomberg L.P.

EXHIBIT 6.23. Wheat—December 1989, Daily (Tweezers Top)

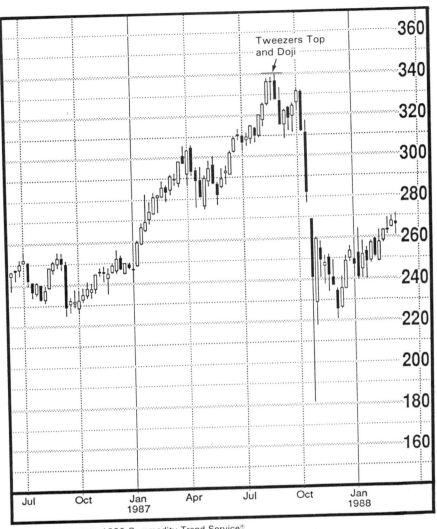

EXHIBIT 6.24. S&P—Weekly
(Tweezers Top)

Source: ©Copyright 1990 Commodity Trend Service®

BELT-HOLD LINES

The belt hold is an individual candlestick line which can be either bull-ish or bearish. The *bullish belt hold* is a strong white candlestick which opens on the low of the day (or with a very small lower shadow) and moves higher for the rest of the day. The bullish belt-hold line is also called a *white opening shaven bottom*. If, as in Exhibit 6.25, the market is at a low price area and a long bullish belt hold appears, it forecasts a rally.

The *bearish belt hold* (see Exhibit 6.26) is a long black candlestick which opens on the high of the session (or within a few ticks of the high) and continues lower through the session. If prices are high, the appearance of a bearish belt hold is a top reversal. The bearish belt-hold line is sometimes called a *black opening shaven head*.

EXHIBIT 6.25. Bullish Belt Hold   **EXHIBIT 6.26.** Bearish Belt Hold

The longer the height of the belt-hold candlestick line, the more significant it becomes. Belt-hold lines are also more important if they have not appeared for a while. The actual Japanese name for the belt hold is a sumo wrestling term: *yorikiri*. It means "pushing your opponent out of the ring while holding onto his belt." A close above a black bearish belt-hold line should mean a resumption of the uptrend. A close under the white bullish belt-hold line implies a renewal of selling pressure.

Exhibit 6.27 shows how bullish belt-hold line 1 signaled a rally. Belt-hold line 2 is interesting. It confirmed a tweezers bottom since it maintained the prior week's lows. A rally ensued which ended with a harami a few weeks later.

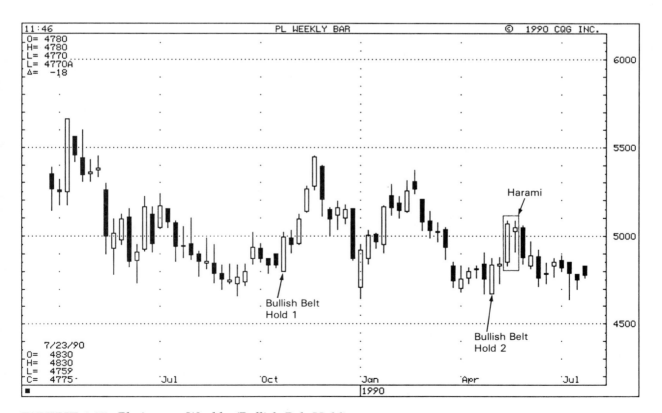

EXHIBIT 6.27. Platinum—Weekly (Bullish Belt Hold)

EXHIBIT 6.28. Cotton—December 1990, Daily (Bearish Belt Hold)

The shooting star was the first sign of trouble in Exhibit 6.28. The next session's bearish belt-hold line confirmed a top. Another bearish belt hold during the following week reflected the underlying weakness of the market.

Exhibit 6.29 is an example of back-to-back bearish belt holds in mid-February. The selloff which ensued, was sharp, but brief as a bullish morning star pattern spelled a bottom.

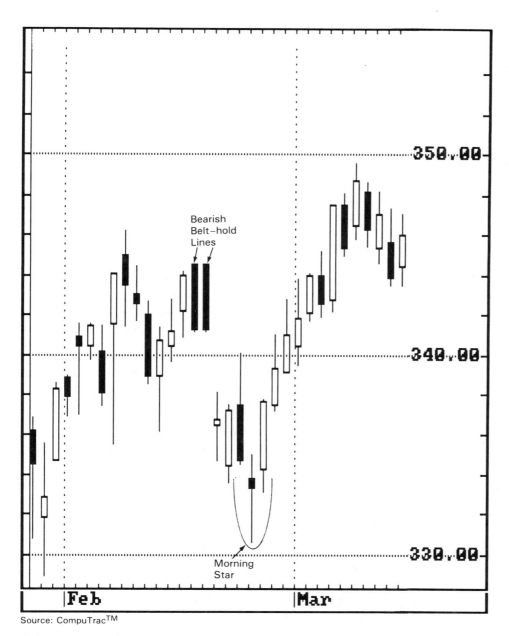

EXHIBIT 6.29. S&P—September 1990, Daily (Bearish Belt Hold)

UPSIDE-GAP TWO CROWS

An upside-gap two crows (what a mouthful) is illustrated in Exhibit 6.30. The upside gap refers to the gap between the real body of the small black real body and the real body preceding it (the real body which precedes the first black candlestick is usually a long white one). The two black candlesticks are the "crows" in this pattern. They are analogous to black crows peering ominously down from a tree branch. Based on this portentous comparison, it is obviously a bearish pattern. An ideal upside-gap two crows has the second black real body opening above the first black real body's open. It then closes under the first black candlestick's close.

The rationale for the bearish aspect of this pattern is as follows: The market is in an uptrend and opens higher on an opening gap. The new highs fail to hold and the market forms a black candlestick. But the bulls can take some succor, at least, because the close on this black candlestick session still holds above the prior day's close. The third session paints a more bearish portrait with another new high and another failure to hold these highs into the close. More negative, however, is that this session closes under the prior day's close. If the market is so strong, why did the new highs fail to hold and why did the market close lower? Those are the questions that the bulls are probably nervously asking themselves. The answers might be that the market may not be as strong as they would like. If the next day (that is, the fourth session) prices fail to regain high ground, then expect lower prices.

There is a related pattern that looks something like an upside-gap two crows. Unlike the upside-gap two crows, it is a bullish in a rising market. As such, it is one of the few candlestick continuation patterns. (Other continuation patterns are discussed in Chapter 7.) It is called a *mat-hold pattern* (see Exhibit 6.31). This pattern occurs in a bull market and is a bullish continuation pattern. The first three candlesticks are similar to the upside-gap two crows but another black candlestick follows. If the next candlestick is white and gaps above the last black can-

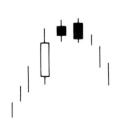

EXHIBIT 6.30. Upside Gap Two Crows

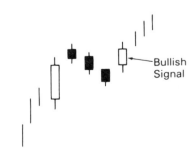

EXHIBIT 6.31. Mat-hold Pattern

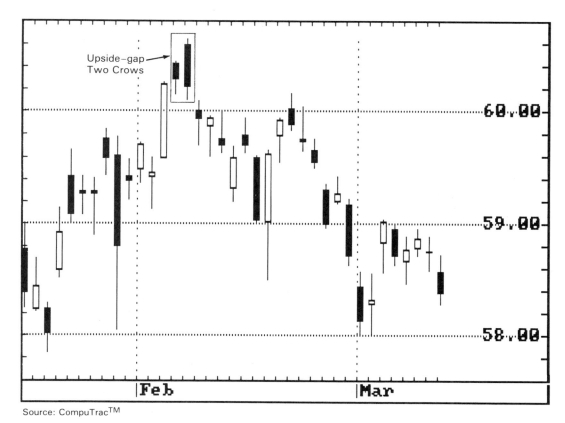

Source: CompuTrac™

EXHIBIT 6.32. Deutschemark—March 1990, Daily (Upside-gap Two Crows)

dlestick's upper shadow or closes above the last black candlestick's high, then buying is warranted. This pattern can have two, three, or four black candlesticks. The upside gap two crows and the mat-hold are relatively rare.

Exhibit 6.32 is a good example of this type of upside-gap two crows pattern. In early February, the two crows flew above a long white candlestick. This pattern called an end to the rally which had begun a month earlier.

In Exhibit 6.33, one can see that on November 27, copper pushed ahead via a long white session. New highs on the two following sessions failed to hold. The second black candlestick session made this into an upside-gap two crows pattern. The market slid until a doji star and a tweezers bottom built a platform for another leg higher.

Exhibit 6.34 is a classic example of the rare mat-hold pattern. A strong white candle followed by a black candlestick that gaped higher. Two more small black candlesticks followed with the white candlestick completing the mat-hold pattern. Note how this pattern is not too much different from the upside-gap two crows (remember the mat hold can also have two, instead of three, small black candlesticks just as the upside-

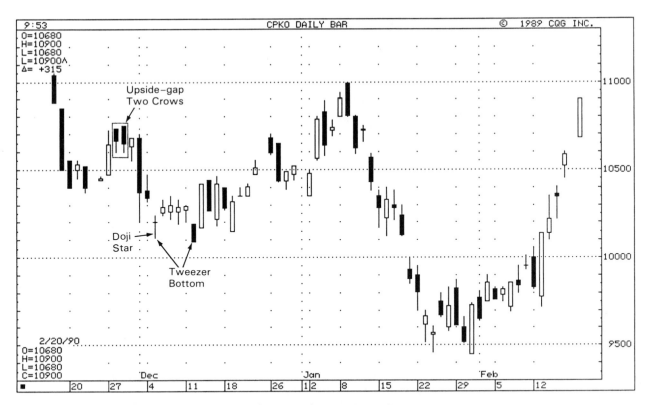

EXHIBIT 6.33. Copper—May 1990, Daily (Upside-gap Two Crows)

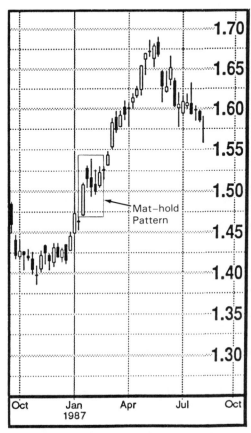

EXHIBIT 6.34. British Pound—Weekly (Mat-hold Pattern).   Source: ©Copyright 1990 Commodity Trend Service®

gap two crows has). The main difference is the appearance of the white candlestick at the end which turns the pattern bullish. Thus, for an upside-gap two crows, I suggest you place a stop on a close above the second black candlestick's high.

THREE BLACK CROWS

The upside-gap two crows consists of two black candlesticks. If there are three declining consecutive black candlesticks it is called *three black crows* pattern (see Exhibit 6.35). The three black crows presage lower prices if they appear at high-price levels or after a mature advance. Three crows are also sometimes called *three-winged crows.* The Japanese have an expression, "bad news has wings." This is an appropriate saying for the three-winged crow pattern. The three crows are, as the name implies, three black candlesticks. Likened to the image of a group of crows sitting ominously in a tall dead tree, the three crows have bearish implications. The three lines should close at, or near, their lows. Each of the openings should also be within the prior session's real body. The analyst would also like to see the real body of the first candlestick of the three crows under the prior white session's high.

Exhibit 6.36 is a good example of a three crows pattern. In mid-June, three black crows appeared. Another three crow pattern shows up a month later in mid July. July's three crows also was a failure at the highs from June's three crows near the 33,000 level. This formed a double top. Exhibit 6.37 is another example of this pattern. June 15 was the first of the three crows. An interesting aspect about these three crows is that the open of the second and third black candlesticks are at, or very near, the close of the prior black candlestick. This is referred to as *identical three crows.* It is regarded as especially bearish, but it is a very rare pattern.

EXHIBIT 6.35. Three Crows

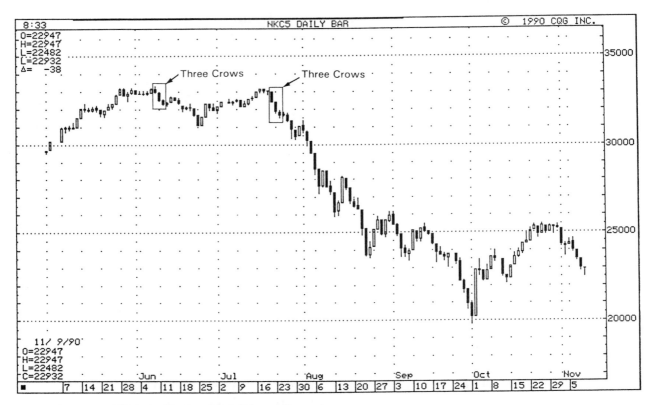

EXHIBIT 6.36. Nikkei—Daily, 1990 (Three Crows)

EXHIBIT 6.37. Dollar Index—September 1990, Daily (Three Crows)

EXHIBIT 6.38. Bullish Counterattack Line

COUNTERATTACK LINES

Counterattack lines are formed when opposite colored candlesticks have the same close. The best way to describe this pattern is by discussing the illustrations in Exhibits 6.38 and 6.39. Exhibit 6.38 is an example of a *bullish counterattack line*. This pattern occurs during a decline. The first candlestick of this pattern is long and black. The next session opens sharply lower. At this point, the bears are feeling confident. The bulls then stage their counterattack as they push prices back up to unchanged from the prior close. The prior downtrend has then been bridled.

The bullish counterattack is comparable to the bullish piercing line. If you remember, the piercing line has the same two-candlestick configuration as that shown for the bullish counterattack pattern. The main difference is that the bullish counterattack line does not usually move into the prior session's white real body. It just gets back to the prior session's close. The piercing pattern's second line pushes well into the black real body. Consequently, the piercing pattern is a more significant bottom reversal than is this bullish counterattack line. Nonetheless, as shown in some examples below, the bullish counterattack line should be respected.

The bullish counterattack line also looks similar to the bearish in-neck pattern (see Chapter 4, Exhibit 4.31). The difference is that the white bullish counterattack line is a longer candlestick than the white candlestick of the in-neck line. In other words, with the counterattack line, the market opens sharply lower and then springs back to the previous close, while the in-neck line opens slightly lower and then moves back to the prior close.

Exhibit 6.39 illustrates the *bearish counterattack line*. It is a top reversal pattern in that it should stall the prior rally. The first candlestick, a long white one, keeps the bullish momentum going. The next session's opening gaps higher. Then the bears come out fighting and pull prices down

EXHIBIT 6.39. Bearish Counterattack Line

to the prior day's close. The bulls' tide of optimism on the second day's opening probably turned to apprehension by the close.

As the bullish counterattack line is related to the piercing line, so the bearish counterattack line is related to the dark-cloud cover. The bearish counter attack, like the dark-cloud cover, opens above the prior day's high. Unlike the dark-cloud cover, though, the close does not go into the prior day's white candlestick. Thus, the dark-cloud cover sends a stronger top reversal signal than does the bearish counterattack line.

An important consideration of these counterattack lines is if the second session should open robustly higher (in the case of the bearish counterattack) or sharply lower (for the bullish counterattack). The idea is that on the opening of the second day of this pattern, the market has moved strongly in the direction of the original trend. Then, surprise! By the close, it moves back to unchanged from the prior session!

On May 29, in Exhibit 6.40, the long white candlestick reinforced the bullish outlook from a rally that started the prior week. Sure enough, on May 30, the market surged ahead on the opening. However, it was downhill from there for the rest of the session. By the close, the market had fallen back to unchanged from the prior close. These two sessions, May 29 and 30, constructed a bearish counterattack pattern.

Exhibit 6.41 shows that a rally terminated with the bearish counterattack line. Exhibit 6.42 shows that the price waterfall, which began with the bearish engulfing line in March 1989, ended with the bullish counterattack a few months later. Remember, all trend reversal indicators, like the counterattack line, tells you is that the trend will change. That does not mean prices will reverse direction. Here is an example of how a bullish reversal pattern signaled that the prior downtrend was over as the trend went from down to sideways. This example also shows that the closes do not have to be identical in order to make the pattern valid. In Exhibit 6.43 one can see how prices eroded from the shooting star until the bullish counterattack line appeared. Another positive feature about this bullish counterattack line is that it was a session which

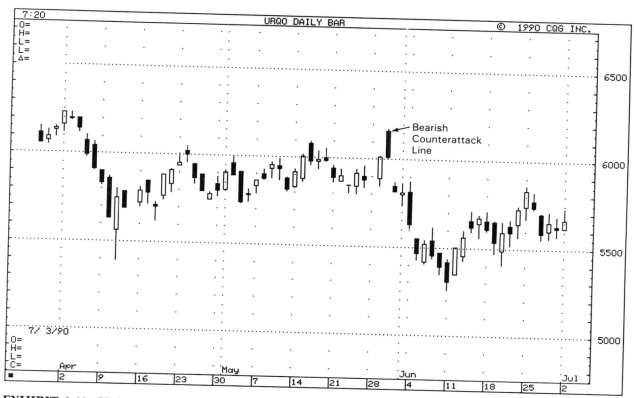

EXHIBIT 6.40. Unleaded Gas—August 1990, Daily (Bearish Counterattack Line)

EXHIBIT 6.41. Yen—Weekly 1990 (Bearish Counterattack Line)

Source: Quick 10E Information Systems

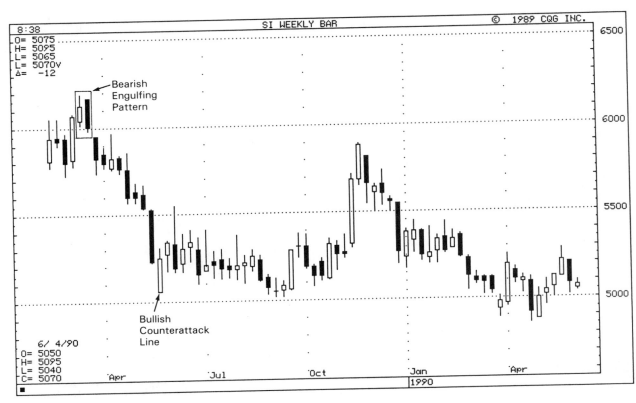

EXHIBIT 6.42. Silver—Weekly (Bullish Counterattack Lines)

EXHIBIT 6.43. Live Cattle—October 1990, Daily (Bullish Counterattack Line)

opened under the late July, early August support area but, nonetheless, the new lows could not be maintained. This showed that the bears could not take control of the market.

THREE MOUNTAINS AND THREE RIVERS

There are a group of longer-term topping and bottoming patterns that include the three mountains, the three rivers, the three Buddha tops, inverted three Buddha, dumpling tops, fry pan bottoms, and tower tops and bottoms. Similar to the Western triple top, the Japanese have a *three mountain top* (see Exhibit 6.44). It is supposed to represent a major top. If the market backs off from a high three times or makes three attempts at a high, it is deemed a three mountain top. The high point of the final mountain should be confirmed with a bearish candlestick indicator (for example, a doji or dark-cloud cover).

If the central mountain of a three mountain top is the highest mountain it is a special type of three mountain called a *three Buddha top* (see Exhibit 6.45). The reason for this name is because, in Buddhist temples, there is a large central Buddha with smaller Buddhas (that is, saints) on both sides. This is a perfect analogy to a head and shoulders pattern. Although the three Buddha top is an analogy to the Western head and shoulders pattern, the theory about the Japanese three Buddha pattern was used over a hundred years before the head and shoulders was known in America. (The earliest I have seen a reference to a head and shoulders pattern in the United States was by Richard Schabacker in the 1930s. For those who are familiar with the Edwards and Magee classic

EXHIBIT 6.44. Three Mountain Tops

EXHIBIT 6.45. Three Buddha Top

EXHIBIT 6.46. Three River Bottom

EXHIBIT 6.47. Inverted Three Buddha

book *Technical Analysis of Stock Trends*, much of the material in that book is based on Schabacker's work. Schabacker was Edward's father-in-law.) It is intriguing how market observers from both the West and the East have come up with the this same pattern. Market psychology is the same the world 'round, or, as a Japanese proverb expresses, "The tone of a bird's song is the same everywhere."

The *three river bottom pattern* (see Exhibit 6.46) is the opposite of the three mountain top. This occurs when the market tests a bottom level three times. The peak of the troughs should be exceeded to confirm a bottom. The equivalent of the Western head and shoulders bottom (also called an *inverted head and shoulders*) is called the *modified three river bottom pattern* or the *inverted three Buddha pattern* (see Exhibit 6.47).

Exhibit 6.48 is an unusual chart in that it has the various manifestations of the three mountain top. They are as follows:

1. Areas 1, 2, and 3 construct a three Buddha pattern because the central mountain is the highest of the three peaks. The top of the third mountain was an evening star line. The selloff which originated with the third mountain concludes at June's morning star pattern.

2. Three price peaks occur at A, B, and C. Some Japanese technicians view the three mountain as three attempts at new highs, like three waves up. The third wave up is supposed to be a crest (the scenario in this instance). Three pushes to new highs and after the third failed push, the bulls surrender. The peak of the third mountain (c) was an evening star.

3. While some Japanese technicians view a three-stage rise as the three mountains, others view the three mountains as repeating tests of the same price peaks. This is what develops at areas C, D, and E. Area D signals a top via a dark-cloud cover; E signals with a hanging man followed by a doji.

Each of the three mountains in Exhibit 6.49 illustrate bearish candlestick evidence. Area 1 is a bearish engulfing pattern, area 2 is a hanging

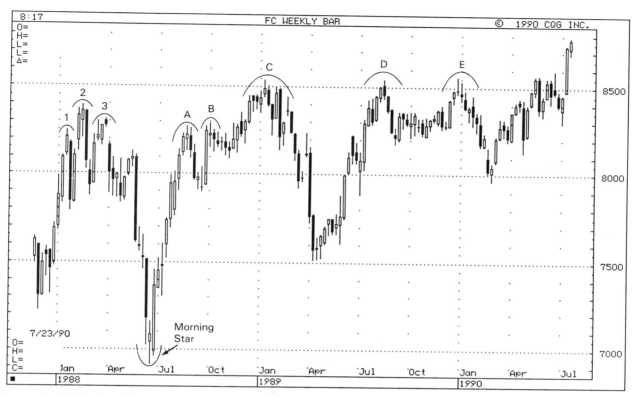

EXHIBIT 6.48. Feeder Cattle—Weekly (Three Mountain Tops)

EXHIBIT 6.49. Live Hogs—August 1990, Daily (Three Mountain Top)

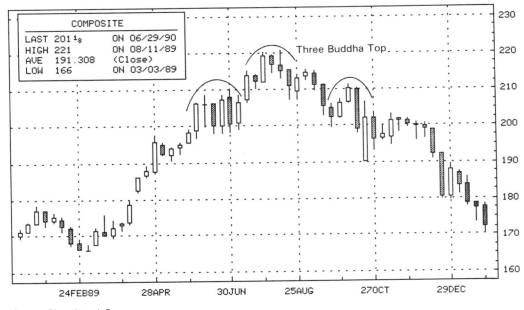

Source: Bloomberg L.P.

EXHIBIT 6.50. CBS—Weekly (Three Buddha Top)

man followed by two doji, and area 3 is another bearish engulfing pattern. Since the central mountain formed the highest peak in Exhibit 6.50, this pattern became a three Buddha pattern. The black real body within the prior white real body formed a harami at the peak of the high central mountain.

As illustrated in Exhibit 6.51, there was an inverted three Buddha pattern in 1988 (that is, similar to an inverted head and shoulders). Each of these bottoms at A, B, and C had a bullish candlestick indication. At A, a hammer appeared. At B, another hammer appeared that was part of a morning star pattern (the morning star rally ended with the dark-cloud cover). At C, a piercing line appeared (it was almost a bullish engulfing pattern). Once the bulls gapped above the downward sloping resistance line, the trend turned up. Gaps are called *windows* by Japanese technicians. (Windows will be discussed at length in the next chapter on continuation patterns.) Because I refer to gaps in this chapter, the reader should note that the Japanese view gaps (that is, windows) as continuation patterns. Thus a gap higher is bullish and a gap lower is bearish. In this example, the gap higher had bullish implications. The price activity from the third quarter of 1989 into the first quarter of 1990 effected a three Buddha top.

In order for the three river bottoms (including this one) to provide a buy signal, there should be a close via a white candlestick above the peaks of the troughs (see Exhibit 6.52). In this case, it would be above

EXHIBIT 6.51. Crude Oil—Weekly (Inverted Three Buddha Bottom and Three Buddha Top)

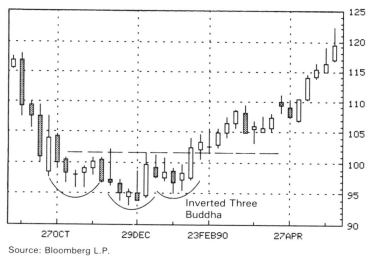

Source: Bloomberg L.P.

EXHIBIT 6.52. IBM—Weekly (Inverted Three Buddha Bottom)

$102. Notice how this $102 then converted to support on the selloff in March.

THE IMPORTANCE OF THE NUMBER THREE IN CANDLESTICK ANALYSIS

The emphasis on triple tops and bottoms by the Japanese probably has to do with the importance of the number three in the Japanese culture. We, as Westerners, would not necessarily see anything special about the three peaks. Our view would be that double tops and, more rarely, tops which have been tested four times can be just as significant as triple tops. But the Japanese think differently. And maybe they can show us a side of Western analysis which we may have overlooked. Intriguingly, there are many pattern and technical concepts based on the number three in Western technical analysis as well as in candlestick charting. The following is a quote from John Murphy's book *Technical Analysis of the Futures Markets:*

> It's interesting to note how often the number three shows up in the study of technical analysis and the important role it plays in so many technical approaches. For example, the fan principle uses three lines; major bull and bear markets have three phases (Dow theory and Elliott Wave Theory); there are three kinds of gaps some of the more commonly known reversal patterns, such as the triple top and the head and shoulders, have three prominent peaks; there are three different classifications of trend (major, secondary, and minor) and three trend directions (up, down, and sideways); among the generally accepted continuation patterns, there are three types of triangles—the symmetrical, ascending, and descending; there are three principle sources of information—price, volume and open interest. For whatever the reason, the number three plays a very prominent role throughout the entire field of technical analysis.[1]

John Murphy was, of course referring to Western technical analysis. But his phrase, "the number three plays a very prominent role" is especially true of Japanese candlestick analysis. In pre-modern Japan, the number three had an almost mystical associations. There is a saying "three times lucky" that expresses this belief. Parenthetically, while the number three is regarded as lucky, the number four is viewed as a foreboding figure. The reason for this belief is easy to ascertain—in Japanese the pronunciation for the number four and the word death are the same.

Some specifics of the frequency of three in candlestick charting are as follows: There are the three white soldiers that presage a rally; the ominous three black crows that portend a price fall; top patterns include the three mountain top and its variation; the three Buddha pattern; the three river bottoms; the three windows (see Chapter 7) which define the extent of a move; the three methods (see Chapter 7); and the three candlestick patterns including the morning and evening stars. The Japanese also believe that if a window (during a rising market) is not closed within three days the market will rally.

DUMPLING TOPS AND FRY PAN BOTTOMS

The *dumpling top* (see Exhibit 6.53) usually has small real bodies as the market forms a convex pattern. When the market gaps down, confirmation of a dumpling top occurs. This pattern is the same as the Western rounded bottom top. The dumpling top should have a downside window as proof of a top.

The *fry pan bottom* (see Exhibit 6.54) reflects a market which is bottoming and whose price action forms a concave design and then a window to the upside opens. It has the same appearance as a Western rounded bottom, but the Japanese fry pan bottom should have a window in an upmove in order to confirm the bottom.

The rounding top and the small real bodies as the market tops out is indicative of dumpling top as seen in Exhibit 6.55. Note how the doji was at the peak of the market with the downside window helping to confirm the dumpling top pattern. The fact the black candlestick after the window was a black belt-hold line was another reason for a bearish outlook. Exhibit 6.56 shows a fry pan bottom whose low points on April 27 and 28 formed a harami pattern. A window in early May substantiated that a fry pan bottom had been put into place.

Exhibit 6.57 illustrates a nicely shaped fry pan bottom. The bullish confirmation came at candlestick 2. Although the market did not form a window between candlestick 1 and 2, the fact that the high for candlestick 1 was $1,000 and the low for candlestick 2 was $997 meant it only

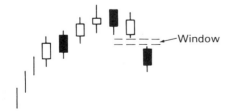

EXHIBIT 6.53. Dumpling Top

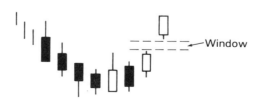

EXHIBIT 6.54. Fry Pan Bottom

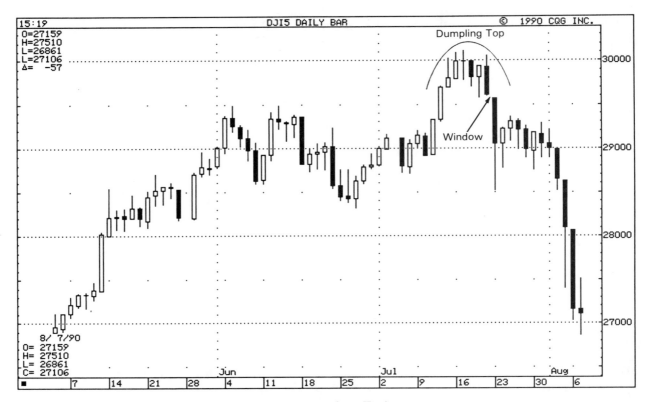

EXHIBIT 6.55. Dow Jones Industrials—1990 (Dumpling Top)

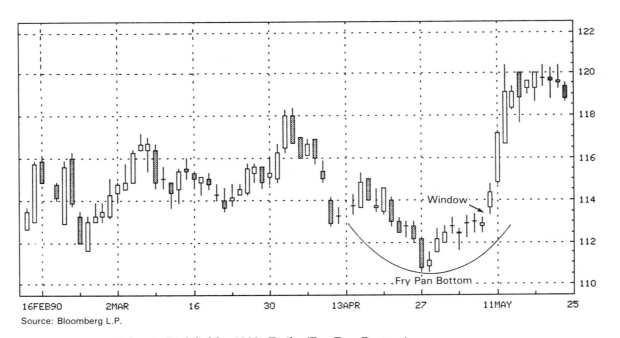

Source: Bloomberg L.P.

EXHIBIT 6.56. Atlantic Richfield—1990, Daily (Fry Pan Bottom)

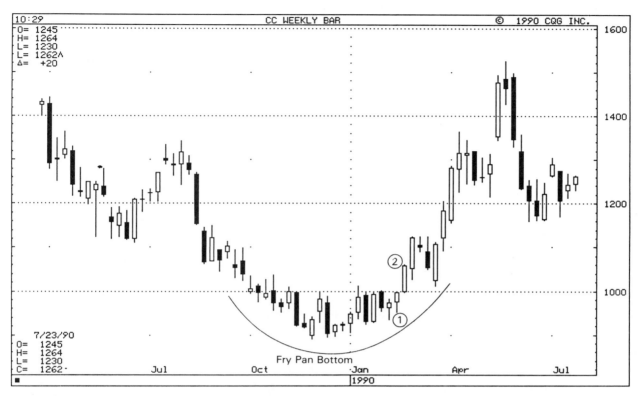

EXHIBIT 6.57. Cocoa—Weekly (Fry Pan Bottom)

missed being a window by 4 ticks. In addition, candlestick 2 was a very strong white belt-hold line.

TOWER TOPS AND TOWER BOTTOMS

The *tower top* is a top reversal pattern. It occurs while the market is in an uptrend and then a strong white candlestick (or a series of white candlesticks) appears. The market's rise then slows and the highs start falling. The tower top is completed with the appearance of one or more large black candlesticks (see Exhibit 6.58). This pattern's long candlesticks resemble tall towers—hence the name.

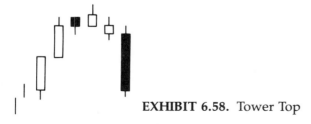

EXHIBIT 6.58. Tower Top

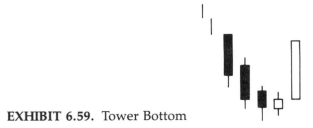

EXHIBIT 6.59. Tower Bottom

The *tower bottom* develops at low price levels. After one or more long black candlesticks there is a short-term lull. Then one or more large white candlesticks emerge. This creates a bottom with towers on both sides (see Exhibit 6.59). That is, long candlesticks on the way down and long candlesticks on the way up.

Exhibit 6.60 shows that a group of strong white candlesticks appeared from first quarter until the second quarter of 1987. Then a series of long black candlesticks surfaced. The tall white candles formed the left tower while the long black ones the right tower. The three black candlesticks were also three black crows.

Exhibit 6.61 illustrates two patterns—the tower bottom and a rare bottom reversal which has not been discussed called the *unique three river*

EXHIBIT 6.60. Cotton—Monthly (Tower Top)

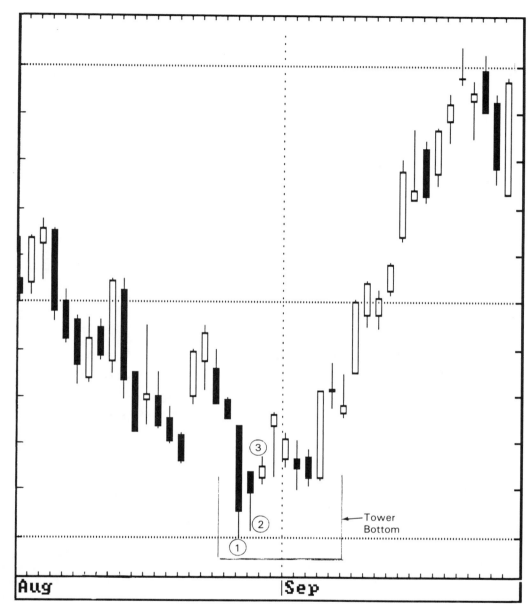

EXHIBIT 6.61. Sugar—May 1990, Daily (Tower Bottom)

bottom. First, I will review the tower bottom. A long black candlestick on August 28, some sideways action via narrow candlesticks, and the long white candlestick September 7 created a tower bottom. The steep price descent on August 28 erected the left tower and the sharp rally, which commenced September 7, erected the right tower. Notice the three candlesticks numbered 1, 2, and 3 on August 28 through August 30. These comprise the extremely rare unique three river bottom (see Exhibit 6.62). Its closest relative in candlesticks is the evening star pattern. The unique three river bottom is a bottom reversal pattern. Its first line is an

EXHIBIT 6.62. Modified Three River Bottom

extended black candlestick, the second line is a black real body candlestick that closes higher than the first candlestick's close, and the third line is a very small real body white candlestick. This last line displays a market whose selling pressure has dried up.

The closest analogy in Western technical terms to the tower reversals would be the spike, or V, reversals. In the spike reversal, the market is in a strong trend and then abruptly reverses to a new trend. The tower top and bottom are similar to the dumpling top and the fry pan bottom. The major differences are that the towers have long real bodies before and after the market turns and the dumpling top and fry pan bottom have windows. The towers usually also have more volatile candlesticks than the dumpling tops or fry pan bottoms. Do not worry about whether a top is a tower top of a dumpling top, or if a bottom is a tower bottom, or a fry pan. All these patterns are viewed as major reversal patterns.

Note

[1]Murphy, John J. *Technical Analysis of the Futures Markets,* New York, NY: New York Institute of Finance, 1986, p. 79.

CHAPTER 7

CONTINUATION PATTERNS

....

運は勇者を助く

"Fate Aids the Courageous"

Most candlestick signals are trend reversals. There are, however, a group of candlestick patterns which are continuation indicators. As the Japanese express it, "there are times to buy, times to sell, and times to rest." Many of these patterns imply a time of rest, a breather, before the market resumes its prior trend. The continuation formations reviewed in this chapter are windows (and patterns which include windows), the rising and falling three methods, and the three white soldiers.

WINDOWS

As discussed earlier, the Japanese commonly refer to a gap as a *window*. Whereas the Western expression is "filling in the gap", the Japanese would say "closing the window." In this section I will explain the basic concepts of windows and then explore other patterns containing windows (gaps). These include the *tasuki gaps,* the *gapping plays,* and *side-by-side white lines.*

A window is a gap between the prior and the current session's price extremes. Exhibit 7.1 shows an open window that forms in an uptrend. There is a gap between the prior upper shadow and this session's lower shadow. A window in a downtrend is displayed in Exhibit 7.2. It shows no price activity between the previous day's lower shadow and the cur-

EXHIBIT 7.1. Window in an Uptrend

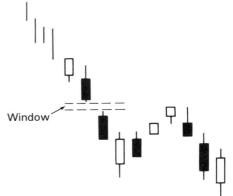

EXHIBIT 7.2. Window in a Downtrend

rent day's upper shadow. It is said by Japanese technicians to go in the direction of the window. Windows also become support and resistance areas. Thus a window in a rally implies a further price rise. This window should also be a floor on pullbacks. If the pullback closes the window and selling pressure continues after the closing of this window, the prior uptrend is voided. Likewise, a window in a declining price environment implies still lower levels. Any price rebounds should run into resistance at this window. If the window is closed, and the rally that closed the window persists, the downtrend is done.

Traditional Japanese technical analysis (that is, candlesticks) asserts that corrections go back to the window. In other words, a test of an open window is likely. Thus, in an uptrend one can use pullbacks to the window as a buying zone. Longs should be vacated and even shorts could be considered if the selling pressure continues after the window closes. The opposite strategy would be warranted with a window in a downtrend.

We see windows 1 and 2 in Exhibit 7.3 amid a rally which originated with the bullish engulfing pattern. A bearish shooting star arose after window 2. The day after this shooting star, the market opened lower and closed the window (that is, filled in the gap). Remembering the concept that corrections go back to the window, this pullback to the window should not be a surprise. If the window is closed and the selling pressure were to continue, the end of the uptrend would be flagged. This did not happen. The selling force evaporated once the window closed. In addition, the support set up at window 1 held. During the week of February 20 the market shuffled its feet. It then retested support at window 2. After this successful test, the market pushed ahead and opened window 3. This was a significant window because it represented a gap above the $1.10 resistance level. This old $1.10 resistance area, once broken,

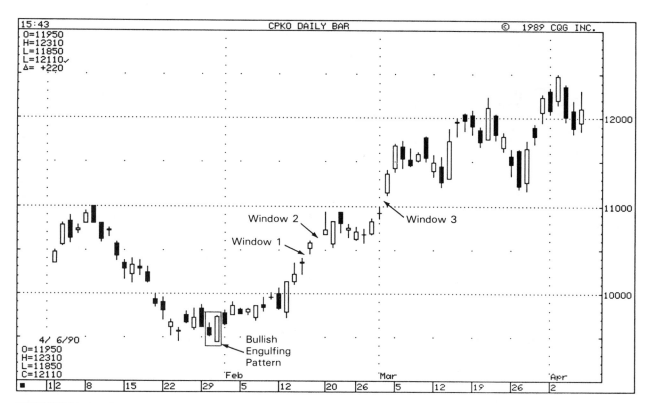

EXHIBIT 7.3. Copper—May 1990, Daily (Windows as Support)

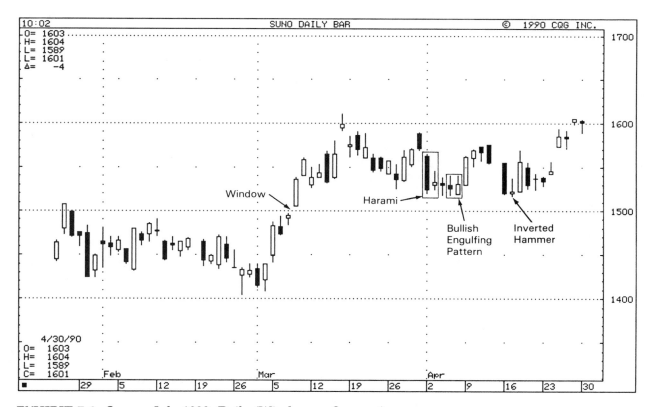

EXHIBIT 7.4. Sugar—July 1990, Daily (Window as Support)

should become support. Add to this the support at the window near this $1.10 area and you have two reasons to expect $1.10 to provide a solid floor. Throughout March, this area did indeed provide a firm footing for the bulls.

The Japanese believe windows from a congestion zone, or from a new high, deserve special attention. See Exhibit 7.4. The early March window above $.15 was a significant break above a month-long congestion zone. Thus there was dual support in the window near $.15. The first was because of the window, the second was because the old resistance area had become support. Notice the solid support this window provided for the next few months. April 2 and 3 comprised a harami. This indicates that the prior trend (in this case, a downtrend) had run out of steam. A bullish engulfing pattern formed a few days later. On April 16 an inverted hammer appeared. Each of these patterns appeared near the window's support at $.15.

In March 1988, a bullish engulfing pattern presaged a rally. (See Exhibit 7.5.) A window opened during the rally. The rally progressed until the bearish counter attack line. The window held as support for five weeks but the persistence of selling after the window closed annulled the uptrend.

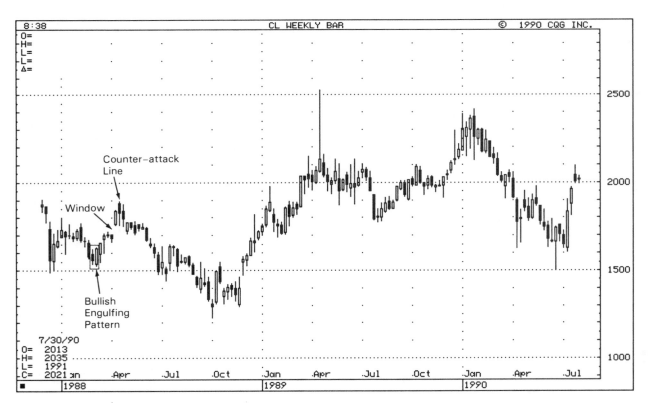

EXHIBIT 7.5. Crude Oil—Weekly (Window as Support)

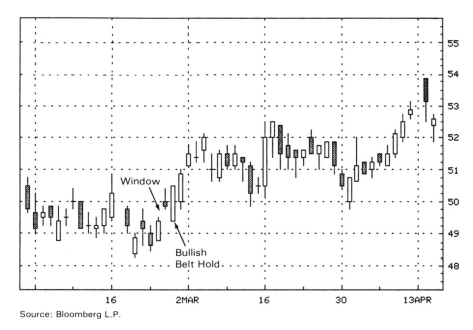

EXHIBIT 7.6. International Paper—Daily 1990 (Window from a Low Price Congestion Area)

Thus far, the focus of this section has been on the use of the window as support or resistance and as a continuation indication. There is another use. (See Exhibit 7.6.) A window, especially if it is made with a small black candlestick from a low price congestion area, can mean a meaningful upside breakout. Exhibit 7.6 illustrates this principle. Throughout February prices were locked in a relatively tight congestion band. Between February 24 and 25, a small upside window opened via a diminutive black candlestick. This window was confirmed as support the next session. On that session (February 26), the market not only held the window as a support but produced the strongest type of candlestick line, a long white candlestick that opens on its low (that is, a bullish belt-hold line) and closes on its high.

A large window appeared in mid-January as indicated by Exhibit 7.7. From late January to late February, there were numerous return moves to this window (corrections go back to the window). Each of these rallies was short circuited when they got near the resistance level created by the window.

Look at the Dow in Exhibit 7.8. The "Crash of '87" created a window in the 2,150 to 2,200 zone. Two criteria were needed to tell us the downtrend was over. The first was to close the large window. The second was for a continuation of the buying force once the window closed. These criteria were met in early 1989.

Exhibit 7.9 is another example of a window creating resistance. The

Continuation Patterns   123

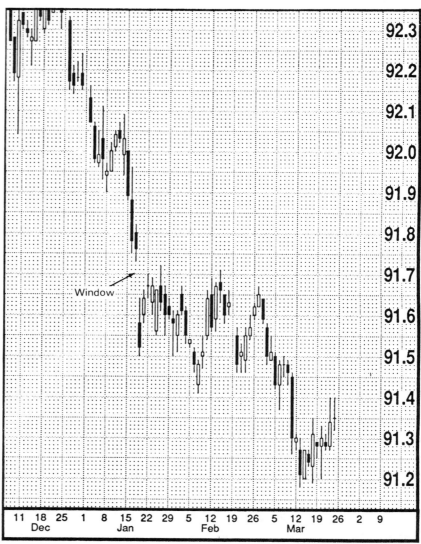

Source: ©Copyright 1990 Commodity Trend Service®

EXHIBIT 7.7. Eurodollar—June 1990, Daily (Window as Resistance)

narrow window 1 in late May implied continuation of the decline. It also became resistance within the next few weeks. Interpreting window 2 offers a chance to underscore the importance of the trend. Real estate agents say the three most important factors about a property are location, location, and location. To paraphrase this, the three most important aspects of the market are trend, trend, and trend. Here, in Exhibit 7.9, we see a market whose major trend is southward.

In this environment, a bullish morning star emerges. Do you buy? No, because the major trend is down! Covering some shorts would be more appropriate. When should nibbling on the long side in this market begin? In this case, it is if the market pushes above $.1164 and buying

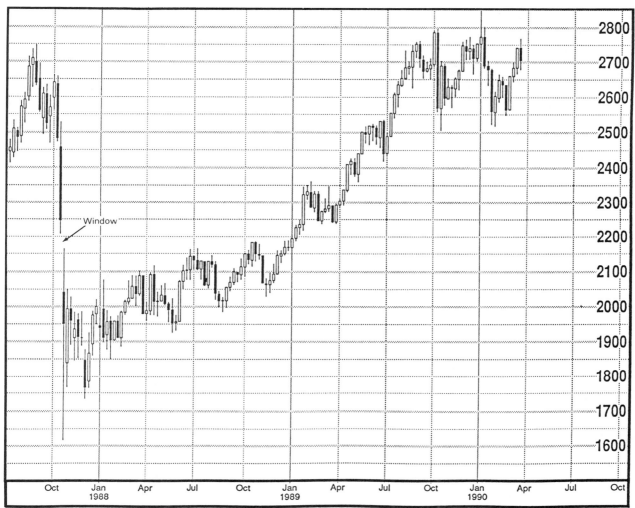

Source: ©Copyright 1990 Commodity Trend Service®

EXHIBIT 7.8. Dow Jones Industrials—Weekly (Window as Resistance)

continued after this level. This is because in mid-July the market formed a window (window 2). The top of the window was $.1164. Until the bulls were able to prove their vigor by pushing prices above this window, going long should be viewed as a high-risk strategy in spite of the morning star. The morning star did act as support on a test of its low a few days after it formed. Yet, after trying for a week the bulls failed in their attempt to close window 2. This told us a new rally was not likely. The moral of this story is that candlesticks, or any other technical tool, should be considered in the context of the prevailing trend.

In Exhibit 7.10, we see that the market headed south after September's hanging man and the black line which engulfed it. The window in late September signaled a continuation of the decline. The window was

EXHIBIT 7.9. Sugar—October 1990, Daily (Windows as Resistance)

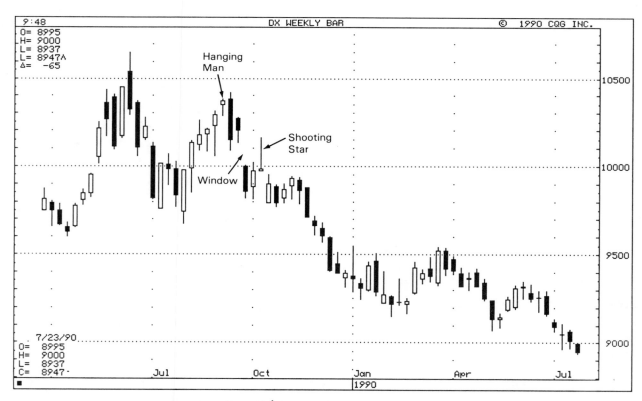

EXHIBIT 7.10. Dollar Index—Weekly (Window as Resistance)

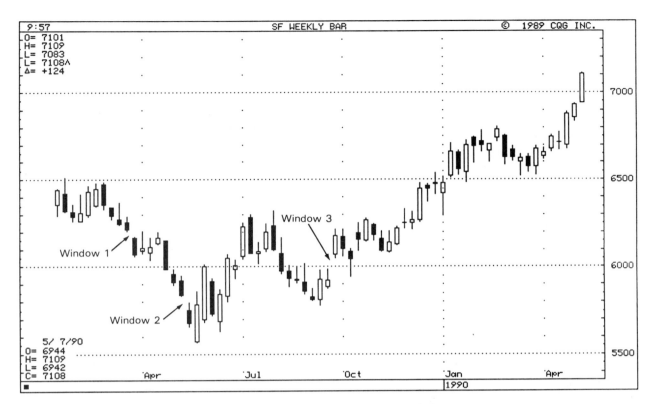

EXHIBIT 7.11. Swiss Franc—Weekly (Windows as Resistance and Support)

closed, but buying steam quickly dissipated as proven by the shooting
star.

There are three windows to discuss in Exhibit 7.11. Window 1 is a
downside window from March 1989. It became a resistance level over the
following few weeks. Window 2 is another downside window which
means more selling pressure will be felt. A long white candlestick a week
after the window formed a bullish engulfing pattern. This was the first
sign of a bottom. The next week, the market closed sharply above the
window. This generated another reason to believe the selling pressure
had dried up. Window 3 is a window in a rally which means to expect
more strength. This window closed in the second week of October, but
not for long as buying pushed prices higher and in the process fashioned
a hammer. Normally hammers are important only during a downtrend
(since they are bottom reversal signals). In this case, it became important
because it reflected a test of the window's support level. If the market
had continued lower after this hammer, the uptrend would have been
nullified.

Exhibit 7.12 shows a series of three windows. Window 1 became
support when the market sold off a few days after the window opened.
Window 2 stopped the rally a month later. Window 3 kept a ceiling on

EXHIBIT 7.12. Gold—December 1990, Daily (Windows and Eight New Record Highs)

all the rally attempts during the week following its opening. Another interesting aspect about the September rally that stalled at window 2 is that the rally, as shown by the numbered days 1 through 8, made eight new higher highs. Candlestick theory states that after about eight to ten new highs or lows, without a meaningful correction, the odds are strong that a significant correction will unfold. Each new high or new low for the move is called a "new record high" or "new record low" by the Japanese. Thus the Japanese will say there are ten record highs or lows, meaning there were a series of ten higher highs or lower lows. If there are, say, eight new highs without a meaningful correction, the Japanese refer to the market by using the expression "the stomach is 80% full." What is interesting about this gold chart is that there were eight record highs. This gave a warning that a top might be near. The fact that after these eight record highs the market was at a resistance area set by window 2 was an extra strong signal to be cautious about the long side of this market.

The enchanted number three makes yet another appearance in Exhibit 7.13. Traditional Japanese technical analysis posits that after three up or down windows, the chances are strong that a top (in the case of three windows in an uptrend) or a bottom (in the case of three win-

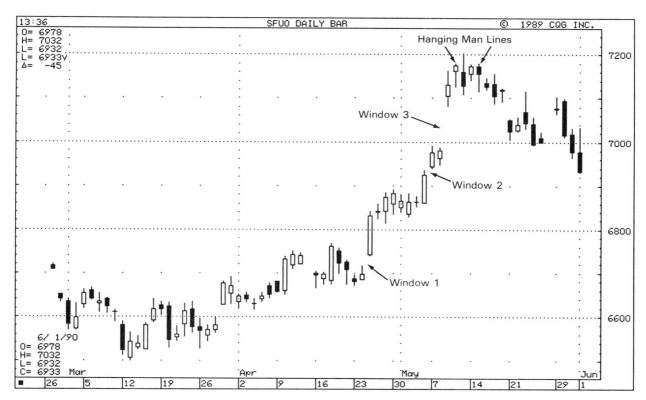

EXHIBIT 7.13. Swiss Franc—September 1990, Daily (Three Windows)

dows in a downtrend) is near, especially if a turning point candlestick pattern or line appears (such as a doji, piercing pattern, or dark-cloud cover) after the third gap. Here we see hanging-man lines after the third window.

In the next few sections, we'll discuss some continuation patterns that have windows as part of their formation. These include the upward and downward gapping tasuki, the high and low price gapping play, and the gapping side-by-side white lines.

Upward- and Downward-Gap Tasuki

The *upside-gap tasuki* (see Exhibit 7.14) is another continuation pattern. The market is in an uptrend. A white candlestick gaps higher and is followed by a black candlestick. The black candlestick opens within the white real body and closes under the white candlestick's real body. The close on the black candlestick day is the buy point. If the market fills in the gap (closes the window) and selling pressure is still evident, the bullish outlook of the upside-gap tasuki is voided. The same concepts would be true, in reverse, for a *downward-gap tasuki* (see Exhibit 7.15).

EXHIBIT 7.14. Upward Gapping Tasuki   **EXHIBIT 7.15.** Downward Gapping Tasuki

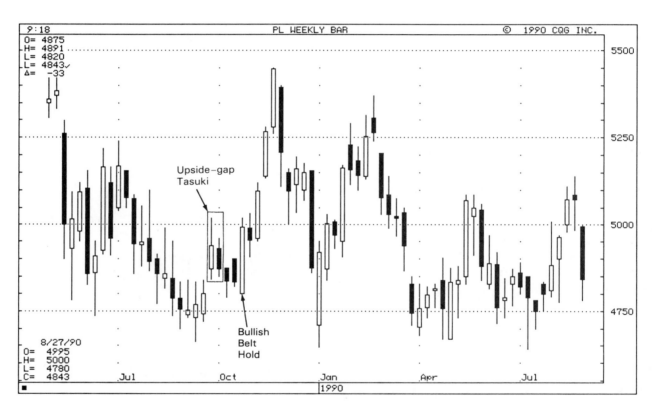

EXHIBIT 7.16. Platinum—Weekly (Upside-gap Tasuki)

The real bodies of the two candlesticks in the tasuki gap be should be about the same size. Both types of tasuki gaps are rare.

Look at Exhibit 7.16 for an example of an upside-gap tasuki. In the last week of September, the market experienced a small upside gap via a white candlestick. The next weekly black candlestick opened in the prior week's real body and closed under that white real body's open. This created an upside-gap tasuki. Note how the small window opened by this pattern provided support in the October pullback. The bullish belt hold signaled the advent of the rally.

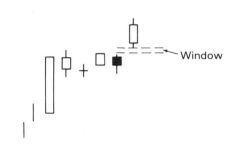

EXHIBIT 7.17. High-price Gapping Play

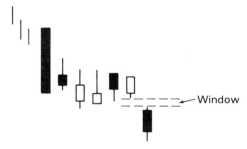

EXHIBIT 7.18. Low-price Gapping Play

High-price and Low-price Gapping Plays

It is normal after a sharp one to two session advance for the market to consolidate the gains. Sometimes this consolidation is by a series of small real bodies. A group of small real bodies after a strong session tells us that the market is undecided. However, if there is an upside gap on the opening (that is, a window) from these small real bodies, it is time to buy. This is *high-price gapping play pattern* (see Exhibit 7.17). It is called this because prices hover near their recent highs and then gaps to the upside.

A *low-price gapping play* is, not surprisingly, the bearish counterpart of the high-price gapping play. The low-price gapping play (see Exhibit 7.18) is a downside window from a low-price congestion band. This *congestion band* (a series of small real bodies) initially stabilized a steep one to two session decline. At first, this group of small candlesticks gives the appearance that a base is forming. The break to the downside via a window dashes these bullish hopes.

Exhibit 7.19 illustrates that in late October/early November, a series of three small real bodies helped digest the gains of the prior tall white candlestick session. When sugar gapped up it completed the first upward-gapping play pattern on this chart. The market rallied until the dark-cloud cover on November 17 and 18. High-price gapping play pattern 2 had a tall white candlestick session, some small real bodies, and then a window. This window converted to support level.

The candlesticks in Exhibit 7.20 sent a bullish signal when the window opened on June 29. This window completed the action needed to form the upward-gapping play. Prior to this gapping play, there was a strong a strong white candlestick on June 11. A group of small candlesticks followed this line. This had the potential to become a high-price gapping play. No upward gap, however, meant a no buy signal.

As shown in Exhibit 7.21, on July 20 and 21 the S&P quickly fell 18 points. It then traded sideways at lower price levels for over a week (for

Source: CompuTrac™

EXHIBIT 7.19. Sugar—May 1990, Daily (High-price Gapping Play)

a gapping play, the consolidation should not last more than 11 sessions). A Japanese broker related to me that one of her clients in Japan (a fund manager who applies candlesticks) obtained a sell signal on August 2 (see arrow at the doji) based on the low-price gapping play pattern.

This shows an aspect about the candlesticks which has been discussed earlier. The techniques and procedures used to interpret the candlestick patterns are guidelines, not hard and fast rules. Here we have an example where the ideals of the low-price gapping play were not exactly meet, yet the Japanese fund manager thought it was close enough to act on. In principle, for a low-price gapping play to be completed the market should gap lower. The low on August 1 was at 355.80 and the high on August 2 was 355.90. Thus there was no gap. Yet it was close enough that the Japanese fund manager got his sell signal on August 2. Note also the sharp decline preceding the small real bodies did not close on the low. Yet, because prices stayed within the lows of the range during the next few sessions, it resembled the low-price gapping play closely enough to provide the Japanese candlestick practitioner with

EXHIBIT 7.20. Soybeans—November 1990, Daily (High-price Gapping Play)

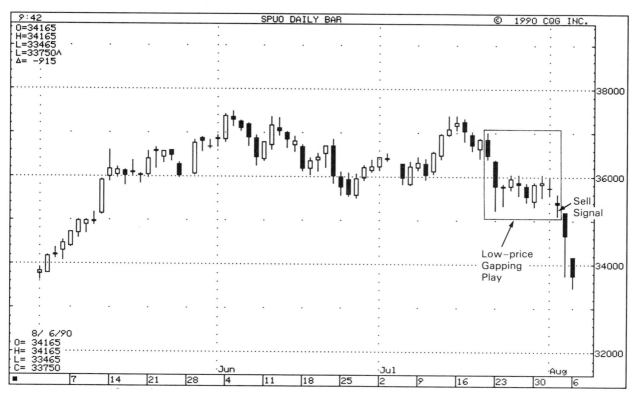

EXHIBIT 7.21. S&P—September, 1990, Daily (Low-price Gapping Play)

a sell signal on August 2. This is an illustration of how candlestick patterns, as with all charting techniques, offer room for subjectivity.

Gapping Side-by-side White Lines

In an uptrend, an upward-gapping white candlestick followed the next session by another similar sized white candlestick with about the same opening is a bullish continuation pattern. This two candlestick pattern is referred to as *upgap side-by-side white lines* (see Exhibit 7.22). If the market closes above the higher of the side-by-side white candlesticks, another leg up should unfold.

The side-by-side white candlesticks described previously are rare. Even more rare are side-by-side white lines which gap lower. These are called *downgap side-by-side white lines* (see Exhibit 7.23). In a downtrend, the side-by-side white lines are also a continuation pattern. That is, prices should continue lower. The reason this pattern is not bullish (as is the upgap variety) is because in a falling market, these white lines are viewed as short covering. Once this short covering evaporates, prices should move lower. The reason that the downgap side-by-side white line pattern is especially rare is because black candlesticks, not white candlesticks, are more natural in a market that lowers gaps. If in a falling market a black candlestick gaps lower and is followed by another black candlestick with a lower close, the market should experience another price decline.

Exhibit 7.24 shows a downgap side-by-side white line pattern in early March. The theory behind this pattern during a downtrend is that it is short covering. Thus it offers only a temporary respite from a falling market. That is what we saw here as the market resumed its drop after a period of consolidation. This is not an ideal downgap side-by-side

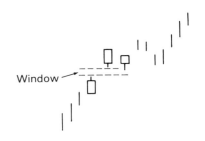

EXHIBIT 7.22. Gapping Side-by-side White Lines in an Uptrend

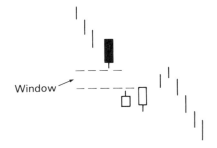

EXHIBIT 7.23. Gapping Side-by-side White Lines in a Downtrend

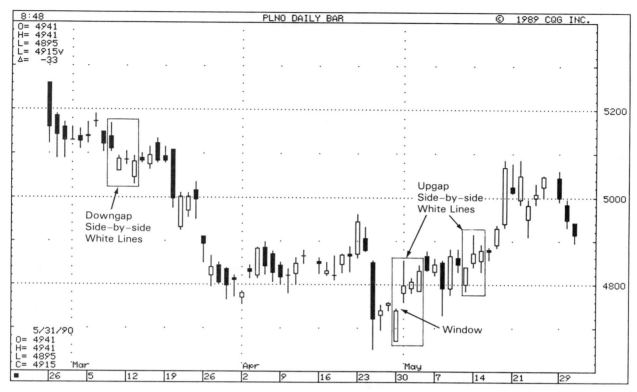

EXHIBIT 7.24. Platinum—July 1990, Daily (Gapping Side-by-side White Lines)

white line pattern since the opens on the white candlesticks were not identical and the white lines were separated by one day. Nonetheless, this is likened to the downgap side-by-side white line pattern.

In addition, Exhibit 7.24 shows two upgap side-by-side white line patterns. This pattern portends bullish implications if it emerges at lower price levels. The first upgap side-by-side white line pattern had three opens at about the same price. Then the market staged a brief pullback on May 8 which marginally broke under the window but sprang right back from there. The second upgap side-by-side white line pattern gave another bullish signal. As should be the case with the upgap side-by-side white lines, they provided a firm footing.

RISING AND FALLING THREE METHODS

These three methods include the *bullish rising three methods* and the *bearish falling three methods*. (Note how the number three again makes an appearance.) These are both continuation patterns. The benchmarks for the rising three methods pattern (see Exhibit 7.25) include:

EXHIBIT 7.25. Rising Three Methods

1. A long white candlestick.
2. This white candlestick is followed by a group of falling small real body candlesticks. The ideal number of small candlesticks is three but two or more than three are also acceptable as long as they basically hold within the long white candlestick's range. Think of the small candlesticks as forming a pattern similar to a three-day harami pattern since they hold within the first session's range. (For this pattern that would include holding within the shadows; for a true harami it would only include the real body.) The small candlesticks can be any color, but black is most common.
3. The final day should be a strong white real body session with a close above the first day's close. The final candlestick line should also open above the close of the previous session.

This pattern resembles the Western bull flag or pennant formation. Yet, the concept behind the rising three methods is from the 1700s. The three methods pattern is considered a rest from trading and a rest from battle. In more modern terms, the market is, with the group of small candles, "taking a breather."

The falling three methods pattern (see Exhibit 7.26) is the bearish counterpart of the rising three methods pattern. For this pattern to occur, the market should be in a downtrend and a long black candlestick should emerge. It is followed by about three small rising candles (usually white) whose real bodies hold within the first candlestick's range (including shadows). The final session should open under the prior close and then close under the first black candlestick's close. After this last

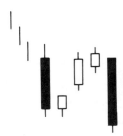

EXHIBIT 7.26. Falling Three Methods

EXHIBIT 7.27. Gold—April 1990, Daily (Rising Three Methods)

black candlestick session, the market should head lower. This pattern resembles a bear flag or pennant formation.

Exhibit 7.27 shows a classic rising three methods pattern. The market is in an uptrend with three downtrending black small real bodies preceded by a white candlestick. The black candlesticks essentially held within the white candlestick's range. The last white candlestick then closes above the first candlestick's close. A factor that may lend more significance to this pattern is if volume on the white (black) sessions for the rising (falling) three method pattern is higher than the small candlestick sessions. Here we see the white session days of the rising three methods pattern had greater volume than on the three small black candlestick sessions.

Exhibit 7.28 is also a rising three methods pattern. When completed, the bonds pushed until they reached the bearish engulfing pattern.

Although the ideal three methods has three small candlesticks following a long white one, Exhibit 7.29 is an example of two small candlesticks. The price action in June 1988 built a tall white candlestick. Black candlesticks that held within this white candlestick's range followed in July and August. September formed another white candlestick which made a new high for the move but failed to close above June's close by

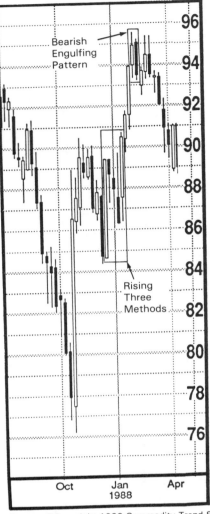

EXHIBIT 7.28. Bonds—Weekly (Rising Three Methods)

Source: ©Copyright 1990 Commodity Trend Service®

only 3 ticks. Normally, we would want to see a higher close. In this case, since the last white candlestick (September) only missed closing above June's close by 3 ticks, this pattern should still be considered a rising three methods pattern with bullish confirmation the next session. A new high close in October gave this confirmation and secured the bullish outlook.

Three small candlesticks held within the first candlestick's high and low range are evident in Exhibit 7.30. These were trailed by another white candlestick. This last white candlestick had the same close as the first one, so we need confirmation. When the next hour opened above the last white candlestick, the bullish confirmation was at hand. Observe how the top of the rising three methods pattern became a support area as tested by the first hour on August 1.

Two examples of this bullish continuation pattern appear in Exhibit

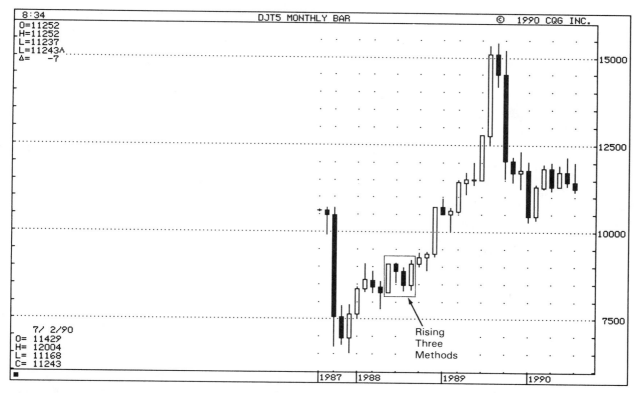

EXHIBIT 7.29. Dow Jones Transportation Monthly (Rising Three Methods)

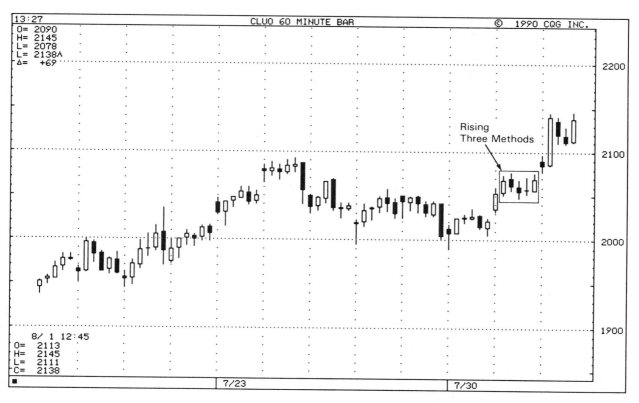

EXHIBIT 7.30. Crude Oil—September 1990, Intra-day (Rising Three Methods)

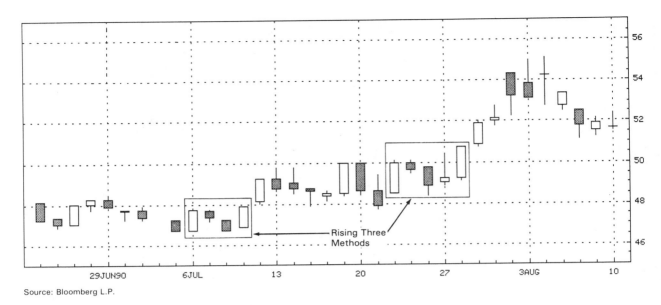

Source: Bloomberg L.P.

EXHIBIT 7.31. Exxon—1990, Daily (Rising Three Methods)

7.31. The first rising three methods pattern, in early July, shows how there can be two candlesticks instead of three, after the first tall white real body. Notice how the two black candlesticks held within the first candlestick's range. Then the last white real body of this pattern opened above the close of the prior session and made a new high close for the move. The second illustration of this pattern in Exhibit 7.31 displays how the color of the real bodies after the first candlestick does not have to be black. As long as the real bodies hold within the first session's range it has the potential to be a three methods pattern. Here the potential was fulfilled as the last long white candlestick closed at a new high.

In March 1989, a window appeared as shown in Exhibit 7.32. Based on the saying that corrections go to the window, one should expect a bounce up to the window. From there the preceding downtrend should resume. After the window, three small real bodies developed. The assault on the window took place on the first week of April. It failed from there. Two weeks later, on the third small white candlestick week, there was another attempt to close the window. This attempt also faltered. The last long black candlestick closed under the first black candlestick's close. This action completed the five candlesticks of the falling three methods.

Exhibit 7.33 is an example with four, instead of three, small real bodies. The key is that the real bodies hold within the first day's range. The last large black candlestick concluded this pattern. Note how *tick volume*™ confirmed the black candlesticks action. That is, tick volume™ expanded with the black candlesticks and shrank with the intervening

EXHIBIT 7.32. Swiss Franc—Weekly (Falling Three Methods)

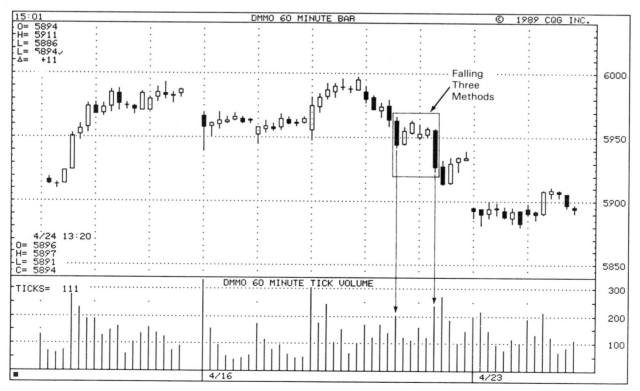

EXHIBIT 7.33. Deutschemark—June 1990, Intra-day (Falling Three Methods)

EXHIBIT 7.34. Copper—July 1990, Intra-day (Incomplete Falling Three Methods)

white candlesticks. We will go into more detail about candlesticks with volume in Chapter 15, including tick volume™.

The intra-day chart in Exhibit 7.34 addresses an important principle—do not act on a formation until that formation is completed. Here, for instance, is an example of an incomplete falling three methods. A lengthy black real body developed during the first hour on April 23. Three uptrending small real bodies then appeared. A long black candlestick follows these small candlesticks. The close on the fifth hour's candlestick was not under the close of the first hour's candlestick. Thus the falling three methods was not completed. If there is bearish confirmation during the next session, the action should still be viewed as confirmation of a bearish falling three methods since the closes of the first and last black candlesticks were so close. In this case, there was no bearish confirmation over the next hour or two.

A doji appeared after the last black real body. This doji, joined with the prior black real body, fashioned a harami cross. This is a reversal pattern which hinted that the immediately preceding downtrend would not persist. In addition, the lows over the next few hours successfully tested all the hourly lows from April 23. Thus, if one anticipated that the falling three methods would be completed, one would have guessed

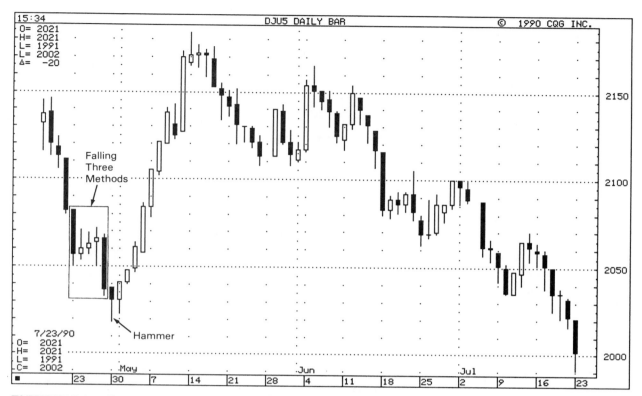

EXHIBIT 7.35. Dow Jones Utilities—1990, Daily (Falling Three Methods).

wrong. Wait until the pattern is formed, or confirmed, before acting on its implications!

Exhibit 7.35 is a classic falling three method whose bearish implication was negated by the hammer. If the hammer was not enough to tell one the downleg was ending more proof was added with the white session following the hammer. This completed a bullish engulfing pattern.

THREE ADVANCING WHITE SOLDIERS

Like much of the candlestick terminology, this pattern has a military association. It is known as the *three advancing white soldiers* (see Exhibit 7.36) or, more commonly, *three white soldiers.* It is a group of three white candlesticks with consecutively higher closes. If this pattern appears at a low price area after a period of stable prices, then it is a sign of strength ahead.

The three white soldiers are a gradual and steady rise with each white line opening within or near the prior session's white real body. Each of the white candlesticks should close at, or near, its highs. It is a

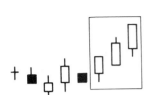
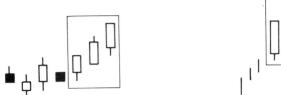

EXHIBIT 7.36. Three Advancing White Soldiers

EXHIBIT 7.37. Advance Block

EXHIBIT 7.38. Stalled Pattern

healthy method for the market to rise (although if the white candlesticks are very extended, one should be cautious about an overbought market).

If the second and third, or just the third candlestick, show signs of weakening it is an *advance block pattern* (see Exhibit 7.37). This means that the rally is running into trouble and that longs should protect themselves. Be especially cautious about this pattern during a mature uptrend. Signs of weakening could be progressively smaller white real bodies or relatively long upper shadows on the latter two white candlesticks.

If the last two candlesticks are long white ones that make a new high followed by a small white candlestick, it is called a *stalled pattern* (see Exhibit 7.38). It is also sometimes called a *deliberation pattern*. After this formation the bull's strength has been at least temporarily exhausted. This last small white candlestick can either gap away from the long white body (in which case it becomes a star) or it can be, as the Japanese express it, "riding on the shoulder" of the long white real body (that is, be at the upper end of the prior long white real body). The small real body discloses a deterioration of the bulls' power. The time of the stalled pattern is the time for the longs to take profits.

Although the advance block and stalled patterns are not normally top reversal patterns, they can sometimes precede a meaningful price decline. The advance block and stalled patterns should be used to liquidate or protect longs (for example, sell covered calls) but not to short. They are generally more consequential at higher price levels.

In Exhibit 7.39, the three white soldiers from a low price level in 1985 projected a rally. There follows two advance block patterns. Advance block 1 has progressively smaller white real bodies in early 1987 which did not bode well for higher prices. A shooting star was the last small white real body of this three candlestick group. The market floundered for the next few months. There was another price push after these doji but the next advanced block pattern gave another warning sign. Advance block 2 formed in mid-1987. The major difference between this three white candlestick pattern and the three white soldiers in advance

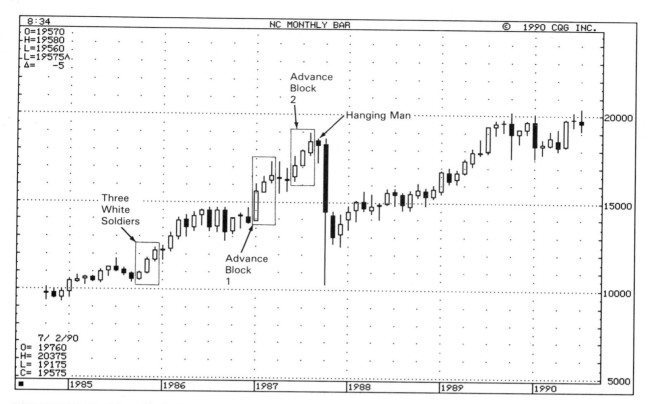

EXHIBIT 7.39. New York Composite—Monthly (Three White Soldiers, Advance Block)

block 1 is that the last white candlestick had a longer upper shadow. It was not very long, but it showed that the market did not have the power to close near the highs. In other words, the lead (that is, advance) soldier had been "blocked." A hanging-man line appeared next month. The soldiers then went into retreat.

There was another reason to be suspicious about more upside after advance block 2. Whereas the three white soldiers in 1985 started from a low price level, the three white candlesticks of the advance block pattern arose after the market had already sustained an extended advance.

In early 1989 (see Exhibit 7.40), stalled pattern 1 temporarily stalled the prior price incline. Additionally, this pattern came after an extended series of white candles.

Stalled pattern 2 only stalled the advance for a couple of weeks. The last small real white body in this deliberation pattern was a hanging man. Once the market closed above the hanging man's high two weeks later, the market was not likely to fall. In early July, the bullish three white soldiers started a meaningful rally. It lasted for seven new highs (that is, seven record highs). Another set of three white soldiers appeared in the third quarter 1989. Because each of these three white candlesticks closed at their high, this pattern had all the earmarks of

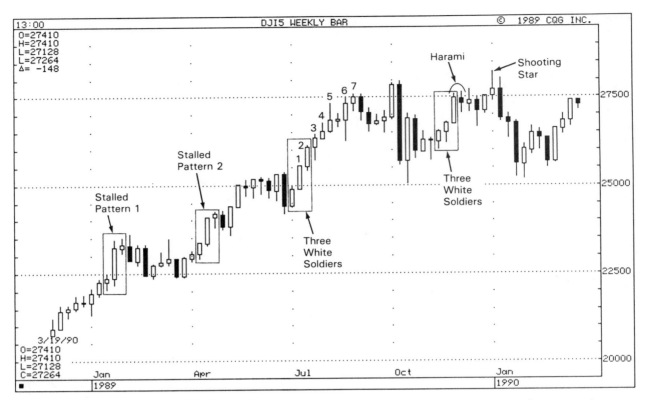

EXHIBIT 7.40. Dow Jones Industrial Average—Weekly (Stalled Patterns and Three White Soldiers)

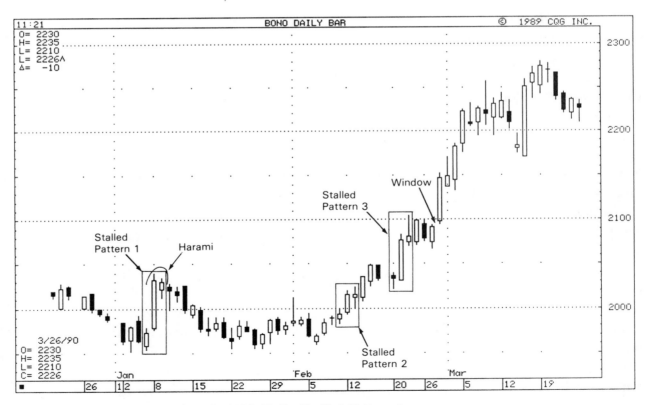

EXHIBIT 7.41. Soybean Oil—July 1990, Daily (Stalled Patterns)

implying another strong rally, similar to the one that had started in July. This was not to be. The week after the third white candlestick of this group, a small real body emerged. This formed a harami and told us the prior uptrend had run into trouble. The shooting star a few weeks later confirmed problems at these highs.

Exhibit 7.41 illustrates three stalled patterns. Pattern 1 also formed a harami which short circuited the rally. Stalled pattern 2 failed to keep the rally in check, while stalled pattern 3 contained a shooting star. Stalled pattern 3 induced a trend change as the market went from up, to sideways for a few weeks. Remember that the stalled pattern is not usually a trend reversal, it often means a time of deliberation before the market decides its next trend. In the case of stalled pattern 3, a window opened after the congestion band completing a bullish high-price gapping play. This indicated a resumption of strength.

SEPARATING LINES

In Chapter 6, we examined the counterattack line. Remember, this is a white or black candlestick line with the same close as the previous opposite color candlestick and it is a reversal signal. Whereas the counterattack line has the same close, the separating lines in Exhibit 7.42 have the same open as the previous opposite color candlestick. The *separating line* is a continuation pattern.

During a market rise, a black real body (especially a relatively long one) would be cause for concern if you are long. The bears might be gaining control. However, if the next session's opening gaps higher to open at the previous black session's opening price, it shows that the bears lost control of the market. If this white candlestick session then closes higher, it tells us the bulls have regained control and the prior price rise should continue. This is the scenario which unfolds with the

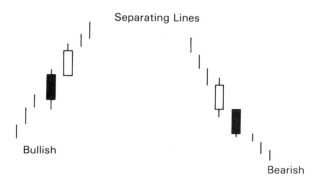

EXHIBIT 7.42. Bullish and Bearish Separating Lines

bullish separating line as shown in Exhibit 7.42. The white line should also be a bullish belt hold (that is, open on the low of the session). The opposite would be true with the bearish separating line in exhibit 7.42. This is viewed as a bearish continuation pattern.

CHAPTER 8

THE MAGIC DOJI

· ·

窓から槍

"A sudden danger"

As described in Chapter 3, a *doji* is a candlestick in which the opening and closing prices are the same. Examples of doji lines are shown in Exhibits 8.1 through 8.3. The doji is such a significant reversal indicator that this chapter is devoted solely to its manifestations. In prior chapters, we have seen the power of a doji as a component of some patterns. These included the *doji star* (see Chapter 5,) and the *harami cross* (see Chapter 6).

EXHIBIT 8.1. Doji   **EXHIBIT 8.2.** Long-legged Doji (Rickshaw Man)   **EXHIBIT 8.3.** Gravestone Doji

THE IMPORTANCE OF THE DOJI

The perfect doji session has the same opening and closing price, yet there is some flexibility to this rule. If the opening and closing price are within a few ticks of each other (for example, a ¼ cent in grains or a few thirty-seconds in bonds, and so on), the line could still be viewed as a doji. How do you decide whether a near-doji day (that is, where the open and close are very close, but not exact) should be considered a doji? This is subjective and there are no rigid rules but one way is to look at a near-doji day in relation to recent action. If there are a series of very small real bodies, the near-doji day would not be viewed as significant since so many other recent periods had small real bodies. One technique is based on recent market activity. If the market is at an important market junction, or is at the mature part of a bull or bear move, or there are other technical signals sending out an alert, the appearance of a near-doji is treated as a doji. The philosophy is that a doji can be a significant warning and that it is better to attend to a false warning than to ignore a real one. To ignore a doji, with all its inherent implications, could be dangerous.

The doji is a distinct trend change signal. However, the likelihood of a reversal increases if subsequent candlesticks confirm the doji's reversal potential. Doji sessions are important only in markets where there are not many doji. If there are many doji on a particular chart, one should not view the emergence of a new doji in that particular market as a meaningful development. That is why candlestick analysis usually should not use intra-day charts of less than 30 minutes. Less than 30 minutes and many of the candlestick lines become doji or near doji (except for the very active markets such as bond and S&P futures).

DOJI AT TOPS

Doji are valued for their ability to call market tops. This is especially true after a long white candlestick in an uptrend (see Exhibit 8.4). The reason for the doji's negative implications in uptrends is because a doji represents indecision. Indecision, uncertainty, or vacillation by buyers will not maintain an uptrend. It takes the conviction of buyers to sustain a rally. If the market has had an extended rally, or is overbought, and then a doji surfaces (read "indecision"), it could mean the scaffolding of buyers' support will give way.

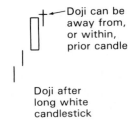

EXHIBIT 8.4. Doji Following a Tall White Candlestick

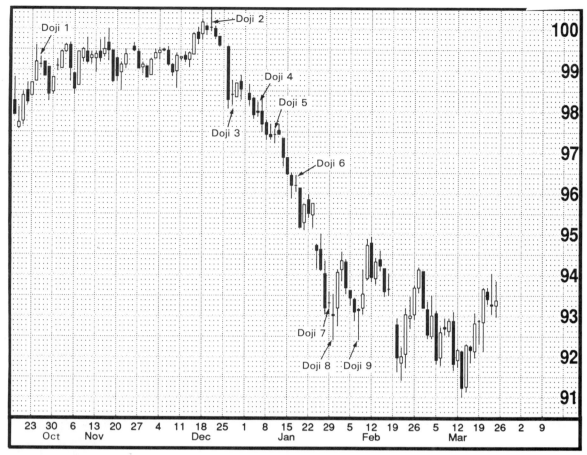

Source: ©Copyright Commodity Trend Service®

EXHIBIT 8.5. Bonds—June, 1990, Daily (Doji at Tops)

Yet, as good as doji are at calling tops, based on experience, they tend to lose reversal potential in downtrends. The reason may be that a doji reflects a balance between buying and selling forces. With ambivalent market participants, the market could fall due to its own weight. Thus, an uptrend should reverse but a falling market may continue its descent. Because of this, doji need more confirmation to signal a bottom than they do a top. This is examined on Exhibit 8.5.

As seen in Exhibit 8.5, after doji 1, the bond's uptrend changed to a lateral band. The market summit was at doji 2. Doji 2 was a long-legged doji. A long-legged doji means a doji with one or two very long shadows. Long-legged doji are often signs of a market top. More about them later in this chapter. We can see how important doji 1 and 2 were after uptrends in calling a trend reversal. (The October 31 doji was in the middle of a trading band and thus unimportant.) Once prices broke to the downside, doji 3, 4, 5, 6, and 7 developed. Yet, these doji were not reversals. The market still continued down after they appeared. Only

EXHIBIT 8.6. Wheat—Monthly (Doji at Tops)

when doji 8 and 9 formed a double bottom was there a trend reversal (albeit temporary). Thus there may be less need for confirmation of a top reversal via a doji than for a bottom reversal.

Exhibit 8.6 illustrates that the rally which began in mid-1987, gave its first sign of peaking with doji 1. Another warning flag was hoisted with doji 2, a few months later. The hanging man after doji 2 confirmed the top. A minor rally attempt ended in late 1989 at doji 3. This exhibit exemplifies that confirmation after a doji increases success in projecting a trend reversal. The white candlestick, which appeared a month after doji 1, did not confirm the top hinted at by doji 1. Bearish confirmation came only after doji 2. After doji 2, this verification came in the form of a hanging man and then a long black candlestick. Confirmation of doji 3 as a top came with the next month's long black candlestick session.

The more conservative trading style used, the more important it is to wait for verification of a trend change. How long should one wait for corroboration? It is a trade-off between risk and reward. If one bases one's trading style on waiting for trend reversal corroboration less risk should be involved but, it also could provide less reward. By the time the reversal is substantiated, profit potential may be reduced.

Exhibit 8.7 shows three doji, each after an uptrend. Doji 1 signaled a

EXHIBIT 8.7. Soybeans—July, 1990, Daily (Doji at Tops)

minor top. Doji 2 did not correctly call a reversal, but it was followed the next day by an $.08 decline. Doji 3 is interesting. It is more important than the prior two doji since it followed a series of three long white candlesticks and it formed a harami cross. Doji 3 strongly stressed that the prior uptrend might be over. When it appeared, longs should have taken protective measures (the prior strong uptrend negated short selling). This means that they should either be liquidating some longs, moving up protective stops levels, and/or selling calls.

An intra-day spike higher the next day made it appear that the prediction about the end of the uptrend was going to be wrong. But, on that day, the market sold off sharply toward the close. This action helped confirm the original view that the prior uptrend was about over. The market then went into a congestion phase for the next few weeks. A pattern resembling an evening star then arose. It was not an ideal evening star pattern since the star portion did not gap away from the prior long white real body, yet it presaged a top.

DOJI AFTER A LONG WHITE CANDLESTICK

Exhibit 8.8 shows that a doji after a long white candlestick, especially after a prolonged uptrend, is often a forewarning that a top is near. This exhibit has three examples of this concept:

1. In August 1989, a doji followed two long white candlesticks. After doji 1, the prior uptrend (which began with a bullish hammer from August 22) went from up to sideways.

2. Doji 2, in early November, was preceded by a long white candlestick. When this doji emerged, the minor rally, which preceded it, ended. Within a few days, the Dow had broken under the late October lows.

3. During the last few weeks of 1989, the Dow had a steep advance that pushed above the 2800 level. But look at where the rally was short circuited—after the appearance of doji 3. The fact that this doji came after a long white candlestick meant that the buyers, which were in control the prior day (as proven by the long white candlestick) had lost control. The next day's black candlestick increased the probability that the market had crested. It also completed an evening doji star formation.

In this example, we see another strength of candlestick charting; they provide a signal not obtainable with Western technical analysis techniques. To non-Japanese technicians, if a session's open and close are the same, no forecasting implications are taken. To the Japanese, such a session, especially at the heels of a sharp advance, is a critical reversal sign.

Exhibit 8.9 illustrates a modest rally which began with a hammerlike line in mid-March (the lower shadow was not long enough nor was the real body small enough to be a true hammer), culminated with a doji after a long white line. This doji day was also part of an evening doji star pattern. An "ideal" hammer on April 6 stopped the price decline.

Exhibit 8.10 illustrates that an uptrend that thrusted bonds 7 points higher, ended with a doji following the long white real body. Exhibit 8.11 shows that a rally commenced with the hammer on April 19. It ended on April 23 when a doji appeared after a long white candlestick.

THE LONG-LEGGED DOJI AND THE RICKSHAW MAN

The *long-legged doji* is an especially important doji at tops. As shown in Exhibit 8.2, this doji has long upper and lower shadows, clearly reflect-

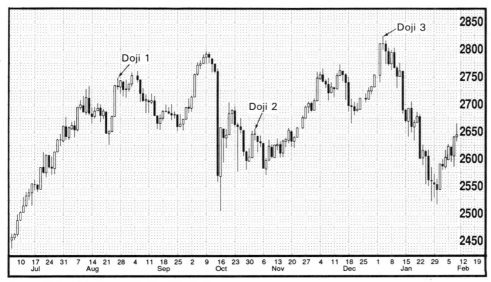

Source: ©Copyright Commodity Trend Service®

EXHIBIT 8.8. Dow Jones Industrials—1989–1990, Daily (Doji after a Long White Candlestick)

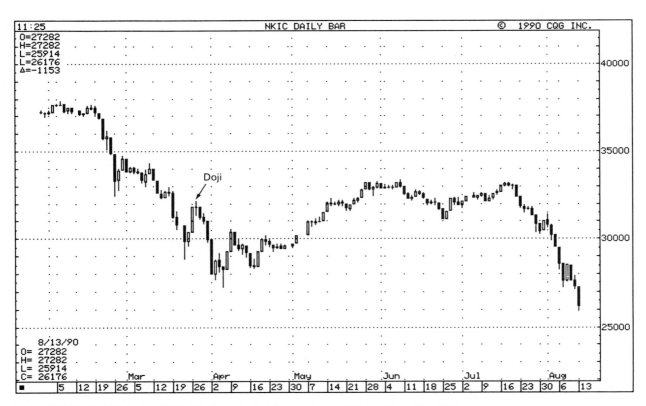

EXHIBIT 8.9. Nikkei—1990, Daily (Doji After a Long White Candlestick)

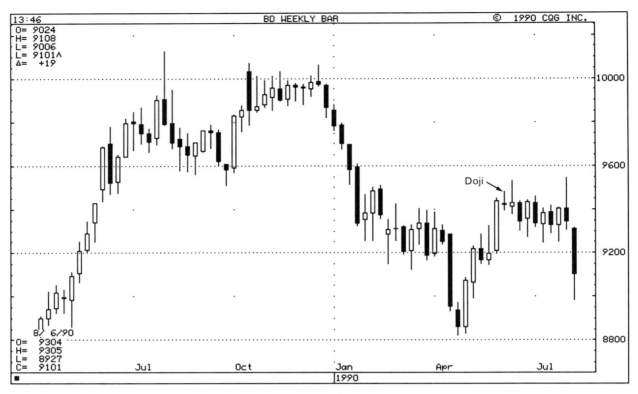

EXHIBIT 8.10. Bonds—Weekly (Doji after a Long White Candlestick)

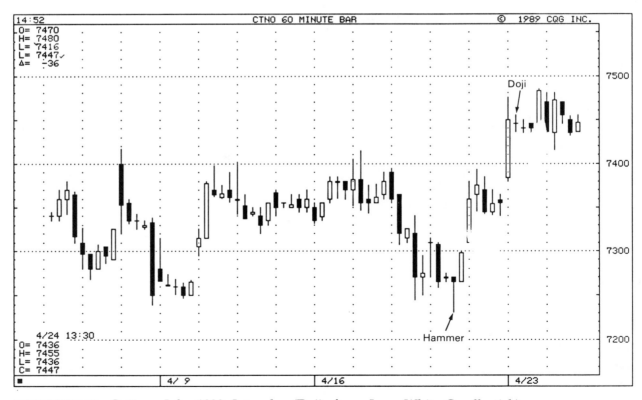

EXHIBIT 8.11. Cotton—July, 1990, Intra-day (Doji after a Long White Candlestick)

ing irresolution. Throughout the session, the market pushed strongly higher, then sharply lower (or vice versa). It then closed at, or very near, the opening price. If the opening and closing are in the center of the session's range, the line is referred to as a *rickshaw man*. If there is a non-doji session with a very long upper and/or lower shadow with a small real body, the line is referred to as a *high-wave line*. A group of high-wave candlesticks are a reversal formation. To the Japanese, very long upper or lower shadows represent a candlestick that has, as they say, "lost its sense of direction."

In Exhibit 8.12, late April and early May trading sessions were marked by a series of doji or near-doji days. These narrow real bodies are an unhealthy sign after a rally. They indicate tired markets. In a rally one likes to see the buyers in control. The long-legged doji (in this case, two rickshaw-man lines) were a major danger sign (although the opening and closing on the first one were not exactly the same, they were close enough to be considered a doji day). These long-legged doji reflects a market that has "lost its sense of direction." This group of small range candlestick days formed a major top. With these bearish candles overhanging the market, we can perhaps jokingly call this the "falling chandelier formation."

EXHIBIT 8.12. Sugar—July, 1990, Daily (Long-legged Doji)

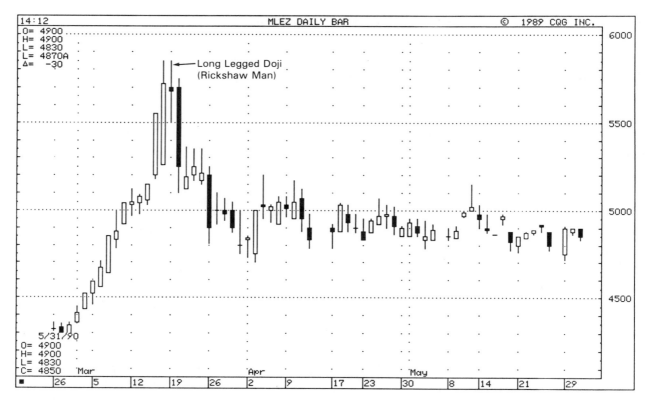

EXHIBIT 8.13. London Lead—1990, Three Month (Long-legged Doji)

Exhibit 8.13 has a strong hint of a peak with the long-legged doji (here the opening and closing were close enough to consider this a doji session). The long-legged doji day also completed a harami pattern and a tweezers top. This confluence of technical factors were forceful clues that the highs were at hand. Exhibit 8.14 illustrates that a price peak in gold was reached with the long-legged doji in January. The long upper shadows in early February confirmed the resistance set by the long-legged doji.

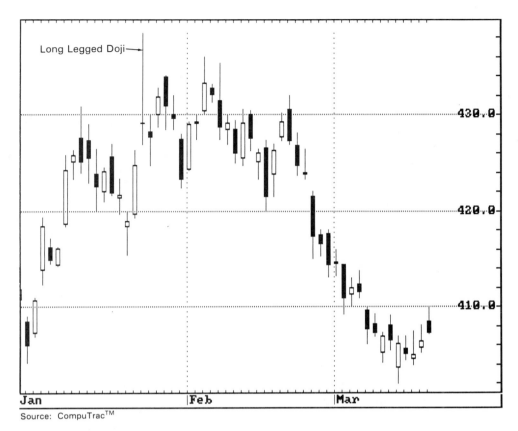

Source: CompuTrac™

EXHIBIT 8.14. Gold—June, 1990, Daily (Long-legged Doji)

THE GRAVESTONE DOJI

The *gravestone doji* (see Exhibit 8.3) is another distinctive doji. It develops when the opening and closing prices are at the low of the day. While it can sometimes be found at market bottoms, its forte is in calling tops. The shape of the gravestone doji makes its name appropriate. As we have discussed, many of the Japanese technical terms are based on military analogies, and in this context, the gravestone doji also represents the graves of those bulls or bears who have died defending their territory.

The reason for the bearish implications of the gravestone doji after a rally can be explained simply. The market opens on the low of the session. It then rallies (preferably to a new high for the move). Then trouble occurs for the longs as prices plummet to the day's lows. The longer the upper shadow and the higher the price level, the more bearish the implications of the gravestone doji.

Exhibit 8.15 shows that April 11 and 12 are doji days. The second doji

EXHIBIT 8.15. Eurodollar—June 1990, Daily (Gravestone Doji)

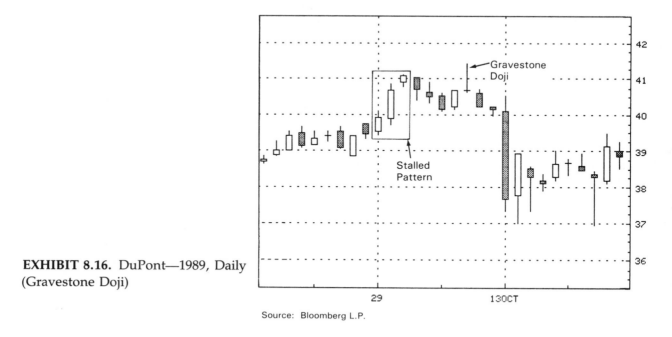

EXHIBIT 8.16. DuPont—1989, Daily
(Gravestone Doji)

Source: Bloomberg L.P.

is the one of most interest. It is a gravestone doji. In this case, it marks the end of the battle for the bulls as the bears take over when the uptrend support line is broken. (This topic of candlesticks with trendlines is examined in detail in Chapter 11.) Exhibit 8.16 illustrates that the gravestone doji on October 8 (the very minor lower shadow does not void this as a gravestone) was especially negative for this stock. On that day, a new high was touched. It was the bulls' chance to propel prices, but they failed. By the close, prices had pulled back to near the daily low. There was trouble at this $41 level before. Beginning on September 29, three candlestick lines developed into a stalled pattern. The gravestone doji confirmed the heavy supply at $41.

Some of you may have noticed that a gravestone doji looks like a shooting star. The gravestone doji, at tops, is a specific version of a shooting star. The shooting star has a small real body, but the gravestone doji—being a doji—has no real body. The gravestone doji is more bearish than a shooting star.

DOJI AS SUPPORT AND RESISTANCE

Doji, especially at significant tops or bottoms, can sometimes turn into support or resistance zones. Exhibit 8.17 shows how the lower shadow

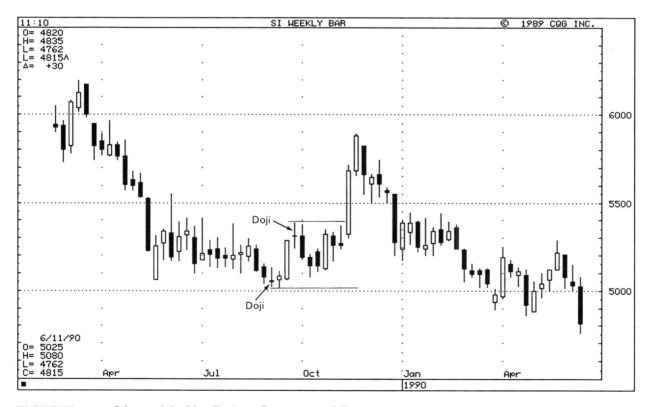

EXHIBIT 8.17. Silver—Weekly (Doji as Support and Resistance)

EXHIBIT 8.18. Soybeans—July, 1990, Intra-day (Doji as Resistance)

of the doji week in September 1989 became a support area. The doji star top in late September became a resistance level.

In Exhibit 8.18, the rickshaw man (the real body was small enough to consider it a doji) on the first hour of March 21 gave a clue that the previous uptrend could be reversing. A doji occurring a few hours later give more proof for this outlook. These two doji became a significant resistance area.

THE TRI-STAR

The *tri-star* (see Exhibit 8.19) is a very rare, but a very significant reversal pattern. The tri-star is formed by three doji lines. The middle doji is a doji star. I have yet to see an ideal tri-star, as shown in Exhibit 8.19, but the following examples show the significance of this pattern even in its variations. The reason we are discussing this pattern here, instead of

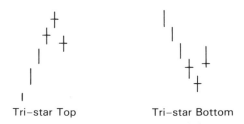

EXHIBIT 8.19. Tri-star Top and Bottom

in the chapter on stars, is because the most important aspect of this pattern is that the lines should be three doji (or near-doji).

Exhibit 8.20 shows that early in the week of September 15 there were two doji followed by a third, small real body candlestick. This variation on a tri-star was the start of a $.15 rally. Exhibit 8.21 shows that in late September 1989, the Dow began a rally that culminated in a series of three doji in early October. Although not an ideal tri-star, the three doji after a 170-point advance was a portentous sign. Notice that the latter two doji also formed a tweezer top.

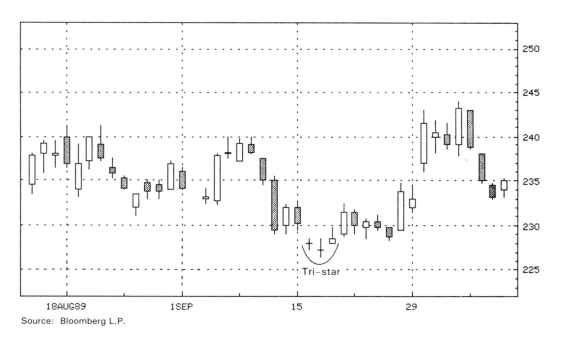

Source: Bloomberg L.P.

EXHIBIT 8.20. Corn—December 1989, Daily (Tri-star Bottom)

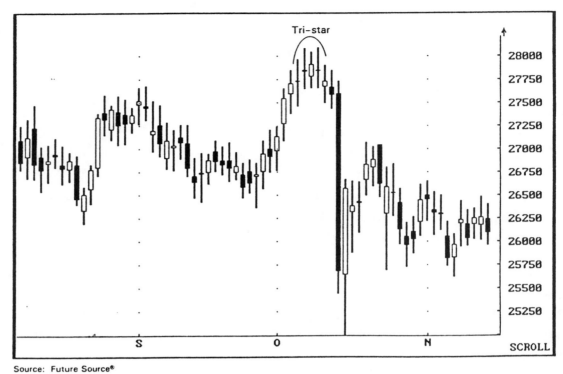

Source: Future Source®

EXHIBIT 8.21. Dow Jones Industrials—1989, Daily (Tri-star Top)

CHAPTER 9

PUTTING IT ALL TOGETHER

....

ちりも積もれば山となる

"The Water of Even a Great Ocean Comes One Drop at a Time"

In Part I of this book, we've examined many candlestick lines and formations. This chapter is a visual summary. The following charts (see Exhibits 9.1, 9.2, and 9.3) have numbered lines and patterns. All are candlestick indicators that have been discussed previously. How would you interpret them? If necessary use the visual Japanese candlestick glossary at the back of the book to help you with your interpretations. My opinion of these candlestick patterns and lines are provided. But, you should decide for yourself.

Remember, the following interpretations are subjective. You may see different indicators than I did, or some where I did not. As with any charting technique, different experiences will give different perspectives. There are no concrete rules, just general guidelines. For example, what if a hammerlike line had a lower shadow only one and one-half times the height of the real body instead of the more ideal version with a lower shadow twice—or even three times—the height of the real body. A purest might say this was not a hammer and ignore it. Others may cover shorts on such a line. Still others might wait for the next session to see what unfolds.

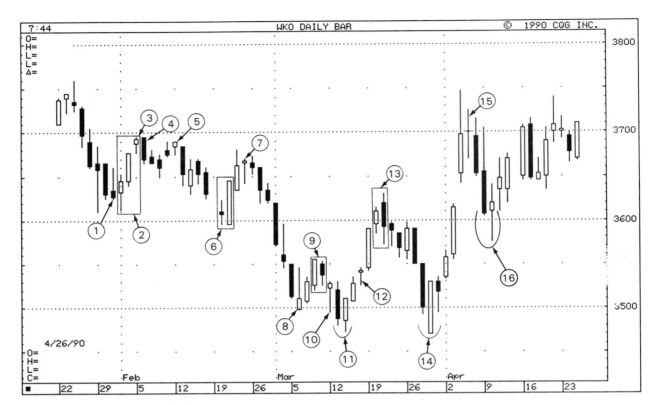

EXHIBIT 9.1. Wheat—May, 1990, Daily (All Together)

Exhibit 9.1 illustrates the following aspects.

1. A bullish inverted hammer confirmed the next session by a higher opening and white candlestick.

2. A stalled pattern implies the market's upward drive has stalled.

3. Adding a bearish hue to the stalled pattern in (2) is the fact that the last line of this pattern is a hanging man.

4. The black candlestick at (4) confirms the hanging man. Combining (3) and (4) provides a tweezer top and a bearish engulfing pattern.

5. Another hanging man.

6. A bullish engulfing pattern and a bullish white belt-hold line were signs of a rally ahead.

7. That is until the hanging-man line appeared. This was almost an ideal hanging man with a very long lower shadow, a small real body and almost no upper shadow. Confirmation of the bearish nature of this line came the next session with lack of upside movement.

8. A bullish inverted hammer confirmed the following session. This was also part of a morning star.

9. The three-day rally that started with the inverted hammer in (8) was halted by this harami pattern.

10. A hammer signaled a possible bottom.

11. A variation on the bullish piercing pattern occurred. Instead of the second white candlestick opening under the first day's low it opens under the first day's close. It then rallies and closes well into the black candlesticks real body.

12. Another hanging man occurs. But this line was not confirmed by the next session since the market gapped higher on the open.

13. A bearish engulfing pattern occurred.

14. Then, a classic piercing pattern presented itself. The second session of this pattern was a bullish belt-hold line that closed on its high. It also successfully tested the lows made in (11).

15. Then, a doji star signaled an end to the rally which started at (14).

16. A harami called the end of the preceding price descent.

Exhibit 9.2 illustrates the following aspects.

1. A tweezers bottom and a white bullish belt hold.

2. A dark-cloud cover.

3. A window which should mean resistance.

4. Then a morning star arose. This morning star is a bit unusual in that the third session was not a long white real body. It, nonetheless, pushed well into the first session's white candlestick. This morning star was also a successful retest of the prior week's lows.

5. The rally that started at (4) ended via a minor tweezers top. This tweezers top stopped at the window from (3).

6. An inverted hammer confirmed the next session. The rally that started with the inverted hammer pushed above the window's resistance.

7. A harami. The prior trend (in this case, the rally) has been put on hold.

8. The bearish implications of the prior large black candlestick session is mitigated by the next day's small real body. These two lines formed a harami. This meant that the immediately preceding move, in this case a downtrend, had run out of steam.

9. The hammer following the harami in (8) was added proof that the prior downtrend was done.

10. A doji star which is a warning of a top.

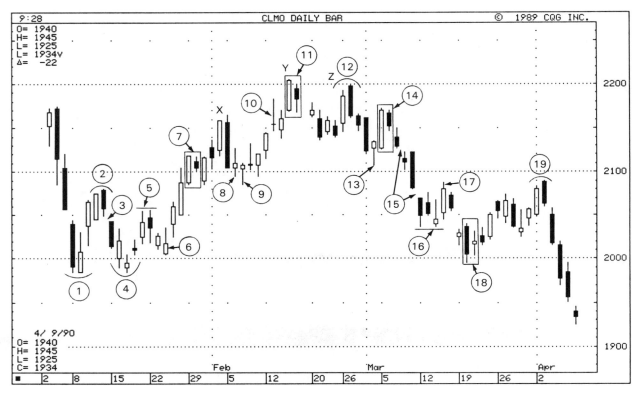

EXHIBIT 9.2. Crude Oil—June, 1990, Daily (All Together)

11. Another warning that the prior uptrend is over occurs thanks to the harami pattern.

12. A dark-cloud cover. The letters X (from early February), Y (in mid-February), and Z (in late February) make up a three Buddha top.

13. A hammer.

14. Another harami. The prior short-term uptrend beginning at the hammer (13) was short circuited with this harami.

15. Two windows which should act as resistance.

16. An inverted hammer. This also made a tweezers bottom.

17. The rally that started at the inverted hammer failed at the resistance level made by an open window in (15).

18. A harami then hinted that the downtrend was over.

19. A dark-cloud cover.

Exhibit 9.3 is a series of top reversal patterns.

1. In mid-May, a harami appears. This increased the chances that the prior uptrend had ended.

2. A lofty white candlestick on June 1 preceded a small white candlestick. This formed a stalled pattern.

3. A bearish engulfing pattern.

4. **and 5.** A doji is followed by a hanging man—not a healthy combination.

6. A hanging-man session.

7. A harami warning that the market has gone from an uptrend to a point of indecision.

8. The indecision soon gave way to conviction by the sellers as shown by the bearish engulfing pattern that immediately followed the harami. This engulfing pattern is an instance where, because the market did not make a new high on the black candlestick day, it was not a reversal day with Western technical methods. Yet, the candlesticks sent out a loud reversal signal.

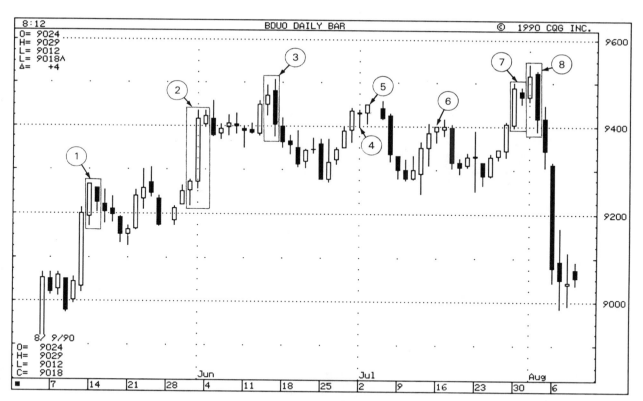

EXHIBIT 9.3. Bonds—June, 1990, Daily (All Together—Top Reversals)

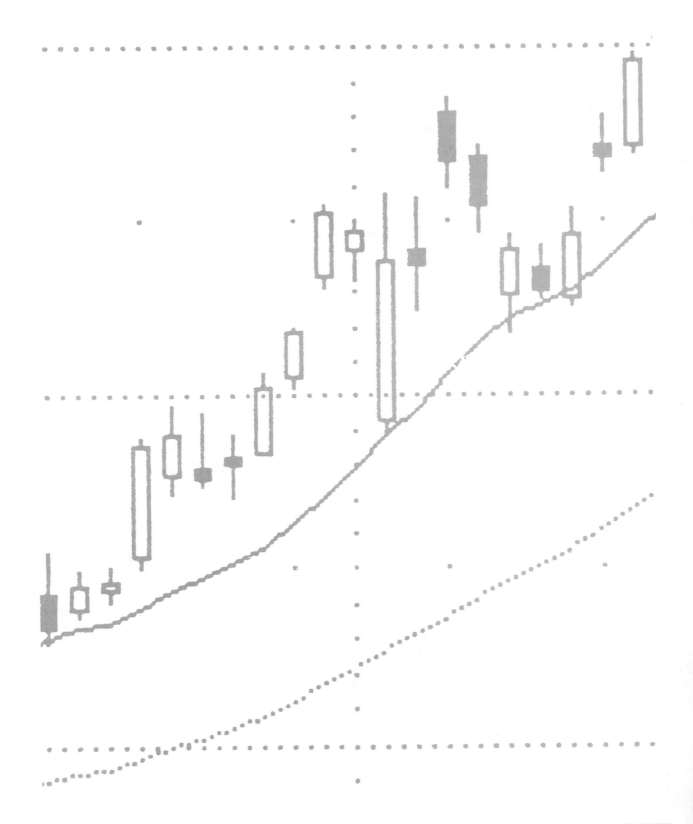

PART 2

THE RULE OF MULTIPLE TECHNICAL TECHNIQUES

千里の道も一歩から

"It is what all eyes see and all fingers point to"

Candlestick methods, by themselves, are a valuable trading tool. But candlestick techniques become even more powerfully significant if they confirm a Western technical signal. This is the focus of Part 2. For example, if a bullish belt-hold line intersects at a long-term support line, there are two reasons for a bullish outlook. The candlestick indicator confirmed a Western technical indicator or, depending on how you view it, the other way around.

This method of looking for confirmation from different technical indicators is called the "Rule of Multiple Techniques" by Arthur Sklarew in his book *Techniques of a Professional Chart Analyst.*[1] This principle states that the more technical indicators that assemble at the same price area, the greater the chance of an accurate forecast.

Part 2 of this book will be based on this "Rule of Multiple Techniques." The remainder of this section's introduction will examine the importance of this idea using two examples of traditional Western technical analysis techniques. Chapter 10 shows how a cluster of candlestick indicators provides a clear sign of an important turning point. Chapters 11 to 17 marry candlesticks to some common Western technical tools. These include trendlines, moving averages, oscillators, and so forth. In each of these chapters, I have detailed how to use candlesticks to supplement traditional Western technical techniques. For novices to technical analysis, or for those who need to refresh their memory on the basics, the introductions to Chapters 11 to 17 offer a broad, and admittedly cursory, explanation of the Western technique reviewed in that chapter. There are many fine books that provide much more detail on these Western techniques.

After these introductions, we'll explore specific examples of how to use the Western technical tool in combination with candlesticks. Since my experience is in the futures markets, the Western techniques with which I join candlesticks are based on futures technical analysis. I will not examine equity technical tools such as advance/decline lines, the ARMS/TRIN index, specialist short sales, and so on. Nonetheless, the concept of using candlesticks as a complimentary tool should be applicable, no matter your technical specialty. Western techniques, when joined with candlesticks, can be a powerfully efficient combination.

EXHIBIT II.1. Gold, Weekly Continuation

EXAMPLES OF THE RULE OF MULTIPLE TECHNICAL TECHNIQUES

This section shows, by example, how a confluence of technical indicators can help predict where important support or resistance may occur. The following examples use Western techniques. The rest of Part 2 addresses candlesticks.

In late October 1989, gold broke above a two-year downtrend resistance line when it closed above $380. This, in combination with the excellent base built in 1989 at $357, was a sign that higher prices were to follow. After gold's breakout in late 1989, *Financial News Network* interviewed me about my technical outlook for gold. I said that we should see a rally, but that this rally should stop at $425 up to $433. In early 1990, gold peaked at $425 before the bear market resumed.

How did I pick this $425 to $433 zone as my target for resistance when gold was trading at that time near $380? By using the rule of multiple technical techniques. There were four separate technical indicators hinting at major resistance at the $425 to $433 region. Refer to Exhibit II.1 as I discuss these four indicators (for this example we will not use candlestick patterns):

1. A 50% retracement of the 1987 high (Area A) at $502 and the 1989 lows (1 and 2) at $357 was $430.

2. The lows, marked 1 and 2 in 1989, were a double bottom. Based on this double bottom, I derived a measured target of $425. (A double bottom measured move is derived by taking the height of the move between the two lows and adding this distance to the intervening high).

3. The late 1988 high was $433.

4. My colleague, John Gambino, who follows Elliott Wave Theory, said gold was in an Elliott fourth wave count. Based on this, rallies in gold should not pierce the prior first wave's low in early 1988 at $425.

These separate technical techniques all pointed to major resistance near the same price area—$425 to $433. By failing to move above the $425 to $433 resistance zone in gold, the bulls could not prove their mettle (pun intended). It was not long before the major downtrend resumed in earnest.

What would have happened if gold went above the upper end of my resistance zone of $433? Then I would have had to change my longer-term bearish prognosis about the market. This is why the technicals can be so valuable. There is always a price where I will say my market view is wrong. In this case, if gold closed above $433 I would have changed by long-term bearish bias.

The market communicates to us by way of its price activity. If this activity tells me I am mistaken in my opinion, I adjust to the market. I am not egocentric enough to believe that the market will adjust to me. That is because the market is never wrong.

In early May, after sugar collapsed (see Exhibit II.2), I thought that sugar could have a temporary bounce from $.14 (that was the bottom a year-long bull channel on a weekly chart as well as the lows in late February/early March). Yet, unless sugar pushed above the $.1515 to $.1520 zone I believed sugar should be viewed as in an intermediate-term bear market. The rally high on May 14 was $.1505.

Where did I get this $.1515 to $.1520 zone as resistance? From identifying four technical indicators that implied strong resistance in that band. Specifically:

1. This was a multi-tested old support level from early March through April. I believed that once this strong support broke, it should become equally strong resistance.

2. The 65-day moving average (which I find useful for many markets)

THE MARKET IS NEVER WRONG

One of my noncandlestick seminars is called the "Techniques of Disciplined Trading Using Technical Analysis." In it, I discuss the importance of a disciplined approach to trading. To convey this idea, I use the word "discipline" as an anagram. For each letter of the word DISCIPLINE I offer a trading rule. For the letter N my rule is "Never trade in the belief the market is wrong."[2]

What do I mean by the expression, "the market is never wrong?" It means do not try to impose your beliefs on the market. For example, if you are firmly convinced crude oil is going to rally, wait until the trend is heading north before buying. Say crude oil is in a bear market. If you buy in the expectation that a bull market will materialize, you are then trying to impose your hopes and expectations on the market. You are fighting the trend. This could be disastrous. You may ultimately be correct in your bullish viewpoint, but by then it may be too late.

As an analogy, imagine you are driving along a one-way street. You notice a steamroller going down this one-way street the wrong way. You stop your car, take out a sign (that you always carry with you) that reads, "Stop, Wrong Way!" and hold it in front of the steamroller. You know the steamroller is going in the wrong direction. But the driver may not see you in time. By the time the steamroller turns around, it could be too late. By then you may be part of the pavement.

So it is with the markets. If you are bucking the trend, your outlook may turn out to be correct. But by then it may be too late. Margin calls in futures may force you out of the position before your expected move occurs. Or, worse, in the end, you may be right, but by then you could be broke.

Do not try to impose your will on the markets. Be a trend follower, not a trend predictor. If you are bullish, jump onto uptrends, if bearish, hop onto downtrends. One of the Japanese books I had translated expresses this idea almost poetically, "buying or selling from the beginning without knowing the character of the market is the same nonsense as a literary man talking about weapons. When faced with a large bull or bear market they are sure to lose the castle; what seems safe is infinitely dangerous. . . . Waiting for just the right moment is virtuous and essential."[3]

intersected near the $.1515 level. (See Chapter 13 for more detail on using moving averages with candlesticks.)

3. Looking at the highs from area A in January and the gap at area B in March, we can see the psychological importance of the $.15 level.

4. A Fibonacci 32% retracement of the move from the $.1627 peak (marked H) to the $.1444 low (marked L) is $.1514. A 32% retracement is where first resistance is sometimes seen after a selloff.

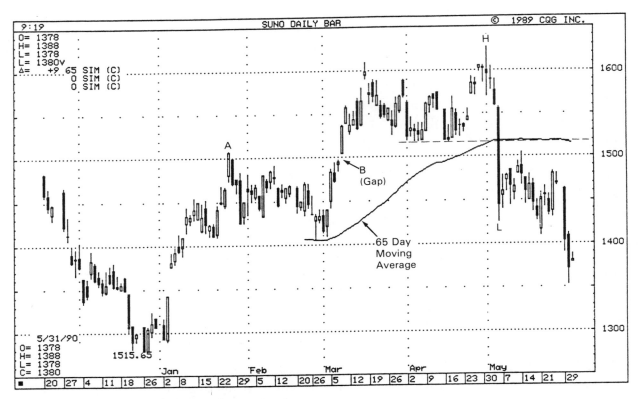

EXHIBIT II.2. Sugar—July, 1990 Sugar, Daily

Notes

[1]Sklarew, Arthur. *Techniques of a Professional Chart Analyst*, Chicago, IL: Commodity Research Bureau, 1990.

[2]For those interested readers, my other rules in the D I S C I P L I N E anagram are:

Don't forget old support and resistance levels (old support becomes new resistance and vice versa).

If . . . then system (*if* the market behaves as anticipated, *then* stay with the trade—otherwise exit).

Stops—always use them.

Consider options.

Intra-day technicals are important.

Pace trades to market environment (change your trading style according to market conditions).

Locals—never forget them.

Indicators—the more the better (the rule of multiple technical techniques).

Never trade in the belief the market is wrong.

Examine the market's reaction to the fundamentals.

[3]*Sakata Goho Wa Furinkazan*, Tokyo, Japan: Nihon Shoken Shimbunsha, 1969, p. 46 (this section translated by Richard Solberg).

CHAPTER 10

A CONFLUENCE
OF CANDLESTICKS

· ·

念には念を入れよ

"Add Caution To Caution"

This chapter explores how a cluster of candlestick patterns or lines that coincide at the same price area can make that level an important market juncture. Exhibit 10.1 shows a confluence of candlestick indicators that foretold a price setback and then another set of candlesticks that called the end of a selloff. In early June, a bearish hanging-man line is immediately followed by another negative technical signal—a doji. Prices then fell until a series of candlestick indicators signaled an important bottom. First, is the hammer. The next day is a bullish engulfing line. A few days later a minor selloff confirmed the solidity of support as the lows of the hammer day were maintained. This second test of the low created a tweezers bottom.

The September hammer in Exhibit 10.2 presaged a rally. In late November, the bonds built three candlestick top reversal indicators that put an end to this rally. They were:

a hanging man;

a doji;

and a shooting star which was the coup de'grace.

Exhibit 10.3 illustrates how an individual candlestick line can give multiple signals. In early April, a long white real body is followed by a small real body with a long upper shadow. The shape of this line is that

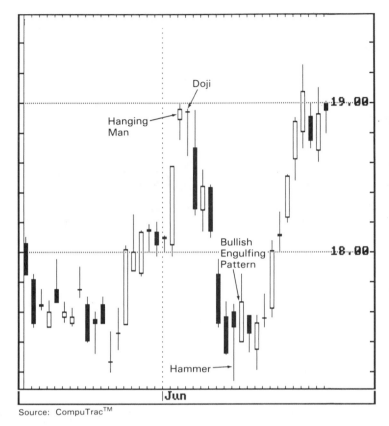

Source: CompuTrac™

EXHIBIT 10.1. Crude Oil—October 1989, Daily (Confluence of Candlesticks)

of a bearish shooting star. This line's small real body (being within the previous day's real body) makes it a harami. Finally, the top of the upper shadow (that is, the high of the day) on the shooting star day was also a failure at the February 1600 highs.

Exhibit 10.4 shows that within a period of a few weeks, this market formed a tweezers bottom, a bullish engulfing pattern, and a hammer. Exhibit 10.5 shows that from mid to late July, a series of bearish candlestick indications occurred including a doji star followed by three hanging-man lines (as shown by 1, 2 and 3). In between hanging-man 1 and 2, a shooting star formed.

Exhibit 10.6 is a bearish candlestick signal within a bearish candlestick signal. The peak of the rally in December was touched by a hanging-man session. This hanging-man session was also the star portion of an evening star formation. Exhibit 10.7 shows that May 9 through 11 delivered a series of top reversal candlestick signals at the $1.12 area. The tall white candlestick on May 9 was followed by a small real body candlestick. This second candlestick was a hanging man. It also, when

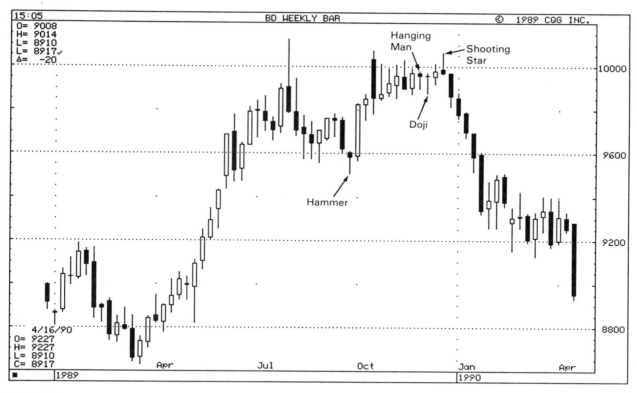

EXHIBIT 10.2. Bonds, Weekly (Confluence of Candlesticks)

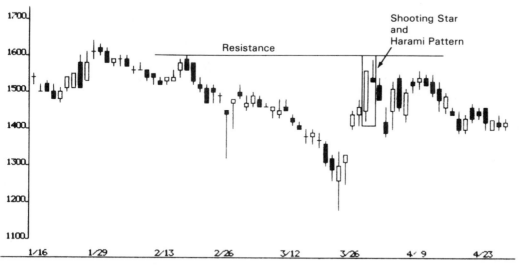

Source: Quick 10-E Informative System

EXHIBIT 10.3. Fujitsu—1990, Daily (Confluence of Candlesticks)

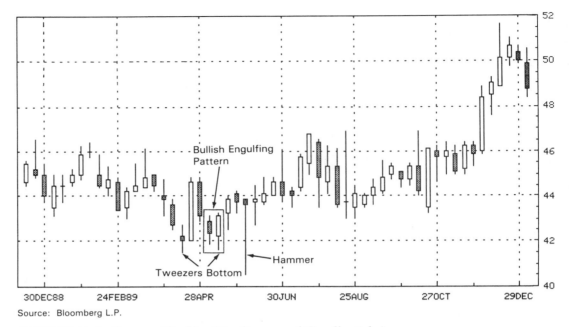

Source: Bloomberg L.P.

EXHIBIT 10.4. Exxon—Weekly (Confluence of Candlesticks)

Source: CompuTrac™

EXHIBIT 10.5. Sugar—October 1989, Daily (Confluence of Candlesticks)

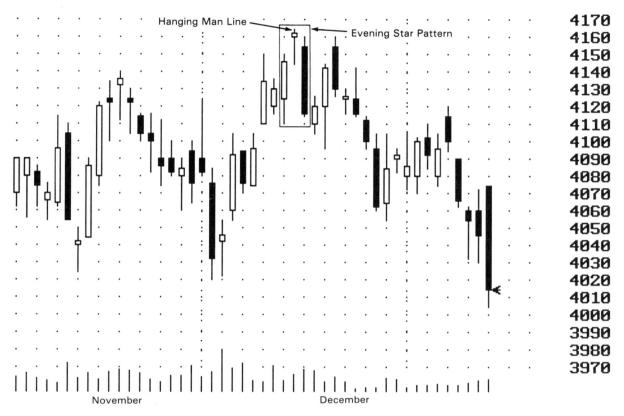

Source: Ensign Software

EXHIBIT 10.6. Wheat—March 1990, Daily (Confluence of Candlesticks)

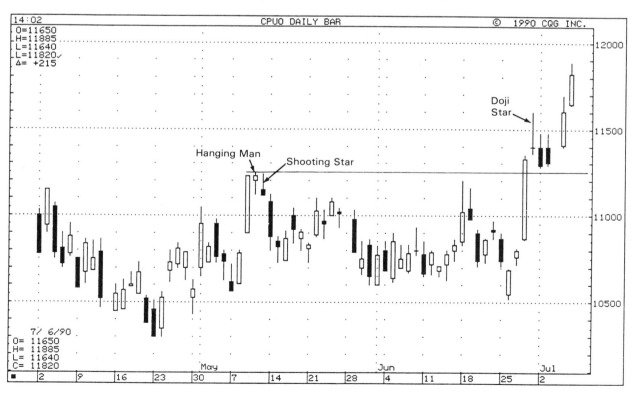

EXHIBIT 10.7. Copper—September 1990, Daily (Confluence of Candlesticks)

EXHIBIT 10.8. British Pound—Weekly (Confluence of Candlesticks)

joined to the prior candlestick, completed a harami pattern. On May 11, another assault at the $1.12 highs occurred. This assault failed via a shooting star line. These three sessions had nearly the same highs. This constructed a short-term top. Thus, within three sessions there were four bearish indications:

a hanging man;

a harami;

a shooting star; and

tweezers top.

The market backed off from these highs. The $1.12 price became significant resistance as evidenced by the bulls' failure to punch above it during mid-June's rally. This $1.12 level was important for another reason. Once broken on the upside on June 28, it converted to pivotal support. Observe the doji star that arose after the June 28 long white candlestick. We know a doji after a long white candlestick is a top reversal. This means the prior uptrend should end. For two days after the doji, the market showed it was running out of breath since there were two black candlesticks locked in a lateral band. The market had run out of steam—or so it had appeared. Remember the May 9 through 11 resistance area? The lows of the two black candlestick sessions of July 2 and 3 held that old resistance as support. The bears had tried to break the market but they could not. Until that support broke, the back of the short-term bull market which commenced June 26 would not be broken. In this scenario, the confluence of candlesticks which was so important as a top on May 9 through 11 became influential again a few months later as important support.

Exhibit 10.8 illustrates how, in mid-1987, a series of candlestick signals intimated a top. Specifically, within a month there was a hanging man, a doji, and a dark-cloud cover. After the dark-cloud cover, the market sold off and, in the process, opened a window. This window became resistance on the brief rally just before the next leg lower. The selloff finally ended with the tweezers bottom and the bullish belt-hold line (although the white candlestick had a lower shadow it was small enough to view this line as a bullish belt hold).

CHAPTER 11

CANDLESTICKS WITH TRENDLINES

....

鬼の留守に洗濯

"Make Use of Your Opportunities"

This chapter examines candlestick techniques in conjunction with trendlines, breakouts from trendlines, and old support and resistance areas. There are many ways to determine a *trend*. One method is with the technician's most basic tool—the trendline.

SUPPORT AND RESISTANCE LINES WITH CANDLESTICKS

Exhibit 11.1 shows an upward sloping support line. It is made by connecting at least two reaction lows. This line demonstrates that buyers are more aggressive than sellers since demand is stepping in at higher lows. This line is indicative of a market that is trending higher. Exhibit 11.2 shows a downward sloping resistance line. It is derived by joining at least two reaction highs. It shows that sellers are more aggressive than buyers as evidenced by the sellers willingness to sell at lower highs. This reflects a market that is trending lower.

The potency of a support or resistance line depends on the number of times the line has been successfully tested, the amount of volume at each test, and the time the line has been in force. Exhibit 11.3 has no candlestick indicators that are worth illustrating. It does represent one of the major advantages of candlesticks, though. Whatever you can do with a bar chart, you can do with a candlestick chart. Here we see how a basic

EXHIBIT 11.1. Upward Sloping
Support Line

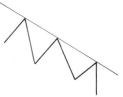

EXHIBIT 11.2. Downward Sloping
Resistance Line

head and shoulders neckline could be drawn on the candlestick chart just as easily as with the bar chart. However, as we will see in the rest of this chapter, the candlesticks provide added depth to trendline analysis.

Exhibit 11.4 illustrates that the lows in late March (near $173) formed a support area that was successfully tested in late April. This successful April test of support had an extra bullish kicker thanks to the candlesticks. Specifically, the three sessions on April 20 to 22 formed a bullish morning star pattern.

EXHIBIT 11.3. Crude Oil—July 1990, Intra-day (Trendlines on Candlestick Charts)

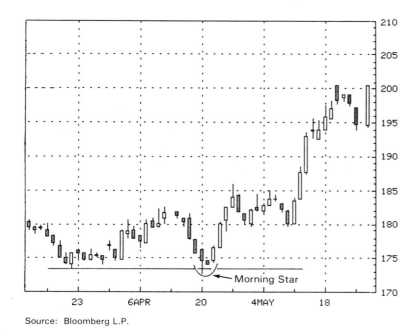

EXHIBIT 11.4. CBS—1990, Daily (Support Line with Candlesticks)

Exhibit 11.5 has a wealth of information about using trendlines with candlestick indicators. That includes:

1. The emergence of support line 1 (late January—early February) shows that the two lows on January 29 and 31 were the initial two points of this line. A third test of this line of February 7 was also a bullish hammer. The combination of these two factors gave a bottom reversal signal. For those who bought at this area, the hammer's low could be used as a protective stop out level.

2. The emergence of support line 2 (mid-January–early March) is more important than support line 1 since it was in effect longer. On March 2, the third test of this line was made by way of a bullish hammer. Since the major trend was up (as shown by the upward sloping support line 2), the bullish hammer and the successful test of support conformed to a buy signal for March 2. Protective sell stops could be positioned under the hammer's low or under the upward sloping support line 2. A puncture of this support line would be a warning that the prior uptrend had stalled. The harami gave the first inkling of trouble.

This example illuminates the importance of stops. As discussed previously, there were numerous reasons to believe that the market was going higher when it tested support line 2 via a hammer. Yet, the mar-

EXHIBIT 11.5. Crude Oil—June 1990, Daily (Support Line with Candlesticks)

ket pulled back. You should be confident when the trade is placed, but always take into account doubt and uncertainty. One of the most important concepts in trading—especially futures, is risk control. The use of stops is synonymous to risk control.

Exhibit 11.6 shows dark-cloud covers 1 and 2 produced a resistance line. Dark-cloud cover 3 intersected at this resistance line and thus confirmed this line's importance as a supply area. Exhibit 11.7 shows that there was a rally (not shown) that stopped at A. This area provided a preliminary resistance area at .6419. A long-legged doji arose at B. The fact that this doji also surfaced near the resistance level set by A was a reason to be cautious. Points A and B gave the first two points of a resistance line. Traders who use hourly charts would thus look for failed rallies near this line to take appropriate action—especially if they got a confirmatory bearish candlestick indicator. At C, there was a long-legged doji (like the one at B) near the resistance line. The market then backed off. At D, the white candlestick with a long upper shadow was a shooting star. It failed at the resistance line. This white candlestick was immediately followed by a black candlestick that engulfed it. These two candles constituted a bearish engulfing pattern.

Exhibit 11.8 shows two engulfing patterns where pattern 1 was a

THE IMPORTANCE OF PROTECTIVE STOPS

Technicals should be used to set up risk/reward parameters. As such they will provide the analyst with a mechanism for a risk and money management approach to trading. Defining risk means using protective stops to help protect against unanticipated adverse price movements. If stops are not used, the analyst is not taking advantage of one of the most powerful aspects of technical analysis.

A stop should be placed at the time of the original trade; this is when one is most objective. Stay in the position only if the market performs according to expectations. If subsequent price action either contradicts or fails to confirm these expectations, it is time to exit. If the market moves opposite to the chosen position you may think, "why bother with a stop—it is just a short-term move against me." Thus you stubbornly stay with the position in the hope the market will turn in your direction. Remember two facts:

1. all long-term trends begin as short-term moves; and
2. there is no room for hope in the market. The market goes its own way without regard to you or your position.

The market does not care whether you own it or not. The one thing worse than being wrong is staying wrong. Lose your opinion, not your money. Be proud of the ability to catch mistakes early. Getting stopped out concedes a mistake. People hate to admit mistakes since pride and prestige get involved. Good traders will not hold views too firmly. It has been said that famous private investor Warren Buffet has two rules:

1. capital preservation; and
2. don't forget rule 1.

Stops are synonymous with rule 1. You have limited resources. These resources should be maximized, or at a minimum, preserved. If you are in a market that has moved against your position, it is time to exit and find a better opportunity. Think of a stop as a cost of doing business.

Since so much of the Japanese candlestick terminology is grounded on military terminology, we will look at stops in this context as well. Each trade you make is a battle. And you will have to do what even the greatest generals have to do—make temporary, tactical retreats. A general's goal is to preserve troops and munitions. Yours is to save capital and equanimity. Sometimes you must lose a few battles to win the war. The Japanese have a saying, "a hook's well lost to catch a salmon." If you are stopped out, think of it as you would a lost hook. Maybe with the next hook you will catch your prize.

EXHIBIT 11.6. Platinum—Monthly (Resistance Line with Candlesticks)

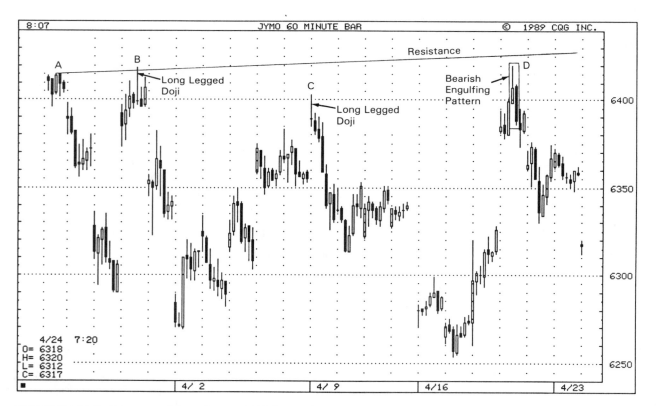

EXHIBIT 11.7. Japanese Yen—June, 1990 Intra-day (Resistance Line with Candlesticks)

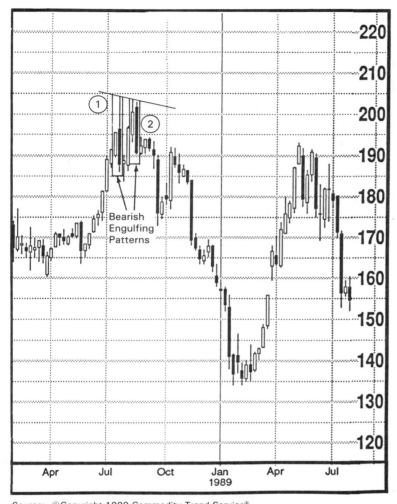

EXHIBIT 11.8. Orange Juice—Weekly (Resistance Line with Candlesticks)

warning to longs. A few weeks later, the second bearish engulfing pattern emerged. The highs on engulfing pattern 2 also were a failure at a resistance line. Exhibit 11.9 shows an upward sloping resistance line. It is a trendline that connects a series of higher highs. While not as popular as the downward sloping resistance line in Exhibit 11.1, it can be a useful device for longs. When the market approaches this kind of line, longs should take defensive measures in anticipation of a pullback. These protective measures could include taking some profits on long positions, moving up a protective stop, or selling calls. Although pullbacks should be temporary (since the major trend is up), the failure from this line could be an early and very tentative indication of the beginning of a new downtrend.

Exhibit 11.10 is a downward sloping support line. This is another type of line not used very often, but can occasionally be valuable for those who are short. Specifically, the downward sloping support line is

Upward Sloping Resistance Line

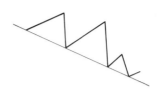

Downward Sloping Support Line

EXHIBIT 11.9. Upward Sloping
Resistance Line

EXHIBIT 11.10. Downward Sloping
Resistance Line

indicative of a downtrend (as gauged by the negative slope). Yet, when the market successfully holds this kind of support line, shorts should take defensive measures in preparation of a price bounce.

In looking at Exhibit 11.11, our first focus is on the downward sloping support line (line A) as previously illustrated on Exhibit 11.10. Connecting lows L_1 and L_2 provides a tentative support line. Candlestick L_3 almost touches this line before prices rebounded. This proved the validity of the support line. The lows at L_4 were not just a successful test of this downward sloping support line, but they formed a bullish piercing pattern. It was time to cover shorts—or at least take defensive measures such as lowering stops or selling puts. It was not time to buy because the major trend was down (as reflected by the bear channel defined by downward sloping line A and the dashed resistance line above line A). In this case, it turned out that the low at L_4 was the start of a powerful bull move that only ended with the appearance, a few months later, of the long-legged doji (a rickshaw man since the opening and closing were in the middle of the range) and the hanging man. Note the second piercing pattern on October 19 and 20.

Next, still looking at Exhibit 11.11, let us look at the upward sloping resistance line (line B) as previously shown in Exhibit 11.9. The price activity from January 15 reflects a market that is creating a series of higher highs. Based on this (and the dashed support line), one can see that there is a bull trend in force. The failure on March 6 at a upward sloping resistance line gave a signal for longs to take protective measures. Notice this third test at this resistance line was a shooting star line with its attendant very long upper shadow and small real body. The three days following the shooting star were hanging-man lines or variations thereof. This combination of factors, a pullback from a resistance line, the shooting star and the hanging-man lines gave clear warnings that the market would soon correct.

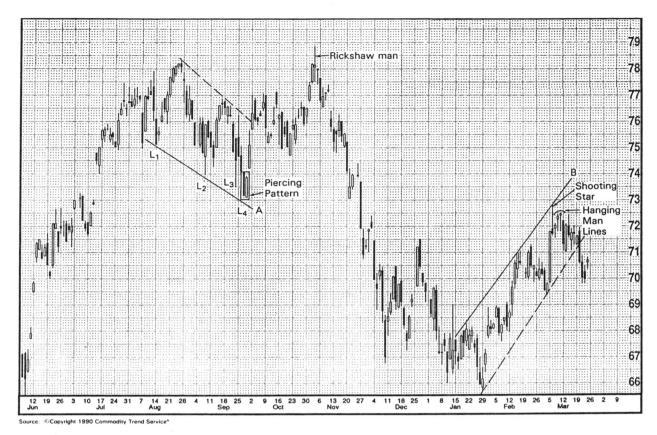

EXHIBIT 11.11. Cotton—May, 1990, Daily (Upward Sloping Resistance Line and Downward Sloping Support Line with Candlesticks)

SPRINGS AND UPTHRUSTS

Most of the time, the markets are not in a trending mode but rather in a lateral range. On such occasions, the market is in a relative state of harmony with neither the bulls nor the bears in charge. The Japanese word for tranquility and calm is "wa." I like to think of markets that are bounded in a horizontal trading zone as being in a state of "wa." It is estimated that markets are in a nontrending mode as much as 70% of the time.[1] As such, it would be valuable to use a trading tool that provides attractive entry points in such circumstances. There is a set of tools which are effective in such environments. They are called *upthrusts* and *springs*. They may be especially useful concepts when employed with candlestick techniques. Upthrusts and springs are based on concepts popularized by Richard Wyckoff in the early 20th century.

As previously mentioned, when the markets are in a state of "wa" they will trade in a quiet, horizontal band. At times, however, the bears

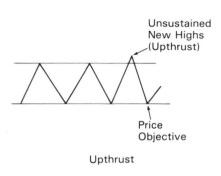

EXHIBIT 11.12. Upthrust

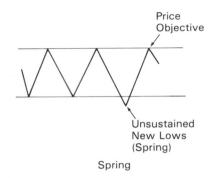

EXHIBIT 11.13. Spring

or bulls may assault a prior high or low level. Trading opportunities can arise on these occasions. Specifically, if there is an unsustained breakout from either a support or resistance level, it can present an attractive trading opportunity. In such a scenario there is a strong probability there will be a return to the opposite side of the congestion band.

There is an unsustained penetration of resistance in Exhibit 11.12. Prices then return back under the old highs which had been "penetrated." In such a scenario, one could short and place a stop above the new high. The price target would be a retest of the lower end of the congestion band. This type of false upside breakout is called an *upthrust.* If an upthrust coincides with a bearish candlestick indicator it is an appealing opportunity to short.

The opposite of an upthrust is the *spring.* The spring develops when prices pierce a prior low. Then prices spring back above the broken support area (see Exhibit 11.13). In other words, new lows could not hold. Buy if prices push back above the old lows. The objective would be for a retest of the congestion zone's upper band. The stop would be under the lows made on the day of the spring. Trading springs and upthrusts is so effective because they provide a clear target (the opposite end of the trading range) and protective stop (the new high or low made with the "false breakout").

Exhibit 11.14 is a good example of upthrusts with candlesticks. Day A marked the high for the move and a resistance level (notice how the hanging-man line the prior day gave warning of the end of the uptrend). The dual lows at L_1 and L_2 defined the lower end of the trading band. There was an upthrust on day B. That is, the prior highs at A were breached, but the new highs did not hold. The failure of the bulls to maintain the new highs at B was a bearish signal. Another negative sign was that day B was also a shooting star. Shooting stars are sometimes part of an upthrust. At such times, it is a powerful incentive to sell. As if a bearish upthrust and a shooting star were not enough to send chills down a bull's back, the day after B a hanging man appeared! With the

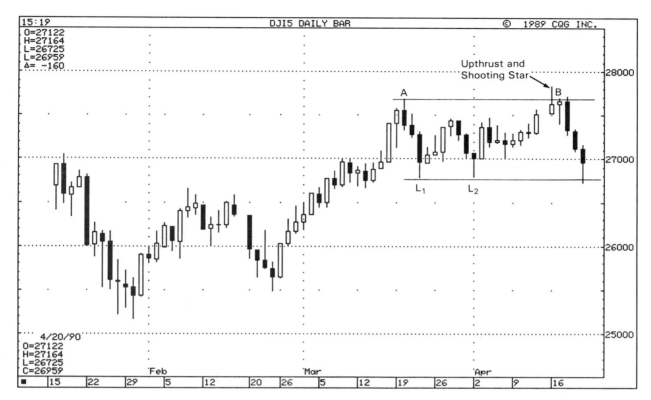

15:19   DJI5 DAILY BAR   © 1989 CQG INC.
O=27122
H=27164
L=26725
L=26959
Δ= -160

Upthrust and
Shooting Star

A   B

L₁   L₂

4/20/90
O=27122
H=27164
L=26725
C=26959

Feb   Mar   Apr
15 22 29 5 12 20 26 5 12 19 26 2 9 16

EXHIBIT 11.14. Dow Jones Industrials—1990, Daily (Upthrust with Candlesticks)

bearish upthrust at B we have a target of the lower end of the lateral band, that is, the lows made by L_1 and L_2.

Exhibit 11.15 shows that on May 1, a new high for the move as the CRB touched 248.44. On May 10, the bulls managed to nudge above this level by about 25 ticks. They were unable to sustain these new highs. This failure was an upthrust. May 10 was also a shooting star. It spelled an end to the prior minor uptrend. Thus, a short sale with a stop above May 10 highs would have been warranted. The objective would be a retest of the lower end of the recent trading range near 245.00.

As shown in Exhibit 11.16, the highs of April 5 overran the early March highs near $5.40. However, the bulls could not defend the new higher territory. This was an upthrust. Verification of the bearish aspect of this upthrust came via the hanging man in the next session. Exhibit 11.17 shows in July 1987, the CRB found a base near 220 via a harami pattern. The lows made by this harami were successfully tested by the following week's long white line which was also a bullish belt hold. In the third quarter of that year, the 220.00 level was temporarily broken. The market then sharply rebounded and, in the process, created a hammer and a spring. The objective based on this spring was a retest of the prior highs near 235.

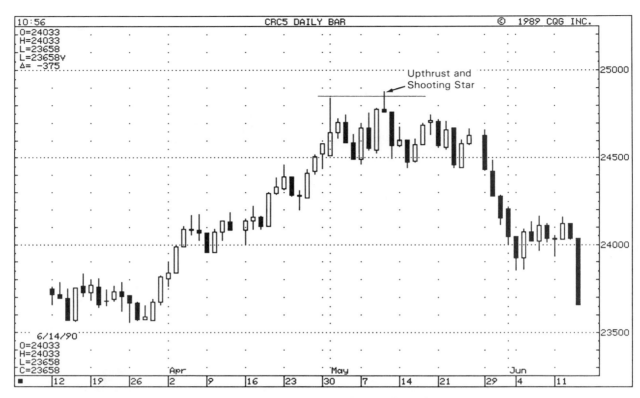

EXHIBIT 11.15. CRB—Cash, Daily, 1990 (Upthrust with Candlesticks)

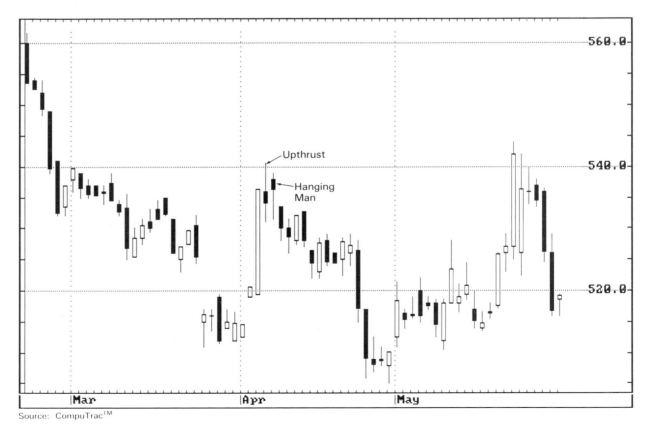

Source: CompuTrac™

EXHIBIT 11.16. Silver—September, 1990, Daily (Upthrust with Candlesticks)

Source: ©Copyright 1990 Commodity Trend Service®

EXHIBIT 11.17. CRB-Cash—Weekly (Spring with Candlesticks)

Exhibit 11.18 indicates that the early January lows were perforated in late February. The failure to hold the lows meant that this was a bullish spring. The day of the spring was also a hammer. This union of bullish signals gave plenty of warning to the technician to look for a return move to the upper end of the January/February band near $78. Interestingly, the rally stopped in mid-March near $78 at an evening doji star formation.

Exhibit 11.19 shows that after a harami, the market slid. It stabilized at hammer 1. This hammer was also a successful test of the prior support near $.50. Another slight pullback occurred on hammer 2. With this bullish hammer, the market nudged marginally under the summer lows (by 25 ticks) but the bears could not maintain these new lows. Thus a spring, complimented by a hammer and a tweezers bottom created noteworthy bullish evidence. Exhibit 11.20 reveals that during the week of March 12, soybeans touched a low of $5.96 formed a bullish engulfing

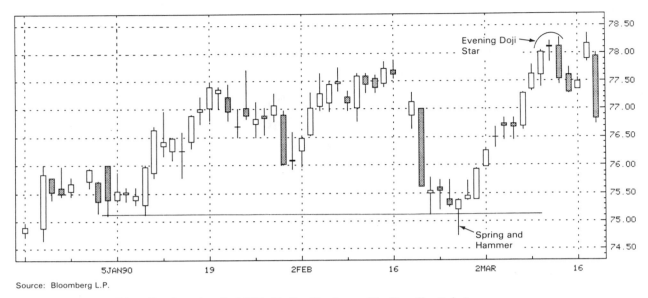

Source: Bloomberg L.P.

EXHIBIT 11.18. Live Cattle—April, 1990, Daily (Spring with Candlesticks)

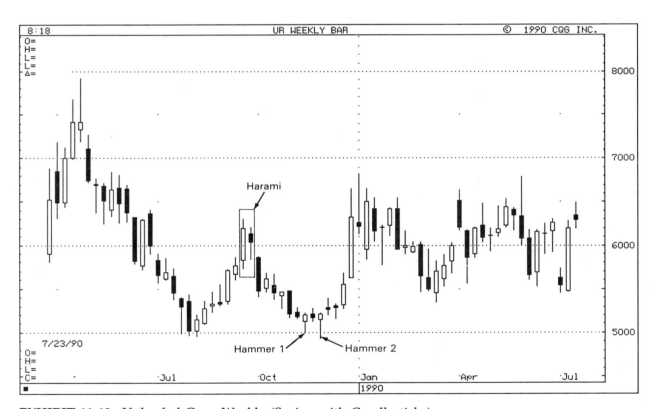

EXHIBIT 11.19. Unleaded Gas—Weekly (Spring with Candlesticks)

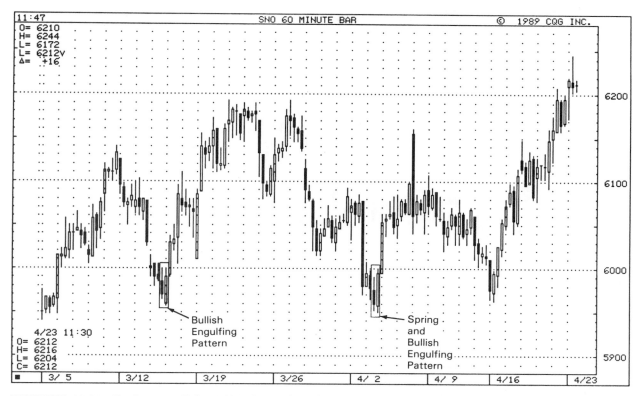

EXHIBIT 11.20. Soybeans—July, 1990, Intra-day (Spring with Candlesticks)

pattern and rallied. On April 3, prices broke this level and made new lows. These new lows failed to hold and created a spring. Furthermore, the lows on that session constructed a bullish engulfing pattern.

Why do springs and upthrusts work so well? To answer this, refer to Napoleon's response when asked which troops he considered best. His terse response was, "those which are victorious."[2] View the market as a battlefield between two sets of troops—the bulls and the bears. The territory they each claim is especially evident when there is a lateral trading range. The horizontal resistance line is the bears' terrain to defend. The horizontal support line is the bulls' domain to defend.

At times there will be "scouting parties" (this is my term and not a candlestick expression) sent by big traders, commercial accounts, or even locals to test the resolve of the opposing troops. For instance, there might be a push by the bulls to try to move prices above a resistance line. In such a battle, we have to monitor the determination of the bears. If this bullish scouting party can set up camp in enemy territory (that is, close above resistance for a few days) then a beachhead is made. New, fresh attacking bull troops should join the scouting party. The market should move higher. As long as the beachhead is maintained (that is, the market should hold the old resistance area as new support), the bull

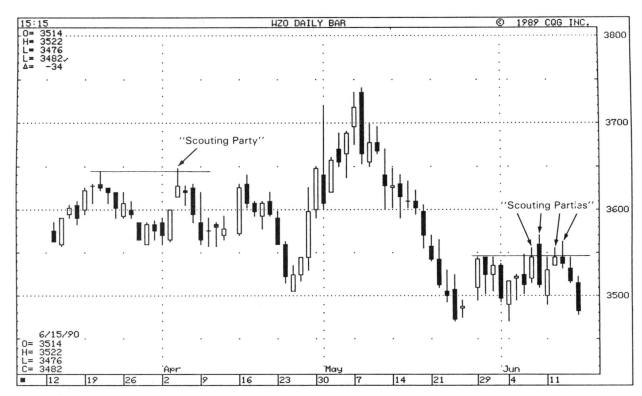

EXHIBIT 11.21. Wheat—December 1990, Daily (Upthrusts and "Scouting Parties")

troops will have control of the market. An example of a "scouting party" is presented in Exhibit 11.21.

In late May, there were highs made at $3.54. Numerous bull scouting parties tried to get a foothold into the bear's terrain above $3.54. They only succeeded in pushing prices above $3.54 intra-day. The bulls could not get a beachhead, that is, a close, into the bears terrain. The bulls then went into retreat. The result? A return to the bottom end of the congestion band near $3.45. A candlestick sign that the bears still had control of the market was the bearish engulfing pattern made in early June. The shooting stars on June 12 and 13 did not help the picture either.

A bullish scouting party also transpired in early April. By failing to hold above the mid-March highs, the bulls had to retreat. The result was a retest of the late March lows. This failure was confirmed by a bearish shooting star.

THE CHANGE OF POLARITY PRINCIPLE

The Japanese have a saying that, "a red lacquer dish needs no decoration." This concept of simple beauty is the essence of a technical principle I frequently use with candlestick charting. It is as simple as it is powerful—old support becomes new resistance; old resistance becomes support. This is what I call the "change of polarity" principle. Exhibit 11.22 shows support converting to resistance. Exhibit 11.23 illustrates prior resistance becoming new support. The potency of this change of polarity is proportional to:

1. the number of times the old support/resistance levels have been tested; and
2. the volume and/or open interest on each test.

The concept behind the change of polarity principle (although not traditionally called that) is an axiom discussed in any basic book on technical analysis. Yet, it is an under utilized gem. To see how universally well this rule works let us briefly look at some examples across the various time horizons and markets.

Exhibit 11.24 shows four occasions in which old resistance converted to new support. Exhibit 11.25 shows how the lows from late 1987 and mid-1988 became an important resistance zone for all of 1989. Exhibit 11.26 illustrates how the old resistance level near 27,000 in 1987, once penetrated, becomes significant support in 1988.

To round out the time horizon (we saw this rule in the prior examples with a daily, weekly and monthly chart) let us look at an intra-day chart (see Exhibit 11.27). From early to mid-July, it was obvious where the resistance level set in—at $.72. Once penetrated on July 23, this $.72 immediately converted to support. Once the July 24 and 25 highs of $.7290 were breached, that level also converted to support.

Exhibit 11.28 shows the usefulness of the change of polarity principle. In late 1989 to early 1990 there was a substantial rally. For the first half of 1990, the market traded in a lateral band with support shown as

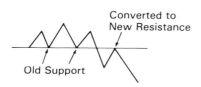

EXHIBIT 11.22. Change of Polarity—Support Converting to Resistance

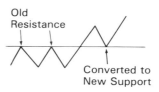

EXHIBIT 11.23. Change of Polarity—Resistance Converting to Support

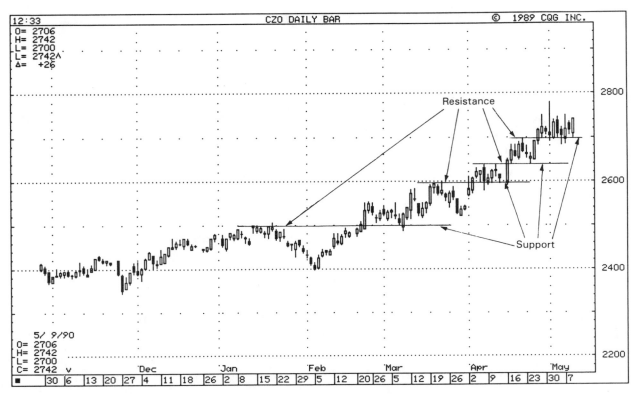

EXHIBIT 11.24. Corn—December 1990, Daily (Change of Polarity)

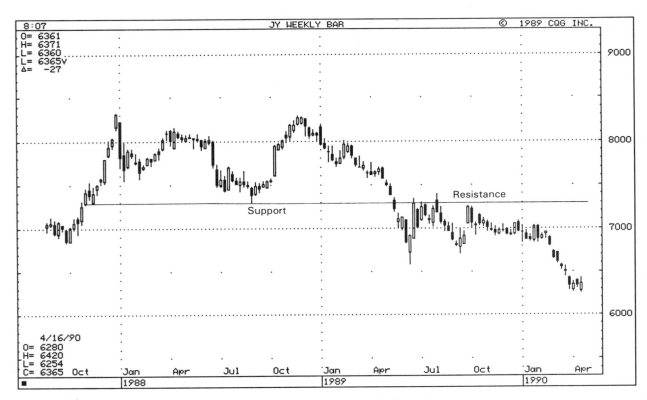

EXHIBIT 11.25. Japanese Yen Futures, Weekly (Change of Polarity)

EXHIBIT 11.26. Nikkei—Monthly (Change of Polarity)

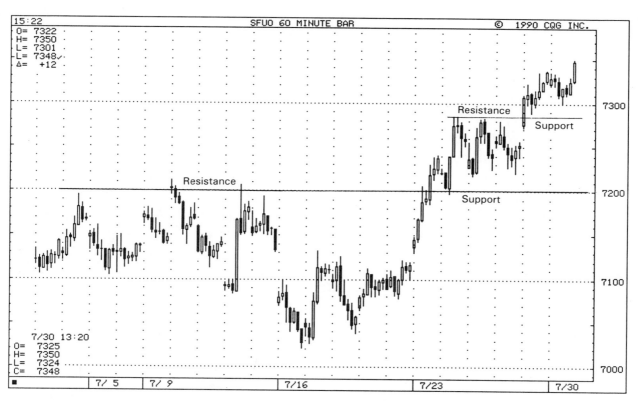

EXHIBIT 11.27. Swiss Franc—September 1990, Intra-day (Change of Polarity)

EXHIBIT 11.28. Orange Juice—Weekly (Change of Polarity)

a dotted line near $1.85. When this level was breached in June 1990, what was next support? The price action from $1.25 to $2.05 was essentially straight up so there was no support evident based on the late 1989 to early 1990 rally. Yet, when $1.85 broke, support was expected near $1.65. Where did I get that figure? Two reasons. The first was that a 50% correction of the prior $.80 rally was near $1.65. The second, and more important reason, was the prior resistance at area A was also near $1.65. That should mean it will now be support. A series of limit-down days comprised the June selloff. This selloff stopped at $1.66.

Pick up just about any chart, be it intra-day, daily, weekly, or longer and the chances are high that you will see examples of this change of polarity in action. Why is something so simple so good? The reason has to do with the raison d'être of technical analysis; to measure the emotions and actions of the trading and investing community. Thus, the better a technical tool measures behavior, the better that tool should work. And the change of polarity principle is so successful because it is based on sound trading psychological principles. What are these principles? It has to do with how people react when the market goes against their position or when they believe they may miss a market move.

Ask yourself what is the most important price on any chart? Is the

highs made for move? The lows? Yesterday's close? No. *The most impor-*
tant price on any chart is the price at which you entered the market. People
become strongly, keenly and emotionally attached to the price at which they
bought or sold.

Consequently, the more trading that transpires at a certain price area
the more people are emotionally committed to that level. What does this
have to do with the fact that old resistance becomes support and old
support becomes resistance? Let us look at the Exhibit 11.29 to answer
this. In late December, a steep selloff culminated at $5.33 (at A). On
another test of this level, there are at least three groups who would consider buying.

Group 1 would be those who were waiting for the market to stabilize
after the prior selloff and who now have a point at which the market
found support—$5.33 (the December 28 lows at area A). A few days
later, a successful test (at B) of this support probably pulled in new
longs.

Group 2 would be those who were previously long but were stopped
out during the late December selloff. On rally B to B1, in mid-January,
some of these old longs who were stopped out would say to themselves
that they were right about silver being in a bull market. They just timed
there original purchase incorrectly. Now is the time to buy. They want
to be vindicated in their original view. They wait for a pullback to support at C to go long again.

Group 3 would be those who bought at points A and B. They also see
the B to B_1 rally and may want to add to their position if they get a "good
price." At area C, they have their good price since the market is at support. Thus more buyers come in at C. Then for good measure another
pullback to D draws in more longs.

Then the problems start for the longs. In late February, prices puncture support areas A, B, C, and D. Anyone who bought at this old support area is now in a losing trade. They will want to get out of their trade
with the least damage. Rallies to where the longs bought (around $5.33),
will be gratefully used by them to exit their longs. Thus, the original
buyers at areas A, B, C, and D may now become sellers. This is the main
reason why old support becomes new resistance.

Those who decided not to liquidate their losing long positions on the
minor rallies in early March then had to go through the pain of watching the market fall to $5. They used the next rally, in early April (Area
E), to exit. Exhibit 11.29 illustrates how support can become resistance.
The same rationale, but in reverse, is the reason why resistance often
becomes support. Do not let the simplicity of the rule fool you. It
works—especially when melded with candlestick indicators. For example look at area E. Notice how the doji after a tall white real body meant

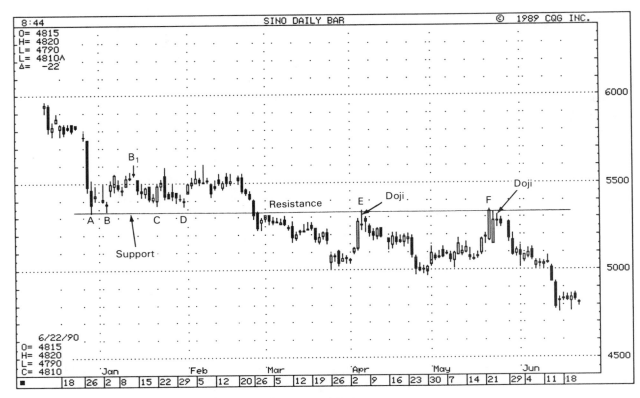

EXHIBIT 11.29. Silver—July 1990, Daily (Change of Polarity)

trouble. This candlestick signal coincided with the resistance line. The same scenario unfolds at F.

In Exhibit 11.30, the highs at A and B then became support in late 1986 and then in 1989. Note how the strength of this support was confirmed twice in 1989 by two consecutive hammer lines.

In September and early October, at areas A and B in Exhibit 11.31, the market maintained a support level near $1,230. Once the bears pulled the market under that level on October 9, this $1,230 then converted to a band of resistance. After the first failure at this new resistance, at C, prices descended until the bullish engulfing pattern. A minor rally then followed. This rally stalled, once again, at the $1,230 level. In addition, there was a dark-cloud cover.

EXHIBIT 11.30. Swiss Franc—Monthly (Change of Polarity with Candlesticks)

EXHIBIT 11.31. Cocoa—December 1990, Daily (Change of Polarity with Candlesticks)

Notes

[1]Colby, Robert W. and Meyers, Thomas A. *The Encyclopedia of Technical Market Indicators,* Homewood, IL: Dow Jones-Irwin, 1988, p. 159.

[2]Kroll, Stanley. *Kroll on Futures Trading,* Homewood, IL: Dow Jones-Irwin, 1988, p. 20.

CHAPTER 12

CANDLESTICKS WITH RETRACEMENT LEVELS

待てば海路の日和あり

"All things come to those who wait"

Markets usually do not trend straight up, nor do they fall vertically downward. They usually retrace some of the advance, or decline, before resuming the prior trend. Some of the more popular retracement levels are the 50% level and the Fibonacci figures of 38% and 62% (see Exhibits 12.1 and 12.2). Fibonacci was a 13th century mathematician who derived a special sequence of numbers. Without getting into too much detail, by comparing these numbers to one another one could derive what is called—not surprisingly—the *Fibonacci ratios*. These ratios include 61.8% (or its inverse of 1.618) and 38.2% (or its inverse of 2.618). This is why the 62% (61.8% rounded off) and the 38% (38.2% rounded off) corrections are so popular. The popular 50% correction is also a Fibonacci ratio. The 50% retracement is probably the most widely monitored level. This is because the 50% retracement is used by those who use Gann, Elliott Wave, or Dow Theory.

Exhibit 12.3 illustrates how well retracements can help predict resistance areas in a bear market. The 50% retracements in gold over the past few years have become significant resistance levels. Let us look at three instances on this chart where 50% retracements melded with candlestick techniques to provide important top reversal signals.

Retracement 1—The highs at A in late 1987 ($502) were made by a bearish engulfing pattern. The selloff which began in late 1987 ended with a piercing pattern at B at $425. Based on a 50% retracement of this selloff from A to B, resistance should occur at $464 (this is figured by taking half the difference between the high at A and the low at B and

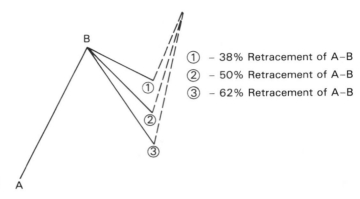

EXHIBIT 12.1. Popular Retracement Levels in an Uptrend

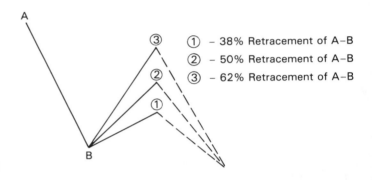

EXHIBIT 12.2. Popular Retracement Levels in a Downtrend

adding this onto the low at B). Thus, at $464 you look for resistance and confirmation of resistance with a bearish candlestick indicator. A bearish engulfing pattern formed at C. At C, the high was $469 or within $5 of the 50% correction. The market began its next leg lower.

Retracement 2—The selloff which began at C ended at the morning star pattern at D. Taking a 50% correction from C's high at $469 to D's low at $392 gives a resistance area of $430. Thus, at that level, bearish candlestick confirmation should appear. Gold reached $433 at area E. During this time (the weeks of November 28 and December 5 (at E)) gold came within $.50 of making a bearish engulfing pattern. Another decline started from E.

Retracement 3—From the high at E to the low at F in 1989 (at $357), prices fell $76. (Interestingly, all three selloffs, A to B, C to D, and E to F fell about $77.) There were no candlestick indicators that called the lows on June 5. The second test of these lows in September came via a hammerlike line.

The next resistance level, a 50% retracement of the decline from E to F, is $395. Not too surprisingly gold surpassed this level. Why wasn't this a surprise? Because, in late 1989, gold pierced a two-year resistance

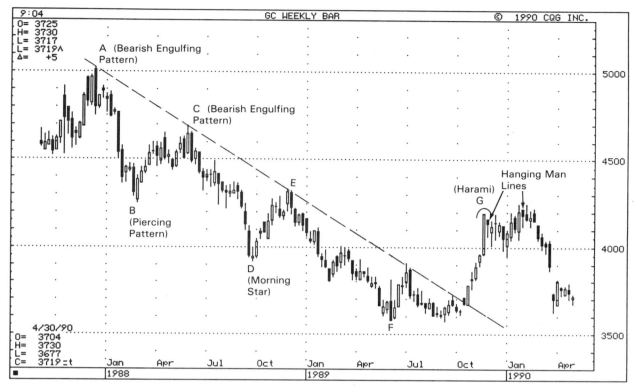

EXHIBIT 12.3. Gold—Weekly (Retracements with Candlesticks)

line. In addition, gold built a solid base in 1989 by forming a double bottom at the $357 level. Thus, we have to look out farther to a 50% retracement of the larger move. This means a 50% retracement of the entire decline from the 1987 high (area A) to the 1989 low (area F). This furnishes a resistance level of $430. Near this $430 level, at $425 on the week of November 20 at area G, the market gave two signs that the uptrend was in trouble. Those signs were a harami pattern and, as part of this pattern, a hanging man. A few weeks later, on the week of January 22, the highs for this move were touched at $425. The following week's price action created another hanging man. Gold declined from there.

Look at Exhibit 12.4. The combination tweezers and harami bottom at $18.58 (A) was the start of a $3.50 rally. This rally terminated at $22.15 (B) with a bearish engulfing pattern. A 50% correction of the A–B thrust would mean support near $20.36. At area C, a bullish piercing pattern formed at $20.15. The market then had a minor rally from C. This rally ran into problems because of the dark-cloud cover at D. Interestingly, D's high at $21.25 was within 10 ticks of a 50% bounce from the prior downleg B–C.

Exhibit 12.5 reveals that a Fibonacci 62% retracement of rally A–B is

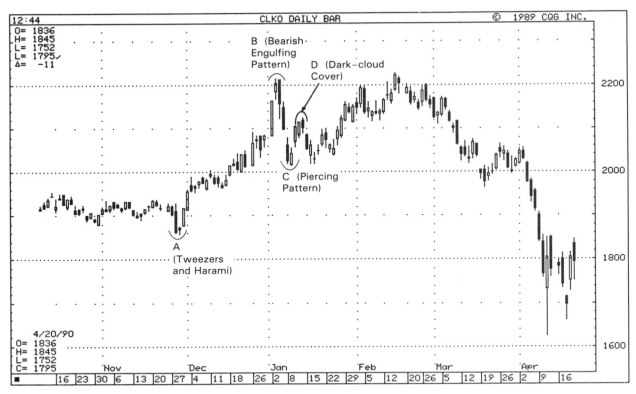

EXHIBIT 12.4. Crude Oil—May 1990, Daily (Retracements with Candlesticks)

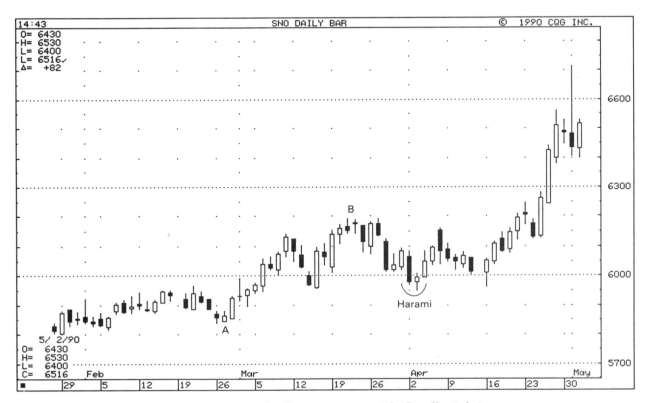

EXHIBIT 12.5. Soybeans—July 1990, Daily (Retracements with Candlesticks)

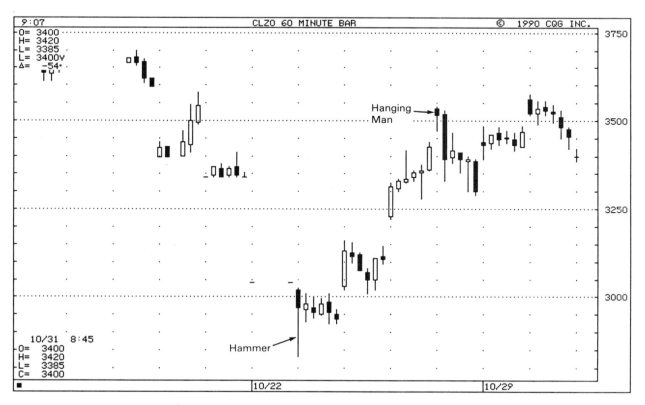

EXHIBIT 12.6. Crude Oil—(a) December 1990 and (b) December 1990 Intra-day

$5.97. This also coincides closely with the old resistance level from late January and February at $5.95. That old resistance converted to support. On the pullback to this level, on April 2 and 3, this $5.97 held as support. These sessions formed a harami pattern that signaled an end to the prior minor downmove. Then, just for good measure, there was an additional test of this support in mid-April, and away went the beans!

Exhibit 12.6a shows from crude oil's July low at L, to its October high at H, there was a $21.70 rally. A 50% retracement of this rally would be at $29.05. Thus, based on the theory that a 50% retracement level from a rally should be support, we should look for a bullish candlestick indicator near that $29.05 area on the brisk selloff from October's high. This is what unfolded. On October 23, after prices touched a low of $28.30, a hammer developed on the daily chart. The market rallied over $5 from that hammer. On the intra-day chart of the price action on October 23 (see Exhibit 12.6b) we see the first hour's action also formed a hammer. Thus, the daily candlestick chart on October 23 and the first hour on the intra-day candlestick chart on October 23 both had hammers. This is a rare, and as we see, significant occurrence. Note how, on the intra-day chart, the brisk rally that began with the hammer ran out of force with the emergence of the hanging man on October 26.

CHAPTER 13

CANDLESTICKS WITH MOVING AVERAGES

....

十人十色

"Ten Men, Ten Tastes"

The *moving average* is one of the oldest and most popular tools used by technicians. Its strength is as a trend-following device which offers the technician the ability to catch major moves. Thus, it is utilized most effectively in trending markets. However, since moving averages are lagging indicators they can catch a trend only after it has turned.

THE SIMPLE MOVING AVERAGE

The most basic of the moving averages is, as the name implies, the *simple moving average*. This is the average of all the price points used. For example, let us say that the last five gold closing prices were $380, $383, $394, $390, and $382. The five-day moving average of these closes would be

$$\frac{(\$380 + \$383 + \$394 + \$390 + \$382)}{5} = \$385.80.$$

The general formula is:

$$\frac{(P1 + P2 + P3 + P4 + P5)}{n}$$

where P1 = the most recent price
P2 = the second most recent price and so on
n = the number of data points

The term "moving" in moving average is applicable because, as the newest data is added to the moving average, the oldest data is dropped. Consequently, the average is always moving as the new data is added.

As seen in the simple moving average example above, each day's gold price contributed ⅕ to the total moving average (since this was a five-day moving average). A nine-day moving average means that each day will only be ⅑ of the total moving average. Consequently, the longer the moving average, the less impact an individual price will have on it.

The shorter the term of the moving average, the closer it will "hug" prices. This is a plus insofar as it is more sensitive to recent price action. The negative aspect is that it has a greater potential for whipsaws. Longer-term moving averages provide a greater smoothing effect, but are less responsive to recent prices.

The more popular moving averages include the four-, nine-, and 18-day averages for shorter-term traders and the 13-, 26-, and 40-week moving averages for position players. The 13- and 40-week moving averages are popular in Japan. The spectrum of moving average users runs from the intra-day trader, who uses moving averages of real-time trades, to the hedger who may focus on monthly, or even yearly, moving averages.

Other than the length of the average, another avenue of analysis is based on what price is used to compute the average. Most moving average systems use, as we did in our gold example, closing prices. However, moving averages of highs, lows, and the mid-point of the highs and lows have all been used. Sometimes, moving averages of moving averages are even used.

THE WEIGHTED MOVING AVERAGE

A *weighted moving average* assigns a different weight to each price used to compute the average. Almost all weighted moving averages are front loaded. That is, the most recent prices are weighted more heavily than older prices. How the data is weighted is a matter of preference.

THE EXPONENTIAL MOVING AVERAGE AND THE MACD

The *exponential moving average* is a special type of weighted moving average. Like the basic weighted moving average, the exponential moving average is front weighted. Unlike other moving averages, though, the exponential moving average incorporates all prior prices used in the data. This type of moving average assigns progressively smaller weights to each of the past prices. Each weight is exponentially smaller than the previous weight, hence, the name exponential moving average.

One of the most popular uses of the exponential moving average is for use in the *MACD* (Moving Average Convergence-Divergence). The MACD is composed of two lines. The first line is the difference between two exponential moving averages (usually the 26- and 12-period exponential moving averages). The second line of the MACD is made by taking an exponential moving average (usually a 9 period) of the difference between the two exponential moving averages used to make the first line. This second line is called the *signal line*. More about the MACD in Exhibits 13.7 and 13.8.

HOW TO USE MOVING AVERAGES

Moving averages can provide objective strategies with clearly defined trading rules. Many of the computerized technical trading systems are underpinned on moving averages. How can moving averages be used? The answer to this is as varied as there are different trading styles and philosophies. Some of the more prevalent uses of the moving average include:

1. Comparing the price versus the moving averages as a trend indicator. For instance, a good gauge to see if a market is in an intermediate-term uptrend could be that prices have to be above the 65-day moving average. For a longer-term uptrend prices would have to be higher than the 40-week moving average.

2. Using the moving average as support or resistance levels. A close above the specified moving average would be bullish. A close below the moving average would be bearish.

3. Monitoring the moving average band (also known as *envelopes*). These bands are a certain percentage above or below the moving average and can serve as support or resistance.

4. Watching the slope of the moving average. For instance, if the moving average levels off or declines after a period of a sustained rise, it may be a bearish signal. Drawing trendlines on the moving averages is a simple method of monitoring their slope.

5. Trading with a dual moving average system. This is addressed in detail later in this chapter.

The examples that follow use various moving averages. They are not based on optimum moving averages. An optimum moving average today might not be the optimum one tomorrow. The moving averages used in this text are widely monitored along with some which are not as widely used but which are based on such tools as Fibonacci numbers. The moving averages used here are not the important point. What is meaningful is how moving averages can be melded with candlesticks.

I like using the 65-day moving average as a broad spectrum moving average. From my experience, it seems to work well in many of the futures markets. Exhibit 13.1 illustrates a 65-day moving average that offered support to the market at areas 1, 2, and 3. Beside the moving average shoring up the market at these points, we see a bullish engulfing pattern at area 1, a hammer and harami at 2, and another hammer-like line at 3.

Exhibit 13.2 reveals that a confluence of technical factors joined on April 2 and 3 to warn alert eyes of trouble ahead. Let us take a look at the specifics:

1. In early March, prices broke under the 65-day moving average. From that point, the moving average became resistance.

EXHIBIT 13.1. Soybeans—July 1990, Daily (Simple Moving Average with Candlesticks)

EXHIBIT 13.2. Crude Oil—June 1990, Daily (Simple Moving Average with Candlesticks)

2. The two candlesticks on April 2 and 3 formed a dark-cloud cover. This dark-cloud cover was also a failure at the moving average's resistance area.

3. April 3 was not only a dark-cloud cover and a failure at a moving average, but it was also within 7 ticks of a 50% retracement of price decline A–B.

Exhibit 13.3 shows that late February's test of the 65-day moving average support line was confirmed with a hammer. The market retested these lows a few days later and, in the process, formed a tweezers bottom.

EXHIBIT 13.3. Sugar—May 1990, Daily (Simple Moving Average with Candlesticks)

DUAL MOVING AVERAGES

There are many ways two moving averages can be used. One way is as an overbought/oversold indicator or oscillator. This indicator is obtained by subtracting the shorter-term moving average from the longer-term moving average. This indicator has plus or minus values. Thus a value above 0 means the shorter-term moving average is above the longer-term moving average. Anything under 0 means the shorter-term moving average is less than the longer-term moving average. In doing this, we are comparing the short-term momentum to a longer-term momentum. This is because, as discussed earlier, the short-term moving average is more responsive to recent price activity. If the short-term moving average is relatively far above (or below), the longer-term moving average, the market is said to be overbought (or oversold).

Another use of two moving averages is to monitor crossovers between the short-term and longer-term moving averages. If the shorter-term moving average crosses the longer-term moving average, it could be an early warning of a trend change. An example would be if a shorter-term moving average crosses above a longer-term moving average. This is a bullish signal. In Japan, such a moving average crossover is called a *golden cross.* Thus, if the three-day moving average crosses above the nine-day moving average it is a golden cross. A *dead cross* in Japan is the opposite. It is a bearish indication which occurs when the shorter-term moving average crosses under the longer-term moving average.

For a short-term overbought/oversold indicator, some technicians monitor the current close in relation to the five-day moving average. (See Exhibit 13.4.) For instance, if copper's five-day moving average is $1.10 and today's close is $1.14, copper would be $.04 overbought. In this example, the lower graph's line is made up of the five-day moving average subtracted from the current close. As can be seen from this chart, when this dual moving average line gets about 400 points (that is, $.04) overbought the market become vulnerable—especially with bearish candlestick confirmation. At time period 1, an overbought reading coincided with a harami; at period 2, it hit another harami; at 3, it hit a doji; and at 4, it hit another harami. A market can relieve its overbought condition by selling off or by trading sideways. In this example, time periods 1 and 3 relieved the overbought situation by easing into a lateral band. Periods 2 and 4 saw selloffs. Overbought markets usually should not be shorted.

EXHIBIT 13.4. Copper—September 1990, Daily (Dual Moving Averages with Candlesticks)

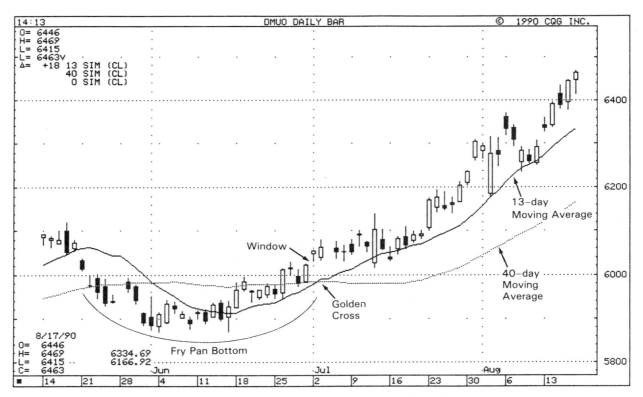

EXHIBIT 13.5. Deutschemark—September 1990, Daily (Dual Moving Averages with Candlesticks)

Instead, they should be used by longs to take defensive measures. The reverse is true in oversold markets.

Two moving averages can be plotted as two lines overlaid on a price chart. As previously mentioned, when the shorter-term moving average crosses above a longer-term moving average it is called a golden cross by the Japanese and is a bullish indication. Exhibit 13.5 has a bullish golden cross and a fry pan bottom. The fry pan bottom was confirmed by the window on July 2. Note how the window became support in the first half of July and how the shorter-term moving average became support as the market rallied.

Dual moving average differences are also used as a divergence vehicle. As prices increase, the technician wants to see the short-term moving average increase relative to the longer-term moving average. This would mean increasing positive values for the moving average difference line. If prices advance and the difference between the short- and long-term moving averages narrows, the market is indicating that the shorter-term momentum is running out of steam. This suggests an end to the price advance.

In Exhibit 13.6, we have a histogram between two moving averages. During time periods 1 and 2, advancing prices were echoed by a

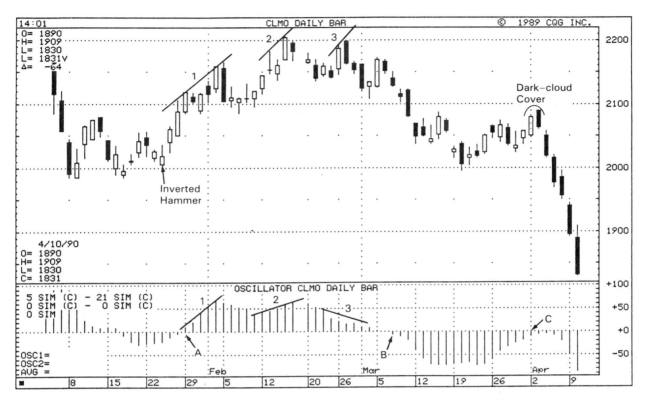

EXHIBIT 13.6. Crude Oil—June 1990, Daily (Dual Moving Averages with Candlesticks)

widening differential between the short- and long-term moving averages. This means the shorter-term moving average is increasing more quickly than the longer-term moving average. This bodes well for a continuation of the uptrend. Time period 3 is where the market experienced problems. The $.50 rally, which began February 23, was mirrored by a narrowing of the moving average differential. This reflects a weakening of the short-term momentum. Add to this the dark-cloud cover and you have a market vulnerable to a price pullback.

The histogram also displays when the short-term moving average crosses above or below the longer-term moving average. When the histogram is below 0, the short-term moving average is under the long-term average. When it is above 0, the short-term average is above the long-term moving average. Thus, an oscillator reading under 0 represents a bearish dead cross; above 0 would be a bullish golden cross.

There was a golden cross at time frame A. A few days before this golden cross there was a bullish inverted hammer. At B, there was a dead cross. At time frame C, prices had rallied but the short-term moving average could not get back above the longer-term moving average (that is, the oscillator remained under 0). In addition, a bearish signal was sent when the dark-cloud cover formed on April 2 and 3.

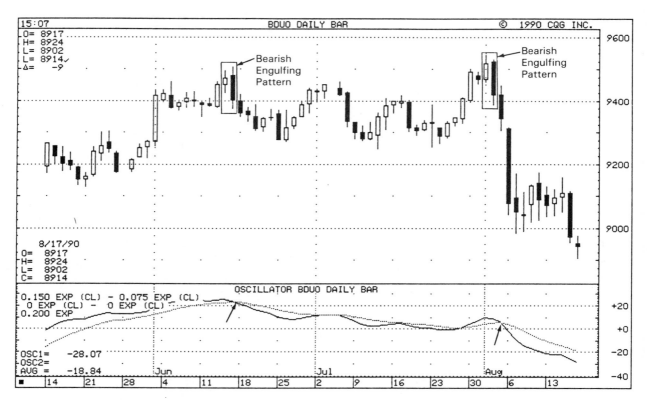

EXHIBIT 13.7. Bonds—September 1990, Daily (MACD with Candlesticks)

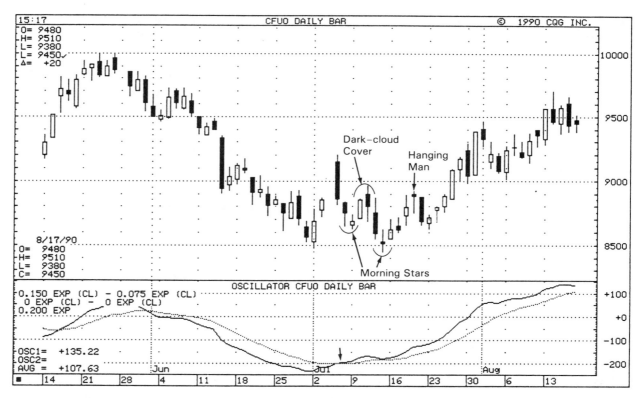

EXHIBIT 13.8. Coffee—September 1990, Daily (MACD with Candlesticks)

The MACD has two lines. They are shown on the lower chart in Exhibit 13.7. The more volatile solid line is the signal line. A sell signal occurs when this signal line crosses below the dashed, less volatile line. In this example, the bearish implications of the two bearish engulfing patterns were corroborated by the bearish crossovers of the MACD indicators (see arrows).

In Exhibit 13.8, the signal line of the MACD pushed above the slower moving line in early July (see arrow). This was a notable clue that the market might be bottoming. Shifting to the candlesticks shows that the first morning star's bullish implications were voided by the dark-cloud cover. The price decline from this dark-cloud cover ended with another morning star. After a temporary set back with the hanging man, the market's upward force gained steam.

CHAPTER 14

CANDLESTICKS WITH OSCILLATORS

....

得手に帆をあげよ

"Let every bird sing its own note"

Pattern recognition techniques are often subjective (this includes candlestick techniques). Oscillators are mathematically derived techniques which offer a more objective means of analyzing the market. They are widely used and are the basis of many computerized trading systems.

OSCILLATORS

Oscillators include such technical tools as the *relative strength index*, *stochastics*, and *momentum*.

As discussed in greater depth later in this chapter, oscillators can serve traders in at least three ways:

1. Oscillators can be used as divergence indicators (that is, when the price and the oscillator move in different directions). They can warn that the current price trend may be stalling. There are two kinds of divergence. A *negative*, or *bearish*, *divergence* occurs when prices are at a new high, but the oscillator is not. This implies the market is internally weak. A *positive*, or *bullish*, *divergence* is when prices are at a new low but the oscillator does not hit a new low. The implications are that the selling pressure is losing steam.

2. As overbought/oversold indicators, oscillators can notify the trader if the market has become overextended and, thus, vulnerable to a correction. Using an oscillator as an overbought/oversold indicator requires caution. Because of how they are constructed, oscillators are mainly applied in lateral price environments. Using an oscillator as an overbought/oversold indicator when a new major trend is about to commence can cause problems. If, for example, there is a break above the top of a congestion band, it could indicate the start of a new bull leg and the oscillator could stay overbought while prices ascend.

3. Oscillators can confirm the force behind a trend's move by measuring the market's momentum. Momentum measures the velocity of a price move by comparing price changes. In theory, the velocity should increase as the trend is underway. A flattening of momentum could be an early warning that a price move may be decelerating.

Use oscillator signals to place a position in the direction of the dominant trend. Thus, a bullish oscillator indication should be used to buy, if the major trend is up, and to cover shorts, if the major trend is down. The same idea applies to a sell signal vis-à-vis an oscillator. Do not short on a bearish oscillator signal unless the prevailing trend is heading south. If it is not, a bearish oscillator signal should be used to liquidate longs.

THE RELATIVE STRENGTH INDEX

The *Relative Strength Index* (RSI)[1] is one of the most popular technical tools used by futures traders. Many charting services plot the RSI and many traders closely monitor it. The RSI compares the relative strength of price advances to price declines over a specified period. Nine and 14 days are some of the most popular periods used.

How to Compute the RSI

The RSI is figured by comparing the gains of up sessions to the losses of the down sessions over a given time frame. The calculations used are dependent only on closing prices. The formula is:

$$RSI = 100 - \left(\frac{100}{1 + RS} \right)$$

where RS = average up points for period/average down points for period

Thus, computing a 14-day RSI entails adding the total gains made on the up days over the last 14 days (on a close-to-close basis) and dividing by 14. The same would be done for the down days. These figures provide the relative strength, (RS). This RS is then put into the RSI formula. This RSI formula converts the RS data so that it becomes an index with a range between 0 and 100.

How to Use RSI

The two main uses of RSI are as an overbought/oversold indicator and as a tool to monitor divergences.

As an overbought/oversold indicator, the RSI implies that the market is overbought if it approaches the upper end of this band (that is, above 70 or 80). At that point, the market may be vulnerable to a pullback or could move into a period of consolidation. Conversely, at the lower end of the RSI range (usually below 30 or 20), it is said to reflect an oversold condition. In such an environment, there is a potential of a short covering move.

As a divergence tool, RSI calculations can be helpful when prices make a new high for the move and the RSI fails to make a concurrent high. This is called a negative divergence and is potentially bearish. A positive divergence occurs when prices make a new low, but the RSI does not. Divergences are more meaningful when RSI oscillator readings are in overbought or oversold regions.

Exhibit 14.1 displays both a bullish positive and a bearish negative RSI divergence which helped these candlestick readings. At the time of the January 24 price low, the RSI was 28%. On January 31, a new price low for the move occurred. The RSI then was 39%. This was noticeably higher than the 28% RSI value of January 24. New price lows and a higher RSI level created a bullish positive divergence. Besides the positive divergence, the white line of January 31 engulfed the prior black candlestick. This built a bullish engulfing pattern.

A doji star arose on March 14. The next session created a candlestick similar to a hanging man. (The lower shadow was not long enough for it to be a classic hanging man, though.) At the time of these potentially bearish candlestick indicators, the RSI was also sending out a warning alert. Specifically, the new price peaks of March 15 and 16 were mirrored by lower RSI readings. This is bearish negative divergence. The market made another price surge on March 21, and although this was a new price high, RSI levels continued to decline. The result was a pullback to the March support area of $1.11.

In Exhibit 14.2 the decline that began with the bearish engulfing pat-

EXHIBIT 14.1. Copper—May, 1990, Daily (RSI with Candlesticks)

tern stopped at the piercing pattern. The constructive outlook implied by this piercing pattern was reinforced by the positive divergence of the RSI. Some technicians also use trendlines with RSI. In this case, the RSI uptrend support line held in spite of new price lows on March 29.

Exhibit 14.2 illustrates another reason to use candlesticks as a compliment to the RSI. Candlesticks may give a bullish or bearish signal before the additional confirmation sometimes needed by the RSI. Specifically, some technicians will view the RSI as giving a bullish signal if two steps occur. The first is the aforementioned positive divergence. The next is that the RSI has to move above its prior high. In this example, that would mean a move above the April 20 RSI level (A). Based on this procedure the bullish signal would have been given at point B. However, by joining the bullish candlestick indication (the engulfing line) with the RSI's positive divergence, the bullish signal would have been apparent a few days earlier.

Doji are a warning signal during uptrends. But, like all technical clues, they can sometimes mislead you. One way to filter out the misleading clues is to add other technical tools. Exhibit 14.3 illustrates the use of the RSI as a tool of confirmation. A bearish shooting star and a set of doji lines appeared in the middle of May (time frame A). These sig-

EXHIBIT 14.2. Wheat—May 1990, Daily (RSI with Candlesticks)

EXHIBIT 14.3. Dow Jones Industrial Average (RSI with Candlesticks)

naled the end of the prior uptrend, at least temporarily, as the market moved into a lateral range for the next few weeks. After this respite, a rally pushed prices to new highs at time frame B. These highs were 100 points above where they were at time frame A. Yet, at time frame B, the RSI was where it was at A. This reflected a flagging of the markets internal strength. The harami at B sounded more warning sirens.

After a 100-point setback from the highs at time frame B, another rally ensued. This rally touched the 3000 level at time frame C. These new highs were sharply above prices at time frame B but the RSI was noticeably less. This bearish divergence at time frame C accompanied with the shooting star, the doji, and the hanging man indicated the internally weak structure of the market, even though prices touched new highs.

STOCHASTICS

The *stochastic oscillator* is another popular tool used by futures technicians. As an oscillator, it provides overbought and oversold readings, signals divergences, and affords a mechanism to compare a shorter-term trend to a longer-term trend. The stochastic indicator compares the latest closing price with the total range of price action for a specified period. Stochastic values are between 0 and 100. A high-stochastic reading would mean the close is near the upper end of the entire range for the period. A low reading means that the close is near the low end of the period's range. The idea behind stochastics is that, as the market moves higher, closes tend to be near the highs of the range or, as the market moves lower, prices tend to cluster near the lows of the range.

How to Compute Stochastics

The stochastic indicator is comprised of two lines; the %K and the %D *lines*. The %K line, called the *raw stochastic* or the *fast %K*, is the most sensitive. The formula for the %K line is:

$$\frac{(\text{Close}) - (\text{Low of } N)}{(\text{High of } N) - (\text{Low of } N)} \times 100 = \%K$$

where   Close = current close
Low of N = low of the range during the period used
High of N = high of the range during the period used

The "100" in the equation converts the value into a percentage. Thus, if the close today is the same as the high for the period under observation, the fast %K would be 100%. A period can be in days, weeks, or even intra-day (such as hourly). Nineteen, fourteen, and twenty-one periods are some of the more common periods.

Because the fast %K line can be so volatile, this line is usually smoothed by taking a moving average of the last three %K values. This three-period moving average of %K is called the *slow %K*. Most technicians use the slow %K line instead of the choppy fast %K line. This slow %K is then smoothed again using a three-day moving average of the slow %K to get what is called the *%D line*. This %D is essentially a moving average of a moving average. One way to think of the difference between the %K and %D lines is too view them as you would two moving averages with the %K line comparable to a short-term moving average and the %D line comparable to a longer-term moving average.

How to Use Stochastics

As mentioned previously, stochastics can be used a few ways. The most popular method is to view it as a tool for showing divergence. Most technicians who monitor stochastics use this aspect of divergence in conjunction with overbought/oversold readings.

Some technicians require another rule. That rule is to have the slow %K line cross under the %D line for a sell signal, or for the slow %K to move above the %D for a busy signal. This is comparable to the bullish (bearish) signal of a faster moving average crossing over (under) the slower moving average. For instance, to get a buy signal, the market must be oversold (25% or less for %D), there is a positive divergence and, the %K line is crossing above the %D line.

Looking at Exhibit 14.4, the doji session of January 3 should give you pause. A doji following a long white candlestick "ain't pretty." The doji session made new price highs as they pushed above the December highs. But stochastics did not echo these price highs with concomitant highs, so this was bearish negative divergence. It was an important affirmation of the bearish signal sent on the doji day.

Besides the divergence, some technicians look for crossovers of the %K and %D lines. See Exhibit 14.5. In mid-1989, copper based out via a hammer. Another series of hammer lines materialized in early 1990. Was this a sign of another base? The answer was more than likely yes because of what the stochastic evidence told us. Hammer B made new lows as it broke under the lows from hammer A. Yet, at hammer B there was a higher stochastic reading than at hammer A. This was a positive divergence. The implications were an abating of selling pressure.

EXHIBIT 14.4. Dow Jones Industrial Average, 1989–1990 (Stochastics with Candlesticks)

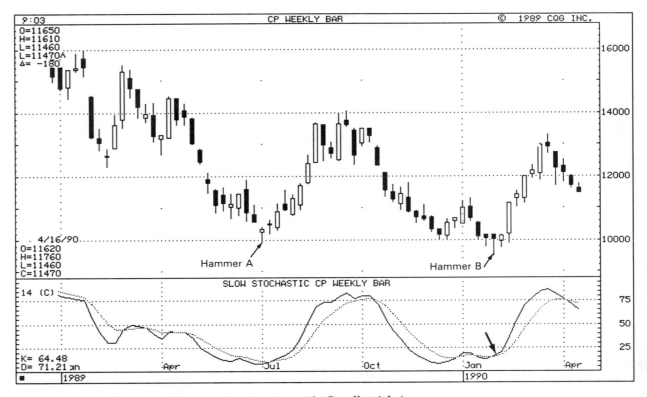

EXHIBIT 14.5. Copper—Weekly (Stochastics with Candlesticks)

There was also a positive crossover as the more volatile, solid %K line crossed above the dotted %D line (see arrow). This crossover is considered more significant if it is from oversold readings (that is, under 25%). That is what occurred here. So, in early 1990, there were a series of hammerlike lines and a positive divergence with a positive crossover during an oversold market. A confluence of technical indicators that were strong clues that the prior downtrend had ended.

As illustrated by Exhibit 14.6, April 12 and 16 formed a dark-cloud cover. The black candlestick session on April 16 pushed prices above the former highs in March. Thus prices were at a new high, but stochastics were not. The dark-cloud cover and the negative divergence were two signs to be circumspect about further rallies. The next downleg was corroborated by a negative crossover when the faster %K line crossed under the slower %D line (as shown by the arrow).

I do not often use candlesticks with British Pound futures because, as can be seen in Exhibit 14.7, many sessions are small real bodies or doji. This is in addition to the frequent gaps induced by overnight trading (this is also true of other currency futures). Nonetheless, at times, there are candlestick signals that bear watching especially when confirmed with other indicators.[2]

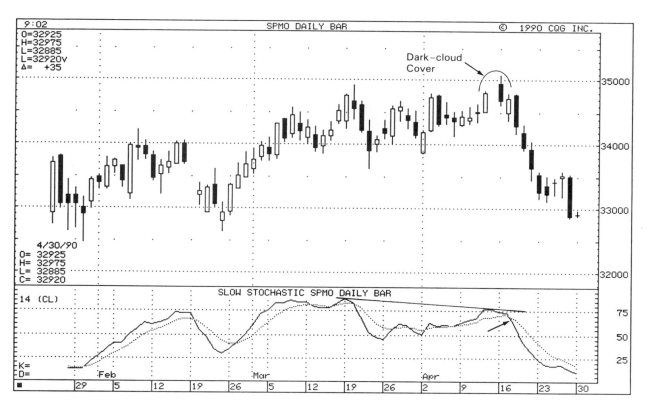

EXHIBIT 14.6. S&P—June 1990, Daily (Stochastics with Candlesticks)

EXHIBIT 14.7. British Pound—June 1990, Daily (Stochastics with Candlesticks)

During the week of March 19, a variation of a morning star arose. Normally, it is best if the third white candlestick of the morning star pattern pushes well into the first session's black body. This white candlestick did not. Before deciding how much importance to place on a variation of a pattern, scan the other technical evidence. At the time of the morning star (or actually its variation), prices touched new price lows; stochastics did not. This was a bullish positive divergence which was soon confirmed when the %K line crossed over the %D line. Consequently, the fact that the morning star pattern was less than ideal should have only given you temporary pause about calling for a bottom. Stochastic indicators provided plenty of added proof to this outlook.

MOMENTUM

Momentum, also called *price velocity*, is a measurement of the difference between the closing price today and the closing price a specified number of days ago. If we use a ten-day momentum we compare today's close to that of ten days ago. If today's close is higher, the momentum is a positive number on the momentum scale. If today's close is lower than that of ten days ago, the momentum is a minus figure. Using the momentum index, price differences (the difference between today's close and that of whatever period you pick) should rise at an increasing rate as a trend progresses. This displays an uptrend with increasingly greater momentum. In other words, the velocity of the price changes is increasing. If prices are rising and momentum begins to flatten, a decelerating price trend is in effect. This could be an early warning that a prior price trend could end. If the momentum crosses under the 0 line, it could be construed as a bearish sign, above the 0 line, as bullish.

Momentum is also handy as an overbought/oversold indicator. For instance, when the momentum index is at a relatively large positive value the market may be overbought and vulnerable to a price pullback. Momentum usually hits its peak before prices. Based on this, a very overbought momentum oscillator could be presaging a price peak.

In Exhibit 14.8, the long-legged doji in January was a warning for the longs to be careful. Further reason for caution was that prices produced new highs on this doji session, yet the momentum was noticeably lower than at the prior high in late November (A). More proof that a downtrend could start was apparent when the momentum fell under 0 in early February.

EXHIBIT 14.8. Gold—June 1990, Daily (Momentum with Candlesticks)

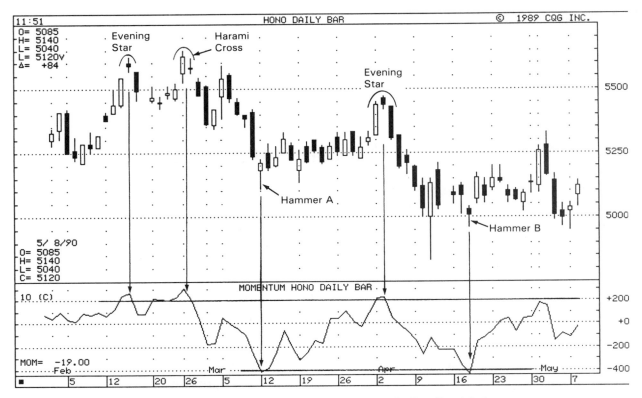

EXHIBIT 14.9. Heating Oil—July 1990, Daily (Momentum with Candlesticks)

Another use of momentum is to provide a yardstick for overbought or oversold levels (see Exhibit 14.9). In this heating oil chart, observe how an oscillator reading of around +200 (that is, the current close is $.02 above the close ten days ago) represents an overbought environment. An oversold state exists for this market when the momentum oscillator is −400 points or $.04 under the close of ten days prior. At the 200-point overbought level, continuation of the prior rally is unlikely and the market should either trade sideways or backoff. The odds of a top reversal with an overbought momentum reading are increased if there is bearish candlestick confirmation. In this regard, in February an overbought momentum level is coupled with an evening star and then a harami cross. Another overbought oscillator in early April joined another evening star pattern. Hammers A and B accompanied the oversold momentum levels in March and April. At these points, further selloffs were unlikely and either sideways action or rallies could unfold to relieve the oversold nature of the market.

Notes

[1]This RSI is different than the relative strength used by equity technicians. The relative strength used by equity technicians compares the relative strength performance of a stock, or a small group of stocks, to the performance of broader market index such as the Dow Jones or the S&P 500.

[2]To help follow the 24-hour foreign exchange markets some Japanese candlestick users will draw a candlestick based on the Tokyo trading session and draw another candlestick line on the U.S. trading session. Thus, for each 24-hour period, there will be two candlesticks. For those who follow the currency futures, the weekly candlestick charts may decrease some of the problems caused by overnight trading.

CHAPTER 15

CANDLESTICKS WITH VOLUME AND OPEN INTEREST

....

一条の矢は折るべく、十条は折るべからず

"A single arrow is easily broken, but not ten in a bundle"

The theory behind *volume* states that the greater the volume, the greater the force behind the move. As long as volume increases, the current price trend should continue. If, however, volume declines as a price trend progresses, there is less reason to believe that the trend will continue. Volume can also be useful for confirming tops and bottoms. A light volume test of a support level suggests a diminution of selling force and is, consequently, bullish. Conversely, a light volume test of a previous high is bearish since it demonstrates a draining of buying power.

Although volume can be a useful auxiliary medium to measure the intensity of a price move, there are some factors with volume, especially as they pertain to futures, that somewhat limit their usefulness. Volume is reported a day late. Spread trading may cause aberrations in volume figures—especially on individual contract months. With the increasing dominance of options in many futures markets, volume figures could be skewed because of option arbitrage strategies. Nonetheless, volume analysis can be a useful tool. This chapter examines some ways volume and candlestick charting techniques can be merged.

VOLUME WITH CANDLESTICKS

Exhibit 15.1 shows how volume and candlestick techniques can help confirm double tops or bottoms. On March 22 (line 1), the market pushed up to the late February highs near 94. Volume at line 1 was 504,000 contracts (all volume figures are total volume for all contract months). For the next few sessions, prices tried to push above this 94 level. The small white real bodies on these days reflected the bulls' lack of fervor. The low volume figures on these small candlestick sessions echoed this. The bulls finally surrendered after a week. In late March, within two days, the market fell two full points.

Next we turn our attention to the tall white candlestick of April 4 (line 2). Could this strong session presage gathering strength by the bulls? The answer is probably not. First, we note the volume on this rally session was a relatively light 300,000 contracts. The long black candlesticks a few sessions before (March 29 and 30) had larger volume. Another sign of trouble appeared with the action following line 2. The next day (line 3) a small real body appeared. Lines 2 and 3 constituted a harami pattern. The implications were that the prior upmove was over. Note also that this small real body day was also a variation on a bearish hanging

EXHIBIT 15.1. Bonds—June 1990, Daily (Volume with Candlesticks)

man (an ideal hanging-man line is at the top of a trading range or an uptrend). The next day, (line 4) there was a final surge to 94. This was a portentous rickshaw man day. In addition, this price push had relatively little force behind it as reflected by the lighter volume (379,000 contracts) compared to the volume on March 22 (504,000 contracts). The light volume test at an old high increased the chance this was a double top. The move under the March 30 low confirmed this as a double top. This double top gave a minimum measured target of 90.

We saw how a light volume test of a high could signal a top, especially when joined with bearish candlestick indications. On this chart we also have a volume/candlestick signal of a bottom. On April 27, there is a doji line. For reasons discussed in Chapter 8, doji days are usually more significant as reversals in uptrends than in downtrends. Yet, with verification, they also should be viewed as a bottom trend reversal. This unfolded in bonds. The importance of the doji on April 27 became amplified when, three days later, another doji appeared. Two doji in themselves are significant, but look at what else occurred during these two doji days. First, there was a tweezers bottom (that is, the lows were nearly the same). Note also the volume on these days. On April 27 volume was 448,000. Volume on May 2, the second doji, was almost half at 234,000 contracts. A light volume test of a support area is bullish. We see the results.

The bullish engulfing pattern, shown in Exhibit 15.2, shows that late April had a white candlestick with the largest volume in the last few months. This forcibly proved the conviction of the bulls. A light volume retest of these lows by a candlestick similar to a hammer confirmed a solid base.

There are many specialized technical tools based on volume. Two of the more popular are *on balance volume* and *tick volume*™.

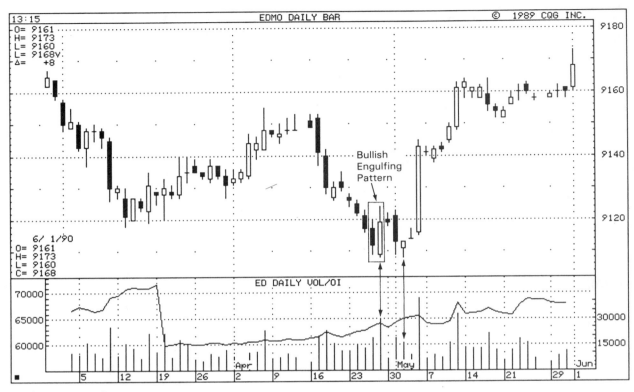

EXHIBIT 15.2. Eurodollars—June 1990, Daily (Volume with Candlesticks)

ON BALANCE VOLUME

On balance volume (OBV) is a net volume figure. When the market closes higher compared to the prior close the volume figure for that day is added to the cumulative on balance volume figure. When the close is lower, the volume for that day is subtracted from the cumulative on balance volume figure.

OBV can be used in a few ways. One way is to confirm a trend. OBV should be moving in the direction of the prevailing price trend. If prices are ascending along with OBV, increased volume is reflected by the buyers, even at higher price levels. This would be bullish. If, conversely, price and OBV are declining, it reflects stronger volume from the sellers and lower prices should continue.

OBV is also used in lateral price ranges. If OBV escalates and prices are stable (preferably at a low price area) it would exhibit a period of accumulation. This would bode well for advancing prices. If prices are moving sideways and OBV is declining it reflects distribution. This would have bearish implications, especially at high price levels.

EXHIBIT 15.3. Silver—July 1990, Daily (OBV with Candlesticks)

OBV with Candlesticks

As illustrated in Exhibit 15.3, the June 13 heavy selloff of silver was followed by a small real body. This harami pattern converted the strong downtrend into a lateral trend. The market traded sideways for the next few weeks. During that time, OBV was ascending reflecting a bullish accumulation. June 25 saw new price lows. These lows did not hold as evidenced by the hammer line formed on that session. The positive divergence in OBV, the failure of the bears to hold the new lows, and the hammer line supplied signs of a near-term bottom.

TICK VOLUME™

In the futures market, volume is reported a day late. As a way to circumvent this problem, many technicians use *tick volume*™ to get a "feel" for volume on an intra-day basis. Tick volume™ shows the number of trades per intra-day period. It does not show the number of contracts per trade.

It would indicate, for instance, a tick volume of 50 trades per hour. We do not know how many contracts were in each trade. They could have been 50 single-lot orders or 50–100 lot orders. In this sense, tick volume is not a true volume figure. It is useful, though, because it is the only means of measuring the volume on a more timely, albeit less accurate, basis.

Tick Volume™ with Candlesticks

The hourly intra-day chart in Exhibit 15.4 shows the usefulness of tick volume™. After a bullish hammer late in the session on May 4, prices moved higher. However, these advancing prices were made on declining tick volume™. This was one sign of lack of conviction by buyers. The other was the short white real bodies. In the first three hours of May 8, there was a sharp price break. These made new lows for the move. The intra-day action late on May 8 provided clues this early morning selloff was to be short lived. After the third hour's long black line, a doji materialized. These two lines formed a harami cross. Then a white body appeared a few hours later which engulfed the prior two black bodies.

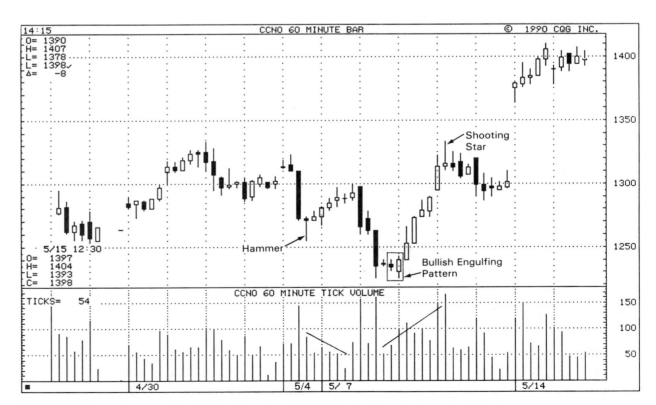

EXHIBIT 15.4. Cocoa—July 1990, Intra-day (Tick Volume™ with Candlesticks)

This was a bullish engulfing pattern that had extra significance since it engulfed two black bodies. The lows made by the white engulfing line also formed a tweezers bottom.

Just in case, another hint of a bottom was needed, tick volume™ substantiated that the buyers were taking control. Prices rose after the aforementioned bullish engulfing pattern. During this rally, volume expanded as did the height of the real bodies. A shooting star and resistance near $1,340 from the prior week, temporarily put a damper on the price ascent. Once the market pushed above the $1,340 resistance level via a window, there was no doubt the bulls were in control.

In Exhibit 15.5, the hammer hour on June 19 furnished a sign that the market may be searching for a bottom. The first hour of June 20 made a new low at $16.62 (line 1). Tick volume™ on this hour was a brisk 324 trades. Another move down to that level, via a long black candlestick (line 2), was made later that session. This time tick volume™ was only 262 trades. The next session, June 21, is the one of the most interest. On the third hour of trading, prices made a new low for the move at $16.57. This new low was made on lighter tick volume™ (249 trades) then the prior two tests (lines 1 and 2). This meant selling pressure was easing. Prices then sprung back and made an hourly hammer line. (From the

EXHIBIT 15.5. Crude Oil—August 1990, Intra-day (Tick Volume™ with Candlesticks)

previous discussion on springs in Chapter 11, you know to look for a retest of the recent high near $17.24.)

OPEN INTEREST

In the futures markets, a new contract is created when a new buyer and a new short seller agree to a trade. Because of this, the number of contracts traded in the futures market can be greater than the supply of the commodity which underlies that futures contract. *Open interest* is the total number of long or short contracts, but not a total of both, which remain outstanding.

Open interest assists in gauging, as does volume, the pressure behind a price move. It does this by measuring if money is entering or exiting the market. Whether open interest rises or falls is contingent on the amount of new buyers or sellers entering the market as compared to old traders departing.

In this section, our focus will be on the importance of price trends accompanied by rising open interest. The major principle to keep in mind is that open interest helps confirm the current trend if open interest increases. For example, if the market is trending higher and open interest is rising, new longs are more aggressive than the new shorts. Rising open interest indicates that both new longs and new shorts are entering the market, but the new longs are the more aggressive. This is because the new longs are continuing to buy in spite of rising prices.

A scenario such as building open interest and falling prices reflects the determination of the bears. This is because rising open interest means new longs and shorts entering the market, but the new short sellers are willing to sell at increasingly lower price levels. Thus, when open interest rises in an uptrend, the bulls are generally in charge and the rally should continue. When open interest increases in a bear trend, the bears are in control and the selling pressure should continue.

On the opposite side, if open interest declines during a trending market it sends a signal the trend may not continue. Why? Because for open interest to decline traders with existing positions must be abandoning the market. In theory, once these old positions are exited, the driving force behind the move will evaporate. In this regard, if the market rallies while open interest declines, the rally is due to short covering (and old bulls liquidating). Once the old shorts have fled the market, the force behind the buying (that is, short covering) should mean the market is vulnerable to further weakness.

As an analogy, let's say that there is a hose attached to a main water line. The water line to the hose can be shut off by a spigot. Rising open interest is like fresh water pumped from the main water line into the hose. This water will continue to stream out of the hose while the spigot remains open (comparable to rising open interest pushing prices higher or lower). Declining open interest is like closing the spigot. Water will continue to flow out of the hose (because there is still some water in it), but once that water trickles out, there is no new source to maintain the flow. The flow of water (that is, the trend) should dry up.

There are other factors to bear in mind (such as seasonality), which we have not touched upon in this brief review of open interest.

Open Interest with Candlesticks

Exhibit 15.1 on June bonds showed a wealth of information about volume. It also illustrates the importance of rising open interest to confirm a trend. Look again at this bond chart, but this time focus on open interest. Refer to Exhibit 15.1 for the following analysis.

A minor rally in bonds started March 13 and lasted until March 22. Open interest declined during this rally. The implication was that short covering caused the rally. When the short covering stopped, so would the rally. The rally stalled at line 1. This was a rickshaw man session that saw prices fail at the late February highs near 94. Open interest began to rise with the selloff that began on April 9. A rising open interest increase meant that new longs and shorts were entering the market. The bears, however, were the more aggressive in their desire since they were still selling at progressively lower prices. Open interest continued higher throughout the late April decline. When the two doji, on April 27 and May 2, emerged at the 88 ½ level, open interest began to level off. This reflected a diminution of the bears' selling pressure.

Ascending open interest and prices throughout May were a healthy combination as seen in Exhibit 15.6. Not so healthy was the fact that June's rising prices were being mirrored by declining open interest. The implication is that June's rally was largely short covering. This scenario does not bode well for a continuation of higher prices. The shooting star spelled a top for the market and the market erased in four sessions what it had made in about a month.

If there is unusually high open interest coinciding with new price highs it could presage trouble. This is because rising open interest means new short and longs are entering the market. If prices are in a gradual uptrend, stop losses by the new longs will be entered along the price move at increasingly higher prices. If prices suddenly fall, a chain reaction of triggered sell stop loss orders can cause a cascade of prices.

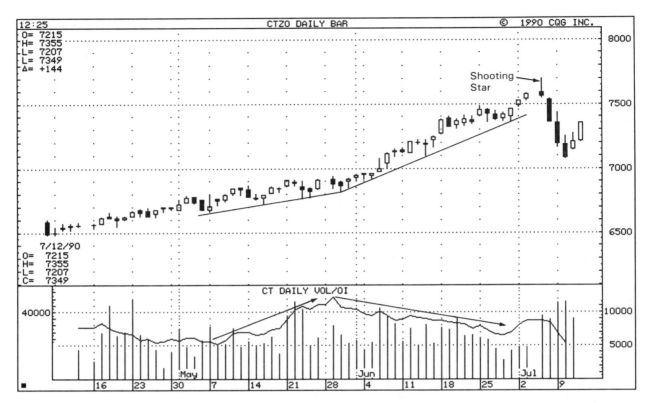

EXHIBIT 15.6. Cotton—December 1990, Daily (Open Interest with Candlesticks)

EXHIBIT 15.7. Sugar—July 1990, Daily (Open Interest with Candlesticks)

Exhibit 15.7 is a good case in point. Sugar traded in the $.15 to $.16 range for two months from early March. Open interest noticeably picked up from the last rally that commenced in late April. It reached unusually high levels in early May. As this rally progressed, sell stops by the new longs were placed in the market at increasingly higher levels. Then a series of doji days gave a hint of indecisiveness and a possible top. Once the market was pressed on May 4, stop after stop was hit and the market plummeted.

The second aspect of this open interest level was that new longs who were not stopped out were trapped at higher price levels. This is because as open interest builds, new longs and shorts are entering the market. However, with the precipitous price decline, prices were at a two-month low. Every one who had bought in the prior two months now had a loss. The longs who bought anywhere near the price highs are in "pain." And judging from the high open interest figures at the highs near $.16, there were probably many longs in "pain." Any possible rallies will be used by them in order to exit the market. This is the scenario that unfolded in mid-May as a minor rally to $.15 meet with heavy selling.

CHAPTER 16

CANDLESTICKS WITH ELLIOTT WAVE

....

車の両輪に於けるが如

"Like both wheels of a cart"

The Elliott Wave Theory of market analysis is employed by a broad spectrum of technical analysts. It is as applicable to intra-day charts as it is to yearly charts. In this introductory section I only scratch the surface of Elliott. Describing Elliott Wave methodology can be, and is, a book in itself.

ELLIOTT WAVE BASICS

The *Wave principle* was discovered by R. N. Elliott early in this century. He noted that, among other aspects, price movements consists of a five-wave upmove followed by a corrective three-wave downmove. These eight waves form a complete cycle as illustrated in Exhibit 16.1. Waves 1, 3, and 5 are called *impulse waves* while waves 2 and 4 are called *corrective waves.* Although Exhibit 16.1 reflects an Elliott Wave count in a rising market, the same concepts would hold in a falling market. Thus, the impulse waves on a downtrending market would be sloping downward and the corrective waves would be upward bounces against the main trend.

Another major contribution of Elliott was his use of the Fibonacci series of numbers in market forecasting. Wave counts and Fibonacci

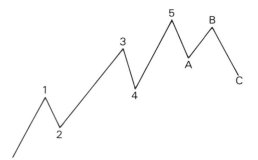

EXHIBIT 16.1. The Basic Elliott Wave Form

ratios go hand in hand since these ratios can be used to project price targets for the next wave. Thus, for example, wave 3 could be projected to move 1.618 times the height of wave 1; a wave 4 could correct 38.2% or 50% of the wave 3 move; and so on.

Elliott Wave with Candlesticks

This chapter illustrated how candlesticks can lend verification to Elliott Wave termination points. The most important waves to trade are waves 3 and 5. Wave 3 usually has the most powerful move. The top of wave 5 calls for a reversal of positions. The wave counts below are with the help of my colleague, John Gambino, who focuses closely on Elliott. Elliott Wave counts are subjective (at least until the wave is over) and as such the wave counts below may not be the same as derived by someone else.

A five-wave count (see Exhibit 16.2a) is discussed wave by wave in the following text. Impulse wave 1 started with the dark-cloud cover in late February. Wave 1 ended at the harami pattern in mid-March. This harami implied that the prior downward pressure was abating. A minor bounce unfolded. Corrective wave 2 was a bounce that ended with another dark-cloud cover. Impulse wave 3 is the major leg down. The extent of this move can be estimated by using a Fibonacci ratio and the height of wave 1. This gives a wave 3 target of $17.60. At $17.60, look for a candlestick signal to confirm a bottom for this wave 3 count. This occurred on April 11. For visual details about April 11, refer to Exhibit 16.2(b) which is the intra-day chart of crude.

On April 11, crude broke in the first hour as it falls $1 from the prior close. At that point, the selloff looks unending. Then some interesting price events occur. The selloff abruptly stops at $17.35—very close to the Elliott count of $17.60. Second, the hourly chart (see Exhibit 16.2(b)) shows that the first hour of trading on this selloff ended as a classic hammer. This potentially bullish indicator is immediately followed by a

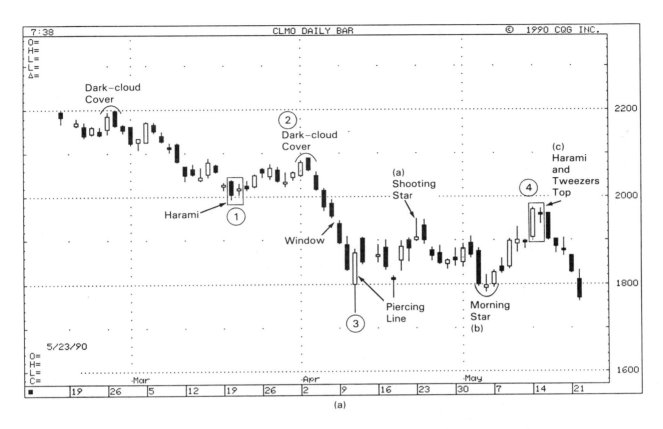

(a)

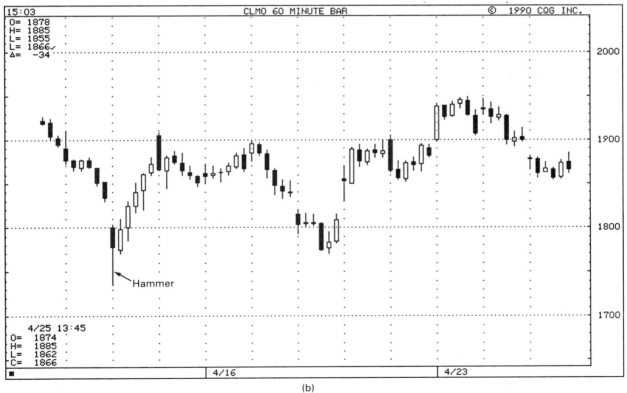

(b)

EXHIBIT 16.2. Crude Oil—June 1990: (a) Daily and (b) Intra-day (Elliott Wave with Candlesticks)

series of strong long white bodies. On this hourly chart the bullish hammer and the ensuing white lines confirmed a bottom for the wave 3 count. The daily chart also provided a bottom reversal signal with a piercing pattern based on the price action of April 10 and 11. We now look for a wave 4 rally.

Corrective wave 4's top should rally but should not move above the bottom of the prior wave 1 according to Elliott Wave theory. In this example, that would be the $19.95. Approaching that level, look for a bearish candlestick cue. That is, indeed, what unfolded. On May 14 and 15, the market stalled under $20 via the harami cross and tweezers top. The wave 4 top was hit.

Interestingly, by breaking wave 4 into its (a), (b), and (c) subcomponents, corroboration by candlestick indicators is apparent. At (a), a shooting star whose highs stopped at a window from early April appears. A morning star at (b) called the bottom. Subcomponent (c) was also the top of wave 4 with its attendant bearish harami cross and tweezers top.

Exhibit 16.3 illustrates that the five impulse waves down began in late December 1989 from 100.16. The wave counts are shown. The bottom of wave 1 formed a harami pattern. The top of wave 2 formed a

EXHIBIT 16.3. Bonds—June 1990, Daily (Elliott Wave with Candlesticks)

dark-cloud cover. Wave 3 did not give a candlestick indication. Wave 4 constituted a harami. The most interesting aspect of this Elliott pattern is the fifth and final downwave. The fifth wave target is derived by taking the height of the third wave and a Fibonacci ratio. This provides a target of 88.08. At the end of April, the low of the move was 88.07. At this low, the candlesticks sent a strong bullish signal based on a tweezers bottom and two doji at this tweezers bottom. Volume also confirmed this bottom. Please refer to Exhibit 15.1 to receive a more detailed description of what happened at this low vis-à-vis the candlesticks and volume.

CHAPTER 17

CANDLESTICKS WITH MARKET PROFILE®

共存共栄

"Existing together, thriving together"

*M*arket *Profile®*, used by many futures traders, presents information about the markets that was previously only available to those in the trading pits. Market Profile® helps technicians understand the internal structure of the markets. It offers a logical, statistically based analysis of price, time, and volume. This section examines only a few of the many tools used by followers of the Market Profile®. Topics such as different types of profile days (that is, normal, trend, neutral, long-term market activity charts, and so on), or the Liquidity Data Bank® will not be discussed here. The goal of this brief introduction is to alert the reader to a few of the unique insights of the Market Profile® and how it can be used in conjunction with candlesticks.

A few of the elements underlying the Market Profile® are:

1. The purpose of all markets is to facilitate trade.
2. The markets are self regulating. The regulating constraints include price, time, and volume.
3. The markets, as they attempt to facilitate trade, will use price probes to "advertise" for sellers or buyers. The reaction to these probes provides valuable clues about the strength or weakness of the market.

The Market Profile® organizes daily action into half-hour periods and assigns a letter to each half-hour period. Thus the "A" period is from

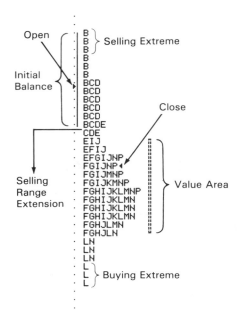

EXHIBIT 17.1. Example of the Market Profile®

8:00 to 8:30 A.M. (Chicago time), "B" is from 8:30 to 9:00 A.M., and so forth. For markets that open before 8:00 A.M. (such as bonds, currencies, and metals), the first half hours are usually designated "y" and "z." Each letter is called a *TPO* (Time-Price Opportunity). The half-hour segment represents the price range that developed over that time period. This is displayed in Exhibit 17.1.

The first hour of trading is labeled as the *initial balance*. This is the time period when the market is exploring the range of trading. In other words, it is the market's early attempt to find value. A *range extension* is any new high or low made after the first hour's initial balance. Exhibit 17.1 establishes a selling range extension, but since there are no new highs after the initial balance, there is no buying range extension.

Value, to those who follow Market Profile®, is defined as the market's acceptance of price over time and is reflected in the amount of volume traded at that price. Thus, time and volume are the key ingredients in determining value. If the market trades briefly at a price, the market is indicating rejection of that price. That is, the market has not found "value." If prices are accepted for a relatively extended time with good volume, it connotes market acceptance. In such a scenario, the market found value. The market's acceptance of price is where 70% of the day's volume occurred (for those familiar with statistics, it is one standard deviation which has been rounded up to 70%). This is defined as the day's *value area*. Thus, if 70% of the volume for trading wheat took place in a $3.30 to $3.33 range, that range would be its value area.

A *price probe* is the market's search for the boundaries of value. How the trading and investing community acts on such price probes can send out important information about the market to Market Profile® users. One of two actions occur after a price probe. Prices can backtrack to the value area or value can relocate to the new price. Acceptance of a new price as value would be confirmed by increased volume and the time spent at that level.

If prices backtrack to value, the market shows a rejection of those prices that are considered unfairly high or low. Quick rejection of a price can result in what is called an *extreme*. An extreme is defined as two or more single TPOs at the top or bottom of the profile (except for the last half hour). Normally, an extreme at the top of the profile is caused by competition among sellers who were attracted by higher prices and a lack of buyers. A bottom extreme is caused by an influx of buyers attracted by lower prices and a dearth of sellers. Buying and selling extremes are noted in Exhibit 17.1.

How the market trades compare to the prior value area also discloses valuable information. Market Profile® followers monitor whether there is initiating buying or selling, or responsive buying or selling. This is identified by determining where the current day's extreme and range extensions are occurring with respect to the prior day's value area. Specifically, buying below the prior day's value area is deemed responsive buying because prices are below value and buyers are responding to what they perceive to be undervalued prices. These buyers expect that prices will return to value.

Sellers at prices below the prior day's value area are said to be *initiating sellers*. This means they are aggressive sellers since they are willing to sell at prices under value. The implication of this is that they believe value will move down. Buying above the prior session's value area is *initiating buying*. These aggressive buyers are convinced that value will move up to price. Otherwise why buy above what is now perceived is as value? Sellers at prices above the prior day's value area are *responsive sellers*. They are responsive to higher prices and expect prices to return to value.

Trading should go in the direction of the initiating group unless price is quickly rejected. Thus, if there is initiating selling activity (extremes and/or range extension), under the previous day's value area on expanding volume, it should have bearish implications.

Market Profile® with Candlesticks

Exhibit 17.2 reveals how a doji on July 2 and a hanging man during the next session were candlestick alerts of a top. What did the Market Pro-

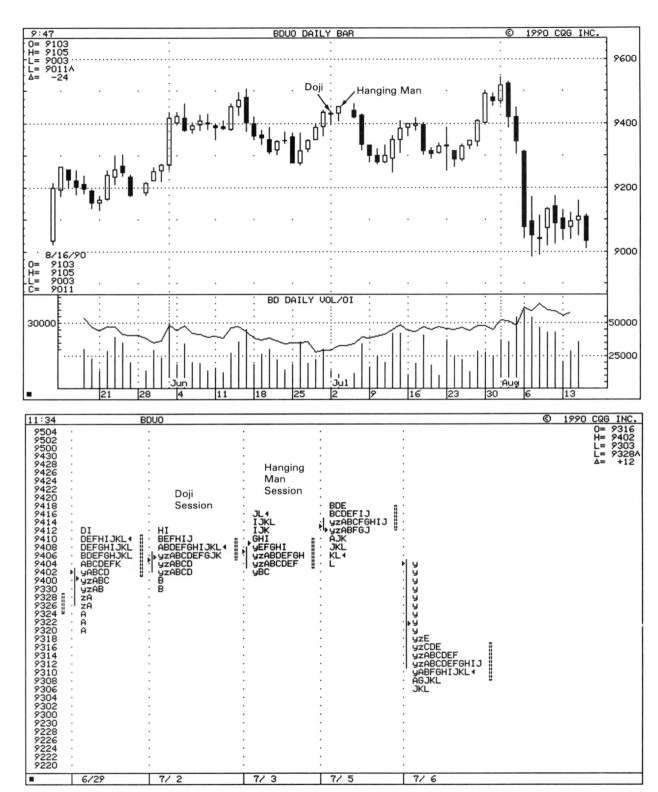

EXHIBIT 17.2. Bonds—June 1990, Daily (Market Profile® with Candlesticks)

file® say during this time period? July 2 had a relatively small value area as compared to the prior session. It was also a light volume session (132,000 contracts as compared to 303,000 the prior session). This hinted that price was having trouble being accepted at these higher rates. In other words, there was lack of trade facilitation. It is also a profile with range extension to both sides. This indicates a tug of war between the bulls and bears.

July 3 was another light-volume session (109,000 contracts) which significantly discounts the bullish developments—an upside range extension and a close at the highs of the day. The next day, July 5, is where the weakness of the market materializes. During the early part of the session, new highs were made for the move. In the process, upside range extensions were also formed. With these range extensions, the market was advertising for sellers. They got them. The market sold off toward the latter part of the session (the J, K, and L periods) to close near the low of the day. The open of July 6 saw initiating selling on the opening since the market opened under the prior day's value area. This showed immediate selling activity. July 6 also displayed increased volume and an initiating selling extreme (that is, single prints at the top of the profile) during the "y" period. This confirmed the market was in trouble.

In this example, we see an important aspect about the hanging man previously addressed; it is only what happens after that line that makes it a bearish indicator. July 3 was the hanging-man day. Here we see the Market Profile® picture of the hanging-man line was giving some positive indications about the market. It was only on the following session, July 5 and especially the morning of July 6, that a top was also verified via Market Profile®.

Exhibit 17.3 shows that July 5 was a very evident shooting star. After this line appeared, cotton plunged for three sessions. Was there anything prior to the shooting star a lá Market Profile® which gave signs of trouble? Yes, there was. From June 29 to July 3 prices advanced but by way of a shrinking value area. This meant less trade facilitation at higher prices. The market was having trouble accepting these new highs as value. In addition, volume, as gauged by the total number of those session's TPO counts, was decreasing (actual volume was light on these sessions. However, since volume is not released until the following day, the TPO count can be used as a gauge of volume). Notice of a top was provided by the shooting star of July 5. The Market Profile® on that session showed a range toward the upside failed to get buying follow-through. Additionally, the entry of sellers attracted by these higher prices drove the market down as indicated by the range extension down and the weak close. These were bearish signs.

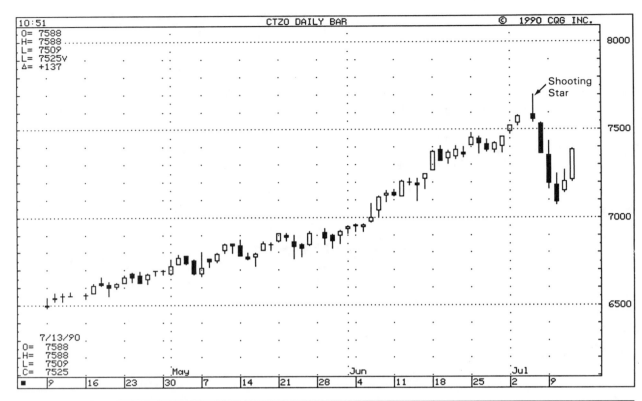

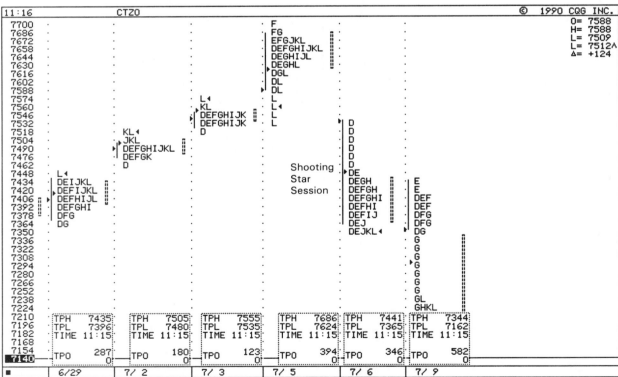

EXHIBIT 17.3. Cotton—December, 1990, Daily (Market Profile® with Candlesticks)

If more proof was needed, all one had to do was wait until the opening of July 6. An initiating selling extreme developed on the opening under the previous day's value area. This confirmed the presence of sellers and difficulty ahead. Thus, the Market Profile® tools confirmed the bearish implications of the shooting star.

There are some interesting similarities between Market Profile® concepts and candlesticks. Wider value areas in Market Profile® usually represent facilitation of trade and, as such, increase the probability for price trend continuation. Thus, in an uptrend, one would like to see widening value areas. Likewise, with the candlesticks, one would like to see a rally via a series of longer and longer white real bodies in order to confirm the power behind the move.

Shrinking value areas in Market Profile® reflect less facilitation of trade and thus less certainty of a continuation of the price move. So it is with the candlestick's advance block or stalled patterns. In those formations, the trend is still up but it takes place by means of shrinking white real bodies. These formations indicate that the prior momentum is running out of steam.

What about a star in candlesticks? A short real body in an uptrend or downtrend would be a sign of decreasing vigor by the bulls (a star in an uptrend) or the bears (a star in a downtrend). So would a small value area after a strong advance (or decline). The small value area would reflect a lack of trade facilitation. They could be a harbinger of a trend change. A hammer's lower shadow might be formed due to a buying extreme in which lower prices induce an influx of buyers. A shooting star's long upper shadow could be the result of a selling extreme in which higher prices attracted strong selling.

CHAPTER 18

CANDLESTICKS WITH OPTIONS

··

合わぬ蓋もあれば合う蓋もあり

"If there is a lid that does not fit, there is a lid that does"

Options, at times, confer advantages over underlying positions. Specifically, options offer:

1. *Staying power*—buying an option limits risk to the premium paid. Options are thus useful when trying to pick tops and bottoms. These are risky propositions, but judicious use of options can help mitigate some of the inherent risks in such endeavors.

2. *The ability to benefit in sideways markets*—by using options, one can profit if the underlying contract trades in a lateral range (by selling straddles or combinations).

3. *Strategy flexibility*—one can tailor risk/reward parameters to one's price, volatility, and timing projections.

4. *Occasionally superior leverage*—for instance, if the market swiftly rallies, under certain circumstances, an out-of-the money call may provide a greater percentage return than would an outright position.

OPTIONS BASICS

Before discussing how candlesticks can be used with options, we'll want to spend some time on option basics. The five factors needed to figure the theoretical value of a futures options price are the *exercise price*, the *time to expiration*, the *price of the underlying instrument, volatility*, and, to a minor extent, *short-term interest rates*. Three of these variables are known (time until expiration, exercise price, and short-term interest rates). The two components that are not known (the forecasted price of the under-lying instrument and its volatility) have to be estimated in order to fore-cast an option price. One should not underrate the importance that volatility plays in option pricing. In fact, at times, a change in volatility can have a stronger impact on option premiums than a change in price of the underlying contract.

Consider as an illustration an at-the-money $390 gold call with 60 days until expiration. If this option has a volatility level of 20%, its the-oretical price would be $1,300. At a 15% volatility, this same option would be theoretically priced at $1,000. Thus, volatility must always be considered since it can so forcefully affect the option premium.

Volatility levels provide the expected range of prices over the next year (volatilities are on an annual basis). Without getting into the math-ematics, a volatility of 20% on, say, gold suggests that there is a 68% probability that a year from now gold's price will remain within plus or minus 20% of its current price. And there would be a 95% chance that a year hence golds's price will remain within plus or minus two times the volatility (that is, two times 20% or 40%) of its price now. For example, if gold is at $400 and volatility is at 20%, there is a 68% chance that its price after one year will be between $320 and $480 (plus or minus 20% of $400) and a 95% probability that it will be between $240 and $560 (plus or minus 40% of $400). Keep in mind that these levels are based on probabilities and that at times these levels are exceeded.

The greater the volatility the more expensive the option. This is due to at least three factors. First, from the speculators' point of view, the greater the volatility, the greater the chance for prices to move into the money (or further into the money). Second, from a hedger's perspective, higher price volatility equals more price risk. Thus, there is more reason to buy options as a hedging vehicle. And, third, option sellers also require more compensation for higher perceived risk. All these factors will buoy option premiums.

There are two kinds of volatility: historic and implied. *Historic volatil-ity* is based on past volatility levels of the underlying contract. It is usu-ally calculated by using daily price changes over a specified number of business days on an annualized basis. In the futures markets, 20 or 30 days are the most commonly used calculations. Just because a futures contract has a 20-day historic volatility of 15% does not mean it will remain at that level during the life of the option. Thus, to trade options it is necessary to forecast volatility. One way to do this is by having the market do it for you. And that is what implied volatility does. It is the market's estimate of what volatility of the underlying futures contract will be over the options's life. This differs from historic volatility in that historic volatility is derived from prior price changes of the underlying contract.

Implied volatility is the volatility level that the market is implying (hence its name). Deriving this number involves the use of a computer but the theory behind it is straightforward. To obtain the option's implied volatility, the five inputs needed are the current price of the futures contract, the option's strike price, the short-term interest rate, the option expiration date, and the current option price. If we put these variables into the computer, using an options pricing formula, the computer will spit back the implied volatility.

Thus, we have two volatilities—historic, which is based on actual price changes in the futures, and implied, which is the market's best guess of what volatility will be from now until the option expires. Some option traders focus on historic volatility, others on implied volatility, and still others compare historic to implied.

OPTIONS WITH CANDLESTICKS

If a strong trending market has pushed volatility levels to unusually high levels, the emergence of a candlestick reversal indicator may provide an attractive time to sell volatility or to offset a long volatility trade. In this regard, the most effective candlestick formations may be those which imply that the market will move into a state of truce between the bulls and bears. These include the harami, counterattack lines, and other patterns discussed in Chapter 6.

Selling volatility could be done in the expectation that with the candlestick's signal, the market's prior price trend will change. If it changes to a lateral band, all other factors being equal (that is, no seasonal volatility factors, no expected economic reports, and so on), volatility could decline. Even if prices reverse, if volatility levels were uncommonly high to begin with, volatility may not increase. This is because the push in volatility may have occurred during the original strong trend.

Candlestick reversal signals may also be useful in helping the technician decide when to buy volatility (or to offset a short volatility trade such as a short strangle or straddle). Specifically, if the market is trading in a lateral band and a candlestick reversal indicator appears, the market could be forecasting that a new trend could emerge. If volatility levels are relatively low at the time of this candlestick reversal, the technician may not only see a new price trend, but also a concomitant rise in volatility. This would be especially likely if there is a confluence of technical indicators (candlesticks and/or Western techniques) that all give a reversal signal near the same price area.

Candlesticks, as tools to predict shifts in volatility, should be viewed in the context that these shifts will most likely be shorter term. That is, if one buys volatility keyed off of candlesticks and volatility does rise, it does not always mean that volatility will remain high until that option expires.

Exhibit 18.1 shows that there were two top reversal warnings in mid-May. The first was a doji after a long white real body. Next, were the three black crows. Historic volatility expanded during the selloff which started from these top reversal formations. The end of this selloff came with early June's harami cross. Then the price trend changed from lower to lateral. Volatility contracted due to this lateral price environment.

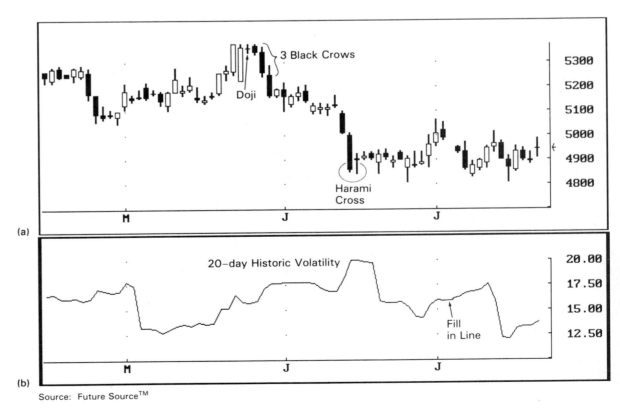

Source: Future Source™

EXHIBIT 18.1. Silver—September 1990, Daily (Candlesticks with Options)

Thus, for those who were riding volatility on the way up, the harami cross could have been viewed as a signal to expect an end to the prior steep trend and, consequently, the possibility of a decline in volatility.

Based on experience, and for various other reasons, candlestick signals seem to work better with historic volatility than with implied volatility. Nonetheless, as shown in Exhibit 18.2, candlesticks, at times, can be useful instruments to assist in forecasting short-term moves in implied volatility. A sharp rally developed in January. During this phase, implied volatility ascended along an uptrend. For much of February, sugar was bounded in a $.14 to $.15 range. In this period of relatively quiet trading, volatility shrank.

On February 26, a hammer appeared (area A in Exhibit 18.2(b)). In addition, this hammer session's lower shadow broke under the support area from late January. This new low did not hold. This demonstrated that the bears tried to take control of the market, but failed. Three trading day's later, on March 2, (area B in Exhibit 18.2(b)) the white candlestick's lower shadow successfully maintained the lows of mid-January. In addition, the March 2 low joined with the hammer to complete a tweezers bottom. The combination of all these bottom reversal indicators sent a powerful signal that a solid base had been built. A significant rally was thus possible. As shown in Exhibit 18.2(b), volatility at areas A and B were at relatively low levels. With a possible strong price rally (based on the confluence of bottom reversal signals discussed above) and low volatility, one could expect any price rallies to be mimicked with expanding volatility. That is what unfolded.

Another use for options and candlesticks is for the risky proposition of bottom and top picking. Just about any book on trading strategies warns against this. But let's face it, we all occasionally attempt it. This is an example of how the limited risk feature of options may allow one to place a trade too risky for an outright future. Exhibit 18.3 is an example of a trade I recommended. I would not have made such a recommendation without the limited risk feature of options.

Cocoa was in a major bull market that started in November 1989 at $900. This exhibit shows the last three waves of an Elliott Wave count. The top of wave 3 was accompanied by the shooting star and the bottom of wave 4 by the bullish piercing line. Based on a Fibonacci ratio, there is a wave 5 target near $1,520. Thus, near $1,520 one should start looking for candlestick confirmation of a top. And in late May, a bearish engulfing pattern emerged after the market touched a high of $1,541. This was close to the Elliott Wave count of $1,520 which signaled a possible top.

I could not resist such a powerful combination of an Elliott fifth wave and a bearish engulfing pattern! Options to the rescue! I recommended

EXHIBIT 18.2. Sugar—July 1990 (a) Daily (Candlesticks with Options) and (b) Implied Volatility

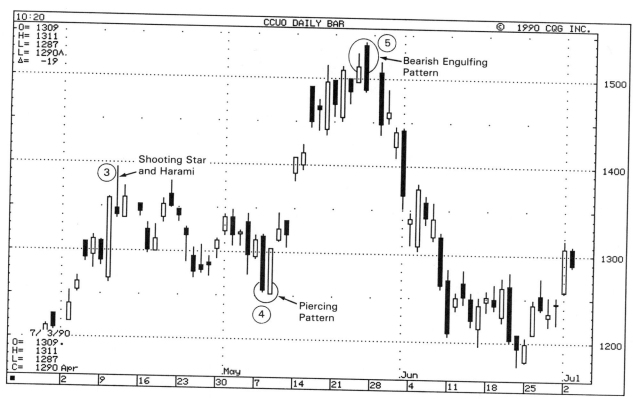

EXHIBIT 18.3. Cocoa—September 1990 Daily (Candlesticks with Options)

a buy of the $1,400 puts (because the major trend was still up, I would have been more comfortable liquidating longs, but unfortunately I was not long during this rally). If I was wrong about a top and cocoa gapped higher (as it did in mid-May), increased volatility could help mitigate adverse price action. As it turned out, this bearish engulfing pattern and Elliott fifth wave became an important peak.

CHAPTER 19

HEDGING WITH CANDLESTICKS

. . . .

転ばぬ先の杖

"Take all necessary precautions"

The days of placing a hedge and then forgetting about it are over. Hedgers are now more sophisticated and technically aware thanks to an increased information stream. Hedgers are consistently deciding when and how much of their cash exposure to hedge. These decisions translate into the bottom line of profitability. In this chapter, we'll examine how candlestick techniques can provide a valuable tool to assist in the decision-making process. This is because many candlestick indicators are trend reversal indicators and, as such, can provide valuable assistance in timing the placement or lifting of a hedge, and when to adjust a hedge.

A *hedger* seeks to offset his current or anticipated cash price exposure by taking an opposite position in the futures or options market. A *short hedger* is one whose underlying cash position is at risk of declining prices. A short hedger, for example, could be a copper producer or a farmer. To help manage this risk of lower prices, the hedger may initiate a short position by selling futures or by buying puts. If prices fall, the decreasing value of their cash position will be at least partially counterbalanced by profits in the futures or options position.

An ultimate user of the cash commodity can become a *long hedger*. Such a hedger is one whose underlying cash position is at risk of rising prices. An example of a long hedger is a shirt manufacturer who has to buy cotton to use in the production of shirts. To assist in managing this risk of higher prices the manufacturer can place a long hedge by buying futures or calls. If prices move up, the higher price needed to purchase the cash commodity would be offset, at least partially, by the gains in the futures or options positions.

In many instances, the underlying cash position may not be fully hedged at one price. The hedger may intend to scale into the hedge position. Thus, the question a hedger must frequently address is what percent of his exposure should be hedged. Candlestick techniques can help answer this question. By exploring the following examples, it should offer insight into how candlesticks can be used to furnish clues as to when to adjust the hedged portion of the cash position.

Candlestick techniques can also be used for those who are 100% hedged. For instance, let's say that you are a corn farmer and the corn market is trending against your cash position (corn prices are falling). This should mean, as a short hedger, your futures hedge position is profitable. If a strongly bullish candlestick reversal formation appears, and you believe prices will rally, you might want to ease back on the hedge. In some instances, early lifting of a profitable hedge may improve cash flow. However, no hedge should be viewed as a strategy to generate profits.

As shown in Exhibit 19.1, an explosive rally unfolded in 1988 as

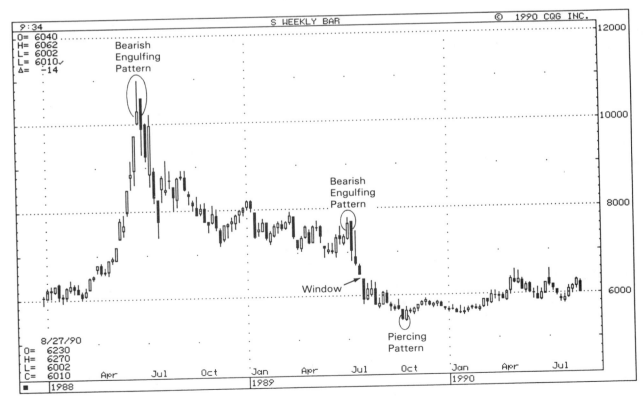

EXHIBIT 19.1. Soybeans—Weekly (Candlesticks with Hedging)

prices nearly doubled from $6 to $11. In mid-1988, near the peak of the rally, the candlesticks gave a reversal signal a lá the bearish engulfing pattern. This would have not been seen as a Western top reversal formation using traditional Western techniques. A top reversal formation would have required a new high for the move and then a close under the prior week's close. The black candlestick session of the engulfing pattern did not create a new high. Thus, while not a Western top reversal pattern, it was a reversal formation with candlesticks. This bearish engulfing pattern, for a soybean farmer, could have been used as a warning to either initiate short hedge positions or, if not already fully hedged, to raise the percentage hedged.

In 1989, another bearish engulfing pattern warned of a top (this also was not seen as a top reversal pattern using Western technicals). Short hedgers could have placed hedge positions here. The window a few weeks later was another bearish candlestick signal which would have told short hedgers to add to their short hedge position (if not already 100% hedged). October's bullish piercing pattern could have been used as a signal to ease back on short-hedge positions. For those looking at a long hedge, the piercing pattern could be used as a signal to initiate such a hedge.

As illustrated in Exhibit 19.2, a confluence of bullish candlestick signals emerged the last week in September and the first week in October in 1988. The most obvious was the bullish engulfing pattern. These two weeks also created a tweezers bottom. Additionally, the white candlestick was a bullish belt hold which closed at its high. It also engulfed the prior five candlesticks. For long hedgers, these would have been signs to start, or add to, their hedges.

In early 1989, the harami cross (an important reversal signal), could have been used by long hedgers to scale back on hedges. Also, the fact that this harami cross was formed by a long white candlestick and a doji would indicate that the market was in trouble. As discussed in Chapter 8, a doji after a long white real body is often a sign of a top.

Exhibit 19.3 explores how a long crude oil hedger could use a candlestick signal to get an early signal of a bottom reversal and then use Western technical tools to confirm a bottom and add to the long hedge. The first tentative bottom reversal clue came with a hammer on July 5. Since this hammer session gapped under the prior lows, it should have not been taken as a bullish sign unless it was confirmed by other bullish indicators during the next few sessions. The next clue was the bullish engulfing pattern which provided bullish confirmation to the hammer. This engulfing pattern was also an extra important bottom reversal signal. This is because the white candlestick on July 9 engulfed not one but two black real bodies. At this point, crude oil end users (that is, long

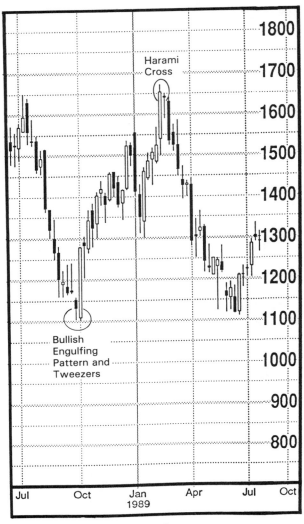

EXHIBIT 19.2. Cocoa—Weekly (Candlesticks with Hedging)

Source: Commodity Trend Service®

hedgers) should have seriously considered placing hedges or adding to their hedge position.

The next clue came when price lows at areas A, B, and C were not confirmed by lower momentum values. This revealed the fact that selling velocity was slowing (that is, experiencing diminishing downside momentum).

The reasons above were more than enough to expect a price bounce, but there is another added feature. A traditional Western falling wedge pattern was broken to the upside about the same time the momentum oscillator crossed into positive territory (see arrow). Based on the falling wedge, there was a target to where the wedge started. This, depending on how one views this wedge, could have been the June high near $19 or the May 18 high near $20. On the piercing of the rising wedge, more long-hedge positions could have been added.

EXHIBIT 19.3. Crude Oil—September 1990, Daily (Candlesticks with Hedging)

We see by this example that candlestick techniques can provide an earlier warning of a trend reversal than with Western technical tools. Also, we see candlestick techniques, in conjunction with Western technical methods, can create a powerful synergy. The more technical signals confirming each other, the greater the likelihood of an accurate call for a trend change.

CHAPTER 20

HOW I HAVE USED CANDLESTICKS

....

備えあれば憂いなし

"A prudent man has more than one string to his bow"

The following are some examples of trades I recommended to the Merrill Lynch system over a month-long period. All of them incorporated some candlestick techniques. Since I track futures, the examples in this chapter are futures oriented. Also, my bias is short term so the examples will be keyed off intra-day and daily charts. Each person has their unique trading style. How you trade is different than how I trade. Thus, I would not expect you to go through all the same thought processes or actions that I did in these trades.

My goal in this chapter is not to provide you with a set of trading rules. It is to show how one person has fused candlestick techniques into their trading methodology. I hope this chapter can start you on the road to incorporating candlesticks into your analysis.

Exhibit 20.1 shows that the neckline of a head and shoulders top was penetrated on May 29. The trend consequently turned down. In Western technical theory, once a head and shoulders neckline is broken you can expect a bounce to that line before selling pressure resumes. During the week of June 11, prices were in the process of approaching this neckline. June 11 was a strong white session. A short sale at that point was not attractive. I needed proof that the rally was running into trouble. The market gave a hint of trouble by way of the next session's small black real body. It signaled that the prior white candlestick's strong session may not continue.

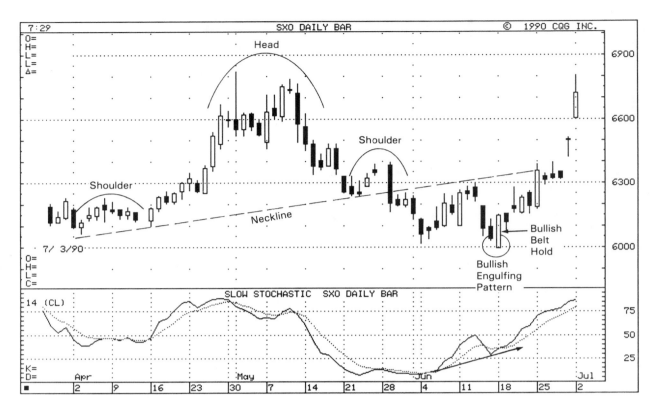

EXHIBIT 20.1. Soybeans—November 1990, Daily

On June 13, I recommended a short at $6.27. The stop was above the neckline at $6.35. The target was $5.90 (this was based on a support area earlier in the year). The short position looked good for the rest of the week as the market tumbled. Then on June 18, the market shouted it was time to cover shorts. The clues were:

1. The tall white candlestick on June 18 engulfed the prior black real body. These two candlesticks formed a bullish engulfing line.

2. The opening on June 18 made a new low for the move by punching under the early June lows. However, prices bounced right back above this early June low. This created a spring in which the lows were broken and not held. Based on this spring, I had targeted a retest of the upper end of the trading range at $6.30.

3. The candlestick on the June 18 was a strong bullish belt-hold line.

4. The new price lows were not validated by lower stochastic levels. This was a positive divergence and it demonstrated that the bears were losing control.

EXHIBIT 20.2. Coffee—September 1990, Daily

The action on June 18 revealed that it was not an environment to be short. I covered my short the following session at $6.12. This is an example of placing a trade mainly based on Western technical analysis, but one which also used some candlestick indicators as reasons to change my mind about the market's trend.

From late May we see a series of lower highs as delineated by the downward sloping resistance line in Exhibit 20.2. This shows the prevailing trend was down. There was support going back to late March and early May near $.92. When, on June 14, coffee broke under these lows it was time to look for an area to short. June 14's long black candlestick showed the force behind the selling pressure. The market was too oversold to short at this time.

The small real body which followed the long black line created a harami pattern. This harami pattern told me not to rush with a short since the prior downtrend had been neutralized. A lateral trading band, or a rally, could unfold. It turned out coffee had a minor rally. The rally stopped right where it was supposed to stop—near $.92. What was so special about $.92 as resistance? Remember the axiom that old support can become resistance. The late March and May lows were near $.92.

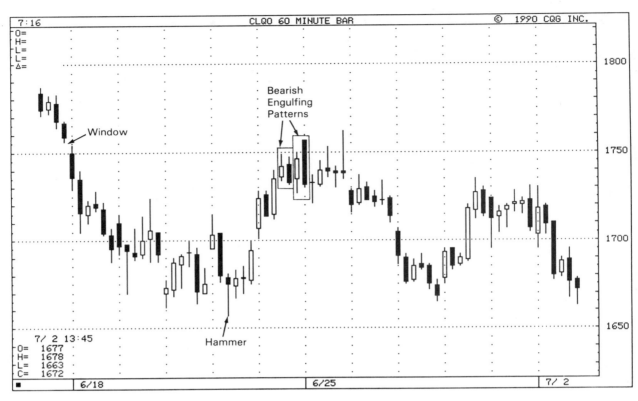

EXHIBIT 20.3. Crude Oil—August 1990, Intra-day

This level became resistance. Once the market backed down from near $.92 on the brief rally, I knew the bears were still in charge. The move on June 20 opened a window. This implied another leg lower. On June

21, when the market failed to move above the window's resistance area, I recommended a short at $.9015 with a stop above the June 20 high of $.9175. The objective was for $.8675 (this was based on support earlier in the year). The market then backed off.

At the time of the chart shown in Exhibit 20.3, crude oil was in a bear market. So I was looking to short on rallies. A rally started on June 21 with the hammer (note how I did not use this bullish hammer as a time to buy. Why? Because the major trend was down). Then, a few days after the hammer, back-to-back bearish engulfing patterns emerged. At that time, I suggested a short sale. There was a small window opened between June 15 and June 18. In the belief that this window would be resistance, I put a stop slightly above it at $17.65. The target was a retest near the hammer lows. A late rally on June 25 quickly backed off from the resistance area made by the bearish engulfing pattern and the window.

Exhibit 20.4 shows that on June 4 a hammer and a successful hold-

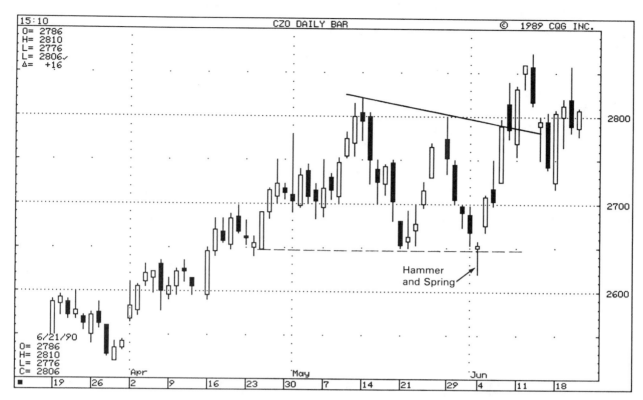

EXHIBIT 20.4. Corn—December 1990, Daily

ing, on a close, of the late April, mid-May lows of $2.65. It was also a bullish spring since prices made new lows for the move but these new lows failed to hold.

Although this was a bullish hammer I needed confirmation the next day before I could recommend to buy since the market was holding the $2.65 support so tenuously. The day after this hammer the market proved itself by opening higher. I recommended a buy at $2.68 with a stop under the support line shown at $2.64. The target was for a test of the downward sloping resistance line at $2.79. The strong session after the hammer day made this into a morning star pattern.

Although the trade in Exhibit 20.5 was not profitable, it is a good example of how candlesticks can help to provide good trade location. The price action on Friday, March 2 gave some buy signals. First, it was a hammer line. Next, this hammer's small real body was inside the prior tall real body creating a harami. This harami meant that the prior minor downtrend was over. Finally, the hammer session's lows took out support from early February, yet these new lows could not hold. In other words, the bears tried to break the market and they could not. It was time to step in and buy.

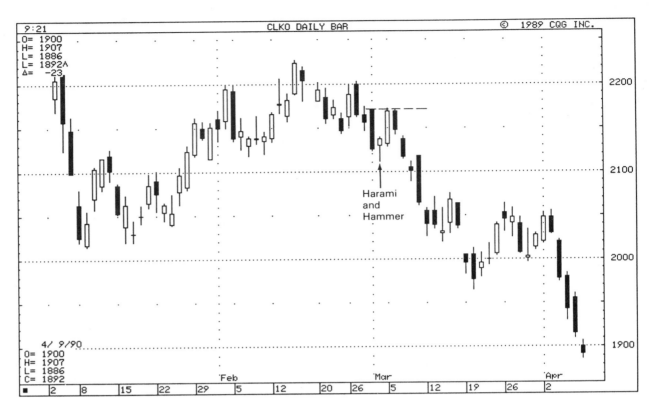

EXHIBIT 20.5. Crude Oil—May 1990, Daily

On Monday, March 5, I suggested a buy at $21.38. The target was a very short-term objective for a retest of the late February highs of $22. Since the target was so close, the stop was proportionally tight under the hammer's low at $21.10. On March 5 and 6, the market moved up to the February 28 and March 1 high's near $21.75. It failed to move above this short-term resistance area. After seeing this failure, I moved the stop up to breakeven. I got stopped out in the pullback on March 7. Once prices pushed under the hammer's lows prices fell in earnest.

CONCLUSION

....

千里の道も一歩より始まる

"Step after step the ladder is ascended"

This book, the result of years of study, research, and practical experience, has hopefully opened new avenues of analysis. After spending some time with candlesticks, I am sure that you, like me, will not trade without the insights they offer.

I do not use bar charts anymore, I only use candlestick charts. But that does not mean I only use candlestick indicators. While the candlesticks are a vital medium of market analysis, I use all the technical tools at my disposal. This is the advantage of candlestick charts. With them you can use candlestick techniques, Western techniques, or a combination of both. For experienced technicians you will find the union of Eastern and Western techniques creates a wonderfully exciting synergy.

Be flexible about chart reading. Where you stand in relation to the overall technical evidence may be more important than an individual candlestick pattern. For example, a bullish candlestick signal in a major bear market should not be used as a buy signal. A bullish candlestick formation, especially when confirmed by other technical signals in a bull market, would be a buying point.

Even though many of you (I hope!) will be using this book as a reference, it does not mean each of you will use its candlestick techniques in the same way. So I am not worried that if others learn these ancient investment techniques they will become invalid. This is because candlesticks, as with all other charting methods, require subjectivity.

Two candlestick analysts are like two doctors who went to the same medical school. Each may have the same knowledge about how the body works, yet each doctor, because of his experiences, philosophies, and preferences may give a particular patient a different diagnosis and treat the patient differently—even if the patient's symptoms are the same. The doctor brings his unique personality and perceptions to the diagnosis. So it is with you and technical analysis. *You are a doctor of the market.* How you read and react to the symptoms of the market's health through candlesticks techniques may not be the same as another candlestick practitioner. How you trade with candlesticks will depend on your trading philosophy, your risk adversity, and your temperament. There are very individual aspects.

In addition, each market has its own unique personality. As the Japanese express it, "The pattern of the market is like a person's face—no two are exactly alike." For example, dark-cloud covers seem to work well in the daily crude oil charts, while hammers appear with relative frequency in weekly copper charts. By studying your market's personality, you can uncover the candlestick formations, and variations of these formations, which appear most and work best for that market.

There is a saying, "Fish for me and I will eat for today, but teach me how to fish and I will eat for the rest of my life." I hope that this book has taught you how to do a little fishing. That what you discovered in reading it can be used to unlock some of the secrets of the candlecharts.

Based on centuries of evolution, candlestick charts are unmatched in their capacity to be used alone or joined with any other technical tool. This means that each of you, from the technical novice to the seasoned professional, can harness the power of candlestick charts.

GLOSSARY A

CANDLESTICK TERMS AND VISUAL DICTIONARY

The descriptions and illustrations below explain and show ideal examples of what the pattern should be like. These "ideal" patterns rarely unfold, therefore, use this glossary as a guidepost, since some subjectivity is required.

Abandoned baby—a very rare major top or bottom reversal signal. It is comprised of a doji star which gaps away (including shadows) from the prior and following sessions' candlesticks. The same as a Western island top or bottom in which the island session is also a doji.

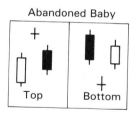

Abandoned Baby

Advance block—a variation on three white soldiers in which the last two soldiers (i.e., white real bodies) display weakening upside drive. This weakness could be in the form of tall upper shadows or progressively smaller real bodies. It signifies a diminution of buying force or an increase in selling pressure.

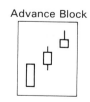

Advance Block

Belt-hold line—there are bullish and bearish belt holds. A bullish belt hold is a tall white candlestick that opens on its low. It is also called a *white opening shaven bottom*. At a low price area, this is a bullish signal. A bearish belt hold is a long black candlestick which opens on its high. Also referred to as a *black opening shaven head*. At a high price level, it is considered bearish.

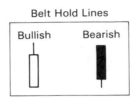

Belt Hold Lines

Bullish   Bearish

Candlestick lines and charts—traditional Japanese charts whose individual lines look like candles, hence their name. The candlestick line is comprised of a real body and shadows. *See* "Real body" and "shadow."

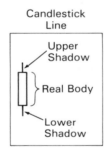

Candlestick
Line

Upper
Shadow

Real Body

Lower
Shadow

Counterattack lines—following a black (white) candlestick in a downtrend (uptrend), the market gaps sharply lower (higher) on the opening and then closes unchanged from the prior session's close. A pattern which reflects a stalemate between the bulls and bears.

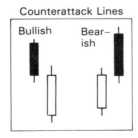

Counterattack Lines

Bullish   Bear–
             ish

Dark-cloud cover—a bearish reversal signal. In an uptrend a long white candlestick is followed by a black candlestick that opens above the prior white candlestick's high. It then closes well into the white candlestick's real body.

Dark–Cloud Cover

Dead cross—a bearish signal given when a short-term moving average crosses under a longer-term moving average.

Deliberation pattern—*see* "Stalled pattern."

Doji—a session in which the open and close are the same (or almost the same). There are different varieties of doji lines (such as a gravestone or long-legged doji) depending on where the opening and closing are in relation to the entire range. Doji lines are among the most important individual candlestick lines. They are also components of important candlestick patterns.

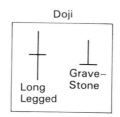

Doji

Long Legged

Grave-Stone

Doji star—a doji line which gaps from a long white or black candlestick. An important reversal pattern with confirmation during the next session.

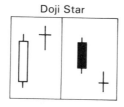

Doji Star

Downside gap tasuki—*see* "Tasuki gaps."

Dumpling tops—similar to the Western rounding top. A window to the downside is needed to confirm this as a top.

Eight or ten new records—after about eight to ten new price highs buying pressure should end. After such an advance, if a bearish candlestick indicator appears, selling is warranted. The opposite occurs after eight or ten new lows.

Engulfing patterns—there is a bullish and bearish engulfing pattern. A bullish engulfing pattern is comprised of a large white real body which engulfs a small black real body in a downtrend. The bullish engulfing pattern is an important bottom reversal. A bearish engulfing pattern (a major top reversal pattern), occurs when selling pressure overwhelms buying pressure as reflected by a long black real body engulfing a small white real body in an uptrend.

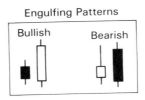

Evening star—a major top reversal pattern formed by three candlesticks. The first is a tall white real body, the second is a small real body (white or black) which gaps higher to form a star, the third is a black candlestick which closes well into the first session's white real body.

Evening doji star—the same as an evening star except the middle candlestick (i.e., the star portion) is a doji instead of a small real body. Because there is a doji in this pattern, it is considered more bearish than the regular evening star.

Falling three methods—see "Three methods."

Fry pan bottoms—similar to a Western rounding bottom. A window to the upside confirms this pattern.

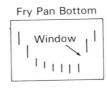

Gapping play—there are two kinds of gapping play:

1. *high-price gapping play*—after a sharp advance the market consolidates via a series of small real bodies near the recent highs. If prices gap above this consolidation it is a buy signal.

2. *low-price gapping play*—after a sharp price decline the market consolidates via a series of small real bodies near the recent lows. If prices gap under this consolidation it is a sell signal.

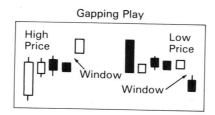

Golden cross—a bullish signal in which a shorter-term moving average crosses above a longer-term moving average.

Gravestone doji—a doji in which the opening and closing are at the low of the session. A reversal signal at tops. Also a reversal signal at bottoms, but only with bullish confirmation the next session. See the illustration under "Doji."

Hammer—an important bottoming candlestick line. The hammer and the hanging man are both the same line, that is a small real body (white or black) at the top of the session's range and a very long lower shadow with little or no upper shadow. When this line appears during a downtrend it becomes a bullish hammer. For a classic hammer, the lower shadow should be at least twice the height of the real body.

Hanging man—an important top reversal. The hanging man and the hammer are both the same type of candlestick line (i.e, a small real body (white or black), with little or no upper shadow, at the top of the session's range and a very long lower shadow). But when this line appears during an uptrend, it becomes a bearish hanging man. It signals the market has become vulnerable, but there should be bearish confirmation the next session (i.e., a black candlestick session with a lower close or a weaker opening) to signal a top. In principle, the hanging man's lower shadow should be two or three times the height of the real body.

Harami—a two candlestick pattern in which a small real body holds within the prior session's unusually large real body. The harami implies the immediately preceding trend is concluded and that the bulls and bears are now in a state of truce. The color of the second

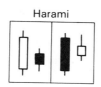

real body can be white or black. Most often the second real body is the opposite color of the first real body.

Harami cross—a harami with a doji on the second session instead of a small real body. An important top (bottom) reversal signal especially after a tall white (black) candlestick line. It is also called a *petrifying pattern*.

Harami Cross

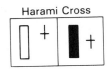

High Waves

High wave—a candlestick with a very long upper or lower shadow and a short real body. A group of these can foretell a market turn.

High-price gapping play—see "Gapping plays."

In-Neck Line

In-neck line—a small white candlestick in a downtrend whose close is a slightly above the previous black candlestick's low of the session. After this white candlestick's low is broken, the downtrend should continue. Compare to on-neck line, thrusting line, and piercing pattern.

Inverted hammer—following a downtrend, this is a candlestick line that has a long upper shadow and a small real body at the lower end of the session. There should be no, or very little, lower shadow. It has the same shape as the bearish shooting star, but when this line occurs in a downtrend, it is a bullish bottom reversal signal with confirmation the next session (i.e., a white candlestick with a higher close or a higher opening).

Inverted Hammer

Inverted three Buddha pattern—see "Three Buddha pattern."

Long-legged doji—a doji with very long shadows. This is an important reversal signal. If the opening and closing of a long-legged doji session are in the middle of the session's range, the line is called a *rickshaw man*. See illustration under "Doji."

Low-price gapping play—see "Gapping plays."

Lower shadow—see "Shadows."

Mat-hold pattern—a bullish continuation pattern. A white candlestick is followed by a small black real body which gaps higher. Then there are two small black candlesticks which are followed by a strong white candlestick (or a candlestick which gaps open above the last black candlestick).

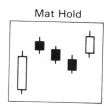

Mat Hold

Morning star—a major bottom reversal pattern formed by three candlesticks. The first is a long black real body, the second is a small real body (white or black) which gaps lower to form a star, the third is a white candlestick that closes well into the first session's black real body.

Morning Star

Morning doji star—the same as a morning star except the middle candlestick is a doji instead of a small real body. Because there is a doji in this pattern it is considered more bullish than the regular morning star.

Morning Doji Star

Morning attack—the Japanese expression for a large buy or sell order on the opening that is designed to significantly move the market.

Night attack—the Japanese expression for a large order placed at the close to try to affect the market.

On-neck line—a black candlestick in a downtrend is followed by a small white candlestick whose close is near the low of the session of the black candlestick. It is a bearish continuation pattern. The market should continue to move lower after the white candlestick's low is broken. Compare to an in-neck line, a thrusting line, and a piercing pattern.

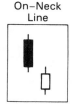

On–Neck Line

Piercing Pattern

Petrifying pattern—another name for the harami cross.

Piercing pattern—a bottom reversal signal. In a downtrend, a long black candlestick is followed by a gap lower during the next session. This session finishes as a strong white candlestick which closes move than halfway into the prior black candlestick's real body. Compare to the on-neck line, the in-neck line, and the thrusting line.

Rain drop—see "Star."

*Real body—*the thick part of the candlestick line. It is defined by the closing and opening prices of the session. When the close is higher than the open, the real body is white (or empty). A black (or filled in) real body is when the close is lower than the opening. See the illustration under "Candlestick lines and charts."

Rickshaw man—see "Long-legged doji."

Rising three methods—see "Three methods."

*Separating lines—*when, in an uptrend (downtrend) the market opens at the same opening as the previous session's opposite color candlestick and then closes higher (lower). The prior trend should resume after this line.

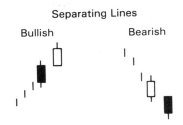

Separating Lines

Bullish   Bearish

*Shadows—*the thin lines above and below the real body of the candlestick line. They represent the extremes of the day. The lower shadow is the line on the bottom of the real body. The bottom of the lower shadow is the low of the session. The upper shadow is the line on top of the real body. The top of the upper shadow is the high of the session. See the illustration under "Candlestick lines and charts."

*Shaven bottom—*a candlestick with no lower shadow.

*Shaven head—*a candlestick with no upper shadow.

Shooting Star

*Shooting star—*a candlestick with a long upper shadow with little, or no lower shadow, and a small real body near the lows of the session that arises after an uptrend. It is a bearish candlestick signal in an uptrend.

*Side-by-side white lines—*two consecutive white candlesticks which have the same open and whose real bodies are about the same size. In an uptrend, if these side-by-side white lines gap higher, it is a bullish continuation pattern. In a downtrend, these side-by-side white lines gapping lower are bearish since they are viewed as temporary short covering. Gapping side-by-side lines are very rare.

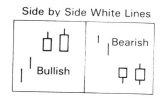

Spinning top—a candlestick with a small real body.

Stalled pattern—a small white real body which is either above the prior long white real body or near its top. Sometimes there is a short white candlestick before the long white one. At the emergence of the stalled pattern, the market's rally should stall. Also called a *deliberation pattern.*

Star—a small real body (i.e., a spinning top) which gaps away from the previous long real body. A star reflects a diminution of the force of the trend preceding the star. Sometimes a star following a long black line in a downtrend is called a *rain drop*.

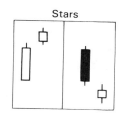

Tasuki gaps—there are downside and upside tasuki gaps. The downside tasuki gap is formed when, in a declining market, a black real body gaps lower. This candlestick is followed by a white candlestick, of about the same size, which opens in the black session's real body and then closes above the black's real body. It is a bearish continuation pattern. The upside tasuki gap is a bullish continuation pattern. It is formed when a white candlestick which gaps higher is followed by a black candlestick of about the same size which opens within the white real body and closes under the white's real body. Tasuki gaps are rare.

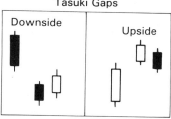

Three Buddha patterns—A three Buddha top is the same as the Western head and shoulders top. In Japanese terms, the three Buddha top is a three mountain top in which the central mountain is the tallest. An inverted three Buddha is the same as the Western inverted head and shoulders. In Japanese terminology, it is a three river bottom in which the middle river is the longest.

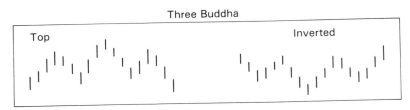

Three Buddha

Three Crows

Three crows—three relatively long consecutive black candlesticks which close near or on their lows. A top reversal at a high price level or after an extended rally.

Three gaps—if a bearish (bullish) candlestick indicator appears after three gaps higher (three gaps lower), buying force (selling pressure) should be exhausted.

Three methods—there are two types. The first is the falling three methods which is a bearish continuation pattern. It is comprised of five lines. A long black real body is followed by three small, usually white, real bodies which hold within the first session's range. Then a black candlestick closes at a new low for the move. The second is the rising three methods which is a bullish continuation pattern. A tall white candlestick preceded three small, usually black, real bodies that hold within the white candlestick's range. The fifth line of this pattern is a strong white candlestick that closes at a new high for the move.

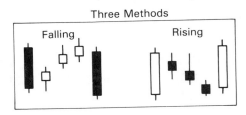

Three Methods

Three mountain top—a longer-term topping pattern in which prices stall at, or near, the same highs. It is also sometimes viewed as three waves up.

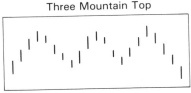

Three Mountain Top

Three river bottom—when the market hits a bottom area three times. When the peak of the intervening valleys is exceeded by a white candlestick or with a gap it is confirmation that a bottom has been put in place.

Three River Bottom

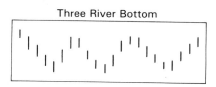

Three white or three advancing soldiers—this is a group of three white candlesticks with consecutively higher closes (with each of the closes near the highs of the session). These three white candlesticks presage more strength if they appear after a period of stable prices and at a low price area.

Three White Soldiers

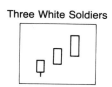

Thrusting line—a white candlestick which closes in the prior black real body, but still under the middle of the prior session's real body. The thrusting line is stronger than an in-neck line, but not as strong as a piercing line. In a downtrend, the thrusting line is viewed as bearish (unless two of these patterns appear within a few days of each other). As part of a rising market it is considered bullish.

Thrusting Line

Towers—there is a tower top and tower bottom. The tower top, a top reversal formation, is comprised of a tall white candlestick followed by congestion and then one or more long black candlesticks. It is a pattern which looks like it has towers on both sides of the congestion

Towers

Top   Bottom

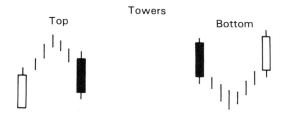

band. A tower bottom is a bottom reversal pattern. A long black candlestick is followed by lateral action. Then the market explodes to the upside via one or more long white candlesticks.

Tri-star—three dojis that have the same formation as a morning or evening star pattern. An extraordinarily rare pattern and a major reversal signal.

Tweezers top and bottom—when the same highs or lows are tested the next session or within a few sessions. They are minor reversal signals that take on extra importance if the two candlesticks that comprise the tweezers pattern also form another candlestick indicator. For example, if both session's of a harami cross have the same high it could be an important top reversal since there would be a tweezers top and a bearish harami cross made by the same two candlestick lines.

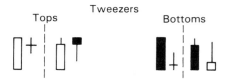

Tweezers

Tops   Bottoms

Unique Three
River Bottom

Unique three river bottom—a rare type of bottom comprised of three lines. The first is a long black real body, the second is a hammer like session with a black real body which makes a new low, and the third candlestick is a small real body.

Upper shadow—*see* "Shadows."

Upside gap tasuki—*see* "Tasuki gaps."

Upside Gap
Two Crows

Upside gap two crows—a three candlestick pattern. The first line is a long white candlestick which is followed by a black real body that gaps higher. The third session is another black real body which opens above the second session's open and closes under the second session's close. It is a top reversal signal.

Window—the same as a Western gap. Windows are continuation patterns. When the market rallies and opens a window, there should be a pullback to that window. The window should be support. If a win-

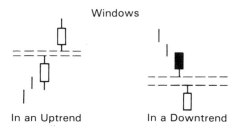

Windows

In an Uptrend   In a Downtrend

dow opens in a selloff, there should be a rally to the window. The window should be resistance. The Japanese expression is that "the market goes to the window."

Yin and yang—the Chinese name of the black (yin) and white (yang) candlesticks.

GLOSSARY B

AMERICAN
TECHNICAL TERMS
....

This glossary clarifies the Western technical terms used in this book. It is not meant to be comprehensive or detailed because this book's focus is on Japanese candlesticks and not Western technical tools.

Bar chart—a graphic representation of price activity. The high and low of the session define the top and bottom of a vertical line. The close for the period is marked with a short horizontal bar attached to the right of the vertical line. The open is marked with a short horizontal bar attached to the left of the vertical line. Price is in on the vertical scale; time is on the horizontal scale.

Blow-offs—a top or bottom reversal. Blow-offs occur after an extended move. Prices, usually with very high volume, sharply and quickly thrust strongly in the direction of the preceding trend. If the market reverses after this action, it is a blow-off.

Breakaway gap—when prices gap away from a significant technical area (i.e., a trendline or a congestion zone).

Breakout—overcoming a resistance or support level.

Change of polarity—when old support converts to new resistance or when old resistance converts to new support.

Confirmation—when more than one indicator substantiates the action of another.

Congestion zone or band—a period of lateral price action within a relatively narrow price band.

Consolidation—the same as a congestion zone. Consolidation, however, has the implication that the prior trend should resume.

Continuation patterns—a pattern whose implications are for a continuation of the prior trend. A flag, for instance, is a continuation pattern.

Crossover—when the faster indicator crosses above (bullish crossover) or below (bearish crossover) the slower indicator. For example, if a five-day moving average crosses under a 13-day moving average it is a bearish crossover.

Divergence—when related technical indicators fail to confirm a price move. For instance, if prices reach new highs and stochastics do not, this is a negative divergence and is bearish. If prices establish new lows and stochastics do not, this is a positive divergence and is bullish.

Downgap—when prices gap lower.

Downtrend—a market that is trending lower as shown by a series of lower highs and/or lower lows.

Double bottom—price action that resembles the letter W in which price declines twice stop at, or near, the same lows.

Double top—price action that resembles a M in which price rallies twice stop at, or near, the same highs.

Elliott Wave—a system of analyzing and forecasting price movements based on the works of R. N. Elliott. The main theory is that prices have five waves in the direction of the main trend followed by three corrective waves.

Exponential moving average—a moving average that is exponentially weighted.

Fibonacci—Italian mathematician who formulated a series of numbers based on adding the prior two numbers. Popular Fibonacci ratios used by technicians include (rounding off) 38%, 50%, and 62%.

Flag or pennant—a continuation formation comprised of a sharp price move followed by a brief consolidation area. These are continuation patterns.

Filling in the gap—when prices go into the price vacuum left by a gap.

Gaps—a price void (i.e., no trading) from one price area to another.

Historical volatility—a calculation that provides an expected range of prices over a specified time. It is based on price changes in the underlying contract.

Implied volatility—the market's forecast of future volatility levels.

Inside session—when the entire session's high–low range is within the prior session's range.

Intra-day—any period shorter than daily. Thus, a 60-minute intra-day chart is based on the high, low, open and close on an hourly basis.

Islands—a formation at the extremes of the market when prices gap in the direction of the prior trend. Prices then stay there for one or more days, and then gaps in the opposite direction. Prices are thus surrounded by gaps which leaves them isolated like an island.

Locals—traders on the floor in the futures markets who trade for their own account.

Market Profile®—a statistical distribution of prices over specific time intervals (usually 30 minutes).

Momentum—the velocity of a price move. It compares the most recent close to the close a specific number of period's ago.

Moving average convergence-divergence (MACD) oscillator—a combination of three exponentially smoothed moving averages.

Neckline—a line connecting the lows of the head in a head and shoulders formation or highs of an inverse head and shoulders. A move under the neckline of a head and shoulders top is bearish; a move above the neckline of an inverse head and shoulders neckline is bullish.

Negative crossover—*see* "Crossover."

Negative divergence—*see* "Divergence."

Offset—to get out of an existing position. Longs are said to liquidate; shorts are said to cover.

On-Balance Volume (OBV)—a cumulative volume figure. If prices close higher than the previous session the volume for the higher close day is added to the OBV. On a day, when the close is lower, the volume for that day is subtracted from the OBV figure. Unchanged days are ignored.

Open interest—futures contracts which are still outstanding. Open interest is equal to the total number of long or short positions, but not a combination of the two.

Oscillator—a momentum line that fluctuates around a zero value line (or between 0 and 100%). Oscillators can help measure overbought/oversold levels, show negative and positive divergence, and can be used to measure a price move's velocity.

Overbought—when the market moves up too far, too fast. At this point the market is vulnerable to a downward correction.

Oversold—when the market declines too quickly. The market becomes susceptible to a bounce.

Paper trading—not trading with real money. All transactions are only imaginary with a record of profit and loss on paper.

Pennant—*see* "Flag."

Positive crossover—*see* "Crossover."

Positive divergence—*see* "Divergence."

Protective stop—a means of limiting losses if the market moves against your position. If your stop level is reached, your position is automatically offset at the prevailing price.

Rally—an upward movement of prices.

Reaction—a price movement opposite to the prevailing trend.

Relative Strength Index—an oscillator developed by Welles Wilder. The RSI compares the ratio of up closes to down closes over a specified time period.

Resistance level—a level where sellers are expected to enter.

Retracement—a price reaction from the prior move in percentage terms. The more common retracement levels are 38%, 50%, and 62%.

Reversal session—a session when a new high (or low) is made for the move and the market then closes under (or above) the prior session's close.

Reversal indicator—*see* "Trend reversals."

Selling climax—when price push sharply and suddenly lower on heavy volume after an extended decline. If the market reverses from this sharp selloff, it is viewed as a selling climax.

Selloff—a downward movement of prices.

Simple moving average—a method of smoothing price data in which prices are added together and then averaged. It is a "moving" average because the average moves. As new price data is added the oldest data is dropped.

Spring—when prices break under the support of a horizontal congestion band and then springs back above the "broken support" area. This is bullish.

Stochastics—an oscillator that measures the relative position of the closing price as compared to its range over a chosen period. It is usually comprised of the faster moving %K line and the slower moving %D line.

Support level—an area where buyers are expected to enter.

Tick Volume™—the number of trades per given intra-day time period.

Time filter—Prices have to stay above, or below, a certain price area for a specific time to confirm that an important technical area has been broken. For example, the market might have to close above a broken resistance level for two days before a long position is placed.

Trading range—when prices are locked between horizontal support and horizontal resistance levels.

Trend—the market's prevalent price direction.

Trend reversals—also called *reversal indicators*. This is a misleading term. More appropriate, and more accurate, would be the term "trend change indicator." It means the prior trend should change. It does not mean prices are going to reverse.

Trendline—a line on a chart that connects a series of higher highs or lower lows. At least two points are needed to draw a trendline. The more often it is tested, and the greater the volume on the tests, the more important the trendline.

Upgap—a gap which pushes prices higher.

Upthrust—when prices break above a resistance line from a laterally trading zone. If these new highs fail to hold and prices pull back under the "broken" resistance line it is an upthrust. It is a bearish signal.

Uptrend—a market that is trending higher.

V bottom or top—when prices suddenly reverse direction forming a price pattern that looks like the letter V for a bottom or an inverted V for a top.

Volume—the total of all contracts traded for a given period.

Weighted moving average—a moving average in which each of the previous prices is assigned a weighting factor. Usually, the most recent data is the more heavily weighted.

BIBLIOGRAPHY

· ·

Analysis of Stock Price in Japan, Tokyo, Japan: Nippon Technical Analysts Association 1986.

Buchanen, Daniel Crump, *Japanese Proverbs and Sayings,* Oklahoma City: University of Oklahoma Press, 1965.

Colby, Robert W. and Thomas A. Meyers, *The Encyclopedia of Technical Market Indicators,* Homewood, IL: Dow Jones-Irwin, 1988.

Dilts, Marion May, *The Pageant of Japanese History,* New York: David McKay, 1963.

Drinka, Thomas P. and Robert L. McNutt, "Market Profile and Market Logic," *Technical Analysis of Stocks and Commodities,* December 1987, pp. 15–18.

Edwards, Robert D. and John Magee, *Technical Analysis of Stock Trends,* 5th ed., Boston: John Magee, 1966.

Hill, Julie Skur, "That's Not What I Said," *Business Tokyo,* August 1990, pp. 46–47.

Hirschmeier, Johannes and Tsunehiko Yui, *Development of Japanese Business 1600–1973,* Cambridge, MA: Harvard University Press 1975.

Hoshii, Kazutaka, *Hajimete Kabuka Chato wo Yomu Hito no Hon (A Book for Those Reading Stock Charts for the First Time),* Tokyo, Japan: Asukashuppansha, 1990.

Ikutaro, Gappo, *Kabushikisouba no Technical Bunseki (Stock Market Technical Analysis),* Tokyo, Japan: Nihon Keizai Shinbunsha, 1985.

Ishii, Katsutoshi, *Kabuka Chato no Tashikana Yomikata (A Sure Way to Read Stock Charts),* Tokyo, Japan: Jiyukokuminsha, 1990.

Kaufman, Perry J. *The New Commodity Trading Systems and Methods,* New York: John Wiley and Sons, 1987.

Keisen Kyoshitsu Part 1 (Chart Classroom Part 1), Tokyo, Japan: Toshi Rader, 1989.

Kroll, Stanley, *Kroll on Futures Trading,* Homewood, IL: Dow Jones-Irwin, 1988.

Masuda, Koh, ed. *Kenkyusha's New School Japanese-English Dictionary,* Tokyo, Japan: Kenkyusha, 1968.

Murphy, John J., *Technical Analysis of the Futures Markets,* New York: New York Institute of Finance, 1986.

Nihon Keisenshi (The History of Japanese Charts), Chapter 2 by Kenji Oyama, pp. 90–102, Tokyo, Japan: Nihon Keisai Shimbunsha, 1979.

Okasan Keisai Kenkyusho, *Shinpan Jissen Kabushiki Nyumon (Introduction to Stock Charts),* Tokyo, Japan: Diamond-sha, 1987.

Sakata Goho Wa Furinkazan (Sakata's Five Rules are Wind, Forest, Fire and Mountain), Tokyo, Japan: Nihon Shoken Shimbunsha, 1969.

Schabacker, Richard W., *Technical Analysis and Stock Market Profits,* New York: The Schabacker Institute.

Seidensticker, Edward G., *Even Monkeys Fall from Trees and Other Japanese Proverbs*, Rutland, VA: Charles E. Tuttle, 1987.

Seward, Jack, *Japanese in Action*, New York: Weatherhill, 1983.

Shimizu, Seiki, *The Japanese Chart of Charts*, trans. Gregory S. Nicholson, Tokyo, Japan: Tokyo Futures Trading Publishing Co., 1986.

Sklarew, Arthur, *Techniques of a Professional Commodity Chart Analyst*, New York: Commodity Research Bureau, 1980.

Smith, Adam, *The Money Game*, New York: Random House, 1968.

Tamarkin, Robert, *The New Gatsbys*, Chicago, IL: Bob Tamarkin, 1985.

Taucher, Frank, *Commodity Trader's Almanac*, Tulsa: Market Movements, 1988.

Technical Traders Bulletin, January 1990, May 1990, June 1990, Rolling Hill Estates, CA: Island View Financial Group Inc., 1990.

Wilder, J. Welles, *New Concepts in Technical Trading Systems*, Greensboro, NC: Trend Research, 1978.

Yoshimi, Toshihiko, *Yoshimi Toshihiko no Chato Kyoshitsu (Toshihiko Yoshimi's Chart Classroom)*, Tokyo, Japan: Nihon Chart, 1989.

Index